Notes of a Provincial Wildfowler

NORTHWESTERN UNIVERSITY PRESS

Studies in Russian Literature and Theory

Founding Editor

Gary Saul Morson

General Editor

Caryl Emerson

Consulting Editors

Carol Avins

Robert Belknap

Robert Louis Jackson

Elliott Mossman

Alfred Rieber

William Mills Todd III

Alexander Zholkovsky

Notes of a Provincial Wildfowler

Sergei Timofeevich Aksakov

TRANSLATED FROM THE RUSSIAN,

INTRODUCED, AND ANNOTATED BY KEVIN WINDLE

Northwestern University Press Evanston, Illinois

Northwestern University Press
www.nupress.northwestern.edu

Copyright © 1998 by Northwestern University Press.
Published 1998. All rights reserved.

Printed in the United States of America

10 9 8 7 6 5 4 3 2 1

ISBN 978-0-8101-2861-3

The Library of Congress has cataloged the original hardcover edition as follows:

Aksakov, S. T. (Sergeĭ Timofeevich), 1791–1859.
[Zapiski ruzheĭnogo okhotnika Orgenburgskoĭ gubernii. English]
Notes of a provincial wildfowler / Sergei Timofeevich Aksakov ; translated from the Russian, introduced, and annotated by Kevin Windle.
p. cm. — (Studies in Russian literature and theory.)
Includes bibliographical references.
ISBN 0-8101-1391-0 (cloth : alk. paper)
1. Fowling—Russia. 2. Birds—Russia. I. Title. II. Series.
SK316.R9A3913 1998
799.2'44'0947—dc21

98-16062
CIP

∞ The paper used in this publication meets the minimum requirements of the American National Standard for Information Sciences—Permanence of Paper for Printed Library Materials, ANSI Z39.48-1992.

CONTENTS

ACKNOWLEDGMENTS

The translator is grateful to Dr. Andrew Durkin of the University of Indiana for his support, encouragement, and valuable advice throughout the duration of this project. The sporadic flow of bird-watching notes between Canberra and Bloomington has provided a lively stimulus.

TRANSLATOR'S INTRODUCTION

In the history of nineteenth-century Russian literature Sergei Timofeevich Aksakov (1791–1859) is more important than is generally realized in the English-speaking world, where his reputation has been overshadowed by those of his great contemporaries. Although his best-known works came late in his career, he was close to the world of letters and the theater from his youth and made a substantial contribution as a drama critic and by his translations from the French of Molière and Boileau. Incongruously perhaps, he was able to enrich his store of literary knowledge during a period of service in the office of the censor, from 1827 until 1832, when he was dismissed. His most spectacular transgression was to permit publication of a satirical work that aroused the ire of the authorities, including Aksakov's master, the head of the Emperor's Third Section, Count Benckendorff.[1]

Sergei Aksakov was born in 1791 in Ufa, a provincial town to the west of the Urals, where his father was a court official in government service. Here and in the neighboring province of Orenburg he spent most of his early childhood until at nine he was sent to school in Kazan', where he later attended the university. After a period in Saint Petersburg and Moscow he spent the greater part of the years 1812 to 1826 managing the family estate in Orenburg province. He then moved with his family to Moscow and entered the office of the censor, which was then expanding its operations in the repressive years following the Decembrist uprising of 1825, and made only rare visits to his beloved Urals and the steppe regions of his youth.

In Moscow he became deeply involved in the world of literature and ideas, the theater and the arts. His acquaintance with other literary figures of the day led him to write his recollections of Gavriil Derzhavin, Aleksandr Shishkov, Nikolai Gogol, and others, providing an invaluable source of background information about these writers. Later his house became a center of Slavophile social thought, when his son Konstantin came to occupy a central position in this school.

In 1843 Aksakov purchased the estate known as Abramtsevo, thirty-five miles to the east of Moscow in beautiful rural surroundings. The estate is now preserved as a museum, partly in remembrance of Aksakov but also commemorating the colony of artists that flourished there in later times. Here he spent most of his remaining years and wrote the works for which he became famous. As his health and eyesight began to fail in the mid-1840s he was obliged to rely increasingly on dictation to produce them.

The first major work to attract a wide readership bore the seemingly unlikely title *Notes on Fishing*, first published in 1847. Readers were quick to notice that although the title was a faithful reflection of the content—Aksakov intended to write only a practical guide to a subject he knew well—there was more to the book than the title announced. His feeling for nature and extraordinary ability to describe it, together with his expert knowledge of botany and wildlife in all its forms, produced a work that had few if any precedents in Russian writing.

A similar if not even greater success attended his *Notes of a Provincial Wildfowler* and his more orthodox autobiographical fiction written in the 1850s, *The Childhood Years of Bagrov's Grandson* and *A Family Chronicle*. While the latter two have long been known in English translation, his shooting and fishing notes have not previously been translated, perhaps because they fall outside the familiar genres of nineteenth-century Russian literature. Yet the fictional and autobiographical writings, for all their charm and merit, produce a somewhat incomplete picture of the man and the writer, since so much of his time was spent in the wilds of his native province with only his shotgun and dog for company. He was a man of wide interests and talents, as much a drama critic as he was a hunter and naturalist, equally at home in the company of Saint Petersburg writers and intellectuals and in solitary reflection on the life of the wild.

In writing of his shooting days in Orenburg he is remembering his youth and reproducing the details he had faithfully recorded in his diaries at the time. His experience in the field reaches back to his childhood, to around the year 1800, and his interest in nature and wildlife endured long after the end of his Orenburg period in 1826. In his *Notes of a Provincial Wildfowler* he shows himself in the gentleman-sportsman tradition to a degree; unlike most of his contemporaries, however, he maintained an abiding interest in wildlife and made a close study of the birds that he shot—that is, most species larger than finches, exception being made for families such as the raptors and corvids. The result is far more than a shooting man's guide to game; rather it is an attempt at a comprehensive guide to local birdlife. His detailed descriptions have all the precision and immediacy of the later British ornithologist Thomas Coward, and his close personal observations on the behavior of various species invite comparison with those of an earlier writer, the English country vicar Gilbert White. White dealt with the natural history of a very small area, the little Hampshire village of Selborne.[2] Aksakov also maintains his focus on a particular area, a much bigger one: the forests, steppes, and marshland of the vast province of Orenburg. Modestly he claims little knowledge of the wildlife beyond its borders, although it is clear that his ornithological knowledge in fact extends far wider.

When first published in 1852, the work enjoyed popularity greatly exceeding the author's expectations, largely because it was the first such book to be written in Russian. It was highly praised by readers as varied but discerning as Turgenev, Nekrasov, Gogol, and Chernyshevsky, and later specialists in the field of ornithology also held it in high regard. It was Turgenev who made the famous comment, "If a black grouse could tell its own story, I am quite sure it would have nothing to add to what Mr Aksakov has told us."[3] On the basis of reviews and correspondence with knowledgeable readers, Aksakov was able to revise and improve the work in two later editions (1853 and 1857), correcting some of his earlier misconceptions—for example, about the roding of the woodcock—and offering different opinions on contentious matters such as the drumming of the snipe (a subject that had earlier exercised Gilbert White's skill as an observer).

It should not surprise us if faults can be found in Aksakov's taxonomy and if he occasionally fails to distinguish species. He was, after all, observing without any visual aids and did not necessarily collect specimens of both sexes of all birds that he saw. There is some confusion regarding the females of divers, grebes, and sawbills, and he does not separate the swans. An added difficulty here is the terminology of the period, which had not yet been standardized. Aksakov used the names then current in his wildfowling milieu. Most of these are in use today but some have been applied to different species. This is particularly true of the ducks, grebes, and divers (loons), as may be seen from a perusal of these terms in the dictionary of a slightly later period by Vladimir Dal'. The occasional gaps in Aksakov's knowledge do not detract from the work, which still provides a fascinating insight into the state of ornithological knowledge in Russia in the mid-nineteenth century.

As a naturalist, Aksakov was very much a man of his time. A love of the natural world meant to many a love of the chase in all its forms and of the meat thus procured for the table. The sense of Russian *dich'* does not correspond exactly to the closest English equivalent "game." It is related to the adjective *dikii* (wild) and it is applied to all forms of wildlife deemed to be edible. It is thus broader than the concept of "game species" in English and few ethical constraints hampered the shooting of birds and animals. Likewise there was no such thing as a "closed season" in which the birds could breed in relative safety. As long as they were present the season was open and the peak of the season was the time when the birds were at their fattest. Apparently nothing in the sportsman's code of ethics proscribed the shooting of sitting birds. The bird was fair game whether in flight, on water, or on land. Aksakov himself describes with more than a tinge of regret the ravages wrought by his shooting confrères and himself on the breeding marshes of the black-tailed godwit.

The Anglo-Saxon reader may need to bear in mind the very different shooting traditions of Continental Europe. It is not only in Russia and not only in the nineteenth century that the indiscriminate shooting of wildlife, particularly migratory birds, reaches devastating proportions.

As Aksakov himself points out, the more respect a hunter has for a particular species of bird, the harder he tries to kill it. His own joy at finding his first little bustard's nest is the greater for being able to rob it of all its eggs. On finding a coot's nest with eggs he takes the nest home with him, while the parent bird pipes in alarm. He tells with pleasure how he shot every bird in the only family of partridges he encountered. The acquaintance whom he quotes at length gives advice on the surest way to hunt down every bird in a covey.

Aksakov is well aware of the paradoxes here and occasionally gives them some emphasis, while speaking of the destruction in which he himself so energetically participated. Only rarely does he recount how his affection for certain species that he has observed caused him to steal away without attempting to shoot them (see Category I, Chapter 17, on the little stint).

The modern reader needs to bear in mind that the concept of conservation had not yet been invented; shocking as Aksakov's attitudes may sometimes appear to naturalists and ecologists of a later age, they do not exclude a deep feeling for the life of the wild or a genuine interest in increasing the store of human knowledge. Aksakov is typically self-deprecating in disclaiming any pretensions to serious science: he repeatedly insists that this work and his fishing notes are not a natural history of all forms of game, "merely the notes of a passionate hunter and observer." It must be acknowledged, however, that his observations as a collector (to use a possibly outdated term) yield a fuller picture of many species than can be obtained by most modern bird-watchers with binoculars. The many hours spent by the dedicated wildfowler in pursuit of his prey, or in patient observation while waiting for the chance to make a kill, yield a wealth of knowledge of behavioral characteristics. We have only to read his account of the feeding habits of the black grouse or the nesting behavior of the black-tailed godwit to appreciate that the extent of his knowledge compares very favorably with that of many field ornithologists. His hunter's eye and his examination of freshly killed specimens yield much detail on seasonal variations in size and weight within species, and by dissecting the birds he obtains detailed information on their diet. But to many readers he will seem at his best in his loving descriptions, feather by feather, of the plumage and physical characteristics of these specimens, in his precision in conveying every tint and every curve of beak or wing.

Aksakov takes a highly individual view of the wildlife he knows so well. Of certain species he is very fond. These include the partridge, for its appearance and its flavor; the crane, whose courtship antics are so entertaining; the wood pigeon, whose conjugal devotion he finds most affecting; and several small sandpipers with endearing habits. (Aksakov's fondness for the wood pigeon would surprise many in western Europe, where the bird is regarded as a pest.) Others he holds in contempt for a variety of personal reasons: the oystercatcher has unattractive plumage, he says, and an unpleasant flavor, even when fat; the tufted duck is also an unappealing bird and one that merits no special attention as game. We learn that most fowlers have no time for the lapwing because it is found everywhere and is very tame. Some species, such as the common merganser (goosander) are practically inedible but still good sport because their habits make them elusive quarry.

Soviet editors and commentators on Aksakov's work were given to pointing out that he set much store by the views, myths, and sayings of the *narod*, the common people. While it is clear that ideological considerations played a role here, it is undoubtedly true that Aksakov had absorbed much peasant lore relating to wildlife and found in it a store of valuable knowledge. Who, after all, would be likely to have a closer knowledge of bird and animal life than the peasant working the land? While no doubt greatly appreciating the factual element, Aksakov is also fond of retailing the folklore attached to some species. His accounts of their lives and habits gain color from the mythology, such as the story of the mating of the black grouse: impregnation is supposedly achieved by the gray-hen consuming the saliva of the male; or of the turtledove: on losing its mate, the surviving member of the pair is so distraught that it commits suicide by plunging to earth from a height.

Humans, other than the author and unnamed drivers, trappers, and informants, do not figure prominently in a work that has as its heroes a large number of species of bird. We do, however, learn something of the class distinctions between types of fowlers and trappers. Though all classes eat their quarry, there are those who kill game for a livelihood, therefore taking as much as they can for sale or consumption, and those whose material need is less acute or nonexistent, for whom shooting is above all a sport. To the latter it is a question of prowess in overcoming, for example, the speed and zigzag flight of a snipe or the wariness of the capercaillie. Aksakov of course is firmly in the category of the sportsmen, though doubtless untypical in the extent and depth of his study of game.

With this work and the earlier *Notes on Fishing*, Aksakov established himself as a leading practitioner of the nascent art of nature writing, a genre that was to be developed in a later period by Mikhail Prishvin, Ivan Sokolov-Mikitov, and Vladimir Soloukhin, among others. It has been a less visible tradition in the turbulent twentieth century than the prose and poetry of massive social upheaval and has not caught the attention of translators to the same extent. Nevertheless it remains well known and well loved by Russian readers and repays serious attention. Aksakov, one of its earliest exponents, has proved the most enduring and abidingly popular.

NOTES

1. Readers interested in learning more about Aksakov's life and work may refer to A. R. Durkin, *Sergej Aksakov and Russian Pastoral* (New Brunswick, N.J., 1983). In Russian the standard work is S. I. Mashinsky, *S. T. Aksakov: zhizn' i tvorchestvo* (Moscow, 1973).

2. A more detailed comparison of Aksakov and White as ornithologists may be found in Kevin Windle, "Sergei Timofeevich Aksakov i Gil'bert Uait: zametki o dvukh literatorakh-ornitologakh," in *Problemy sovremennoi rusistiki*, ed. Antoni Markunas (Poznań, 1995).

3. The comment was made in a review published in *Sovremennik;* see I. S. Turgenev, *Polnoe sobranie sochinenii v 30-ti tomakh* (Moscow, 1980), 4:518.

ON THE TRANSLATION

This translation is based on S. T. Aksakov, *Zapiski ruzheinogo okhotnika Orenburgskoi gubernii*, edited by S. V. Kirikov (Moscow, 1953). Frequent reference has also been made to Sergei Timofeevich Aksakov, *Sobranie sochinenii v piati tomakh*, edited by S. I. Mashinsky (Moscow, 1966). Both these editions use Aksakov's revised edition of 1857. There are no significant discrepancies in the text, but the editorial apparatus differs, each edition providing valuable background information.

Aksakov appended numerous notes to his text, particularly in its later additions, often adding information supplied by his readers. Most of these notes have been preserved, but some have been absorbed into the text and a few (those which were judged to be of little interest to the English-speaking reader) discarded. Notes added by the translator are marked *Trans.* In many cases the translator's notes cite observations made by the editors of the modern Russian editions and the ornithologists K. F. Rul'e and M. A. Menzbir quoted by the editors of these editions.

Aksakov's text has been subjected to a small amount of editing in the translation process, primarily in his Preface. In the original this begins with some fifteen pages devoted to technical details and specifications of shotguns, powder, shot, and cartridges, and to gun-dogs and their training. As he tells us, this section was designed to be of help to the rural wildfowler of the 1850s. Turgenev commented that it was "rather feeble and incomplete" and added that the book proper really began after this. In this translation the Preface has been abridged after the opening paragraphs, the section on guns and dogs removed, and the preceding and following text slightly adjusted to allow for this. At a very few other points a sentence or part of a sentence, usually dealing with Russian terminology, has been omitted.

Aksakov presents a number of problems for the English translator, first, because he is writing about a specialized area of experience to which he has devoted a lifetime of study, and second, because he is famous for the extraordinary range of his vocabulary. This is less the language of the scientist (indeed, certain English terms that can be avoided only with difficulty in the translation, such as "species" and "habitat," smack rather too strongly of modern scientific writing), than that of the educated countryman, born and raised in a rural environment, accustomed from earliest youth to giving everything about him its proper name and intolerant of imprecise usage. When this is coupled with the literary vocabulary of the intelligentsia, as is the case with Aksakov, the range of expression is formidable. The richness of his language and his ability to convey the finest nuances have long been recognized. The variety of specific terms for the tracks left by different animals, particularly hares, is especially daunting. To my knowledge, English, unlike Russian, does not possess a comparable range of terms denoting various types of track.

It is difficult to match either Aksakov's range or his precision in any form of English a hundred and fifty years after the publication of the original. Although the ornithological and botanical terms have equivalents, those relating to various aspects of Russian rural life or descriptions of landscapes often do not. Modern Russian editions of Aksakov's works, such as *Sobranie sochinenii*, edited by S. I. Mashinsky, often provide a glossary of words likely to be unfamiliar to the Russian reader. Readers of the English translation, whether American, British, or Australian, may therefore come across terms that lie outside their everyday vocabulary, but that fill a definite need. I have not hesitated, for instance, to speak of an "alder carr," meaning specifically a stand of alders on marshy ground, rather than a "grove," which seems more appropriate to other species in different terrain. A "fall" of woodcock or other migratory species, meaning its sudden appearance in numbers, or the blackcock's lek (display ground), may be familiar only to ornithologists. This is the vocabulary of the equivalent English genre and to avoid using it would be to give the text an unwanted pallor, of which Aksakov cannot be accused. In most cases the meaning of these terms will emerge clearly from the context; in many cases there is no need for explanatory notes as Aksakov himself explains the less common Russian terms.

The ornithological terms have their own poetry, of which Aksakov is very much aware, as well as their own associations, on which he often comments. These will only rarely match those of the English names. The names "pesochnik" and "little ringed plover" refer to the same bird but they describe it in very different terms; the Russian might be rendered as "sand bird" or "sanderling," if the latter were not the English name of a different species (*Calidris alba;* Russian, *peschanka*). In the translation, of course, standard English names replace the Russian, but in every section the Russian names are also given (those used by Aksakov in addition to the modern names where these differ), as well as the current scientific names. Since Aksakov frequently comments on the meaning and derivation of the Russian names, it has been necessary in many cases to append notes clarifying their associations; in some cases, however, Aksakov's linguistic remarks have been edited in the translation process.

In the translator's notes occasional reference is made to two standard English works that have been useful: W. B. Lockwood, *The Oxford Dictionary of British Bird Names* (Oxford, 1993); and T. A. Coward, *The Birds of the British Isles and Their Eggs*, 3 vols. (London, first published 1920).

When Aksakov gives dates from his diaries or for the arrival and departure of migratory birds, the dates are according to the "Old Style" or Julian calendar then in use. To convert these dates to the "New Style" or Gregorian calendar, twelve days must be added.

Russian names have been transliterated according to a slightly modified form of the Library of Congress system, the usual exceptions being made for names which have become familiar in other forms.

Notes of a Provincial Wildfowler

PREFACE

I first thought I would begin my wildfowling notes by speaking in detail about all aspects of hunting, not only of shooting and game, its haunts and habits in the province of Orenburg, but also of pointers, shotguns, and various accessories and broadly of the technical aspects. Now that I have set to work on it I realize that since I set aside my gun the technical side has greatly advanced and that I have little detailed knowledge of the current state of affairs. Where is the point, for example, of speaking now of certain famous old breeds of dog, of how to rear them and keep them, when the breeds no longer exist, or of training, which has changed because the fowler's requirements have changed? Why speak of the famous fowling pieces of old when they are preserved only as mementos of times past, in the gun-rooms of old wildfowlers?

At the outset, then, I shall speak of those fundamentals that will not change or age and about things that I, with my long experience and passion for the chase and for observation, have noticed. Moreover, my little book may find its way into the hands of country wildfowlers who live far from big cities, people of modest means who cannot afford to order ready-made modern equipment. I confess that I would like my book to be of use to precisely such readers as this. It pleases me to think that my advice on technical aspects, my observations on the habits of game birds, and my notes on shooting itself may be of help to them. It is for them that this Preface is designed.

I do not know who is meant by the words "a real hunter," a phrase I shall not often use: one who pursues mainly marshland game and woodcock, hardly bothering with bustards, partridges, and young blackcocks, and looking with disdain upon all other birds, especially large ones; or one who zealously pursues all kinds of birds according to the season: marshland birds, waterfowl, grassland and forest birds, scorning all difficulties and even finding pleasure in surmounting them? I shall not presume to judge this matter, saying only that I myself always belonged to the latter category, those who could never reside permanently in the capital cities, because it is necessary to travel too far to locate many kinds of birds and subject oneself to great deprivation and effort.

The second of these categories was formerly much more numerous. Now, however, the first is in the majority. The requirements of this majority of today's fowlers regarding the quality of a shotgun are now much changed. It follows that the best of gunsmiths now make guns to meet the current requirements of the majority, that is they make them primarily for shooting smaller game birds. [. . .]

I must repeat a little of what I said in the Foreword to my *Notes on Fishing:* my little book is neither a treatise on shooting nor a natural history of all forms of game. My book is no more and no less than the simple notes of a passionate hunter and observer: sometimes quite full and detailed, sometimes superficial and one-sided, but always written in good conscience. Russia has many hunters, and I do not doubt they will be well disposed.[1] Learned naturalists may fully rely on my words: I never present suppositions as fact and assert nothing that I have not witnessed with my own eyes.

SPRING PASSAGE

The season dearest to the sportsman's heart, and the most poetic, is the spring—the time of the spring passage and return of the game birds. He will have spent the winter glancing with fading heart at his favorite fowling piece hanging idly on the wall, taking it down occasionally and quite unnecessarily to clean the barrels and oil the moving parts. At last the long, monotonous season of blizzards draws to a close. February may have brought huge snowdrifts so deep that you could only walk on a well-trodden path. By late March, however, early in the morning, it is possible to walk without skis on the frozen crust of the snow, which is sometimes so firm that you can drive a team of horses over it. Through the trees you can sometimes creep up on a blackcock as it begins its courtship call; you may stumble unexpectedly upon a hare, either in its spring coat, with black tail and mottled lambskin stripe along its back, or in its pure white winter coat, not yet beginning to turn gray although the molt has begun; or if you pipe on a whistle you may attract a hazel grouse and thus be able to put some fresh unfrozen game on your table. . . .[2]

But the morning frosts of March are treacherous, and so is the crust on the surface of the snow, especially on a fine day. As soon as the sun begins to warm it, it thins and begins to sag, giving muffled cracks like distant gunfire, and will no longer support a man's weight. At every step you sink to the waist in the snow beneath.[3] To stray far from the road is a mistake: you will wear yourself out and take hours to cover one verst. Even if you have skis, hunting on them is very wearisome, as great agility and skill, as well as practice, is needed to control them on uneven surfaces.

Soon the days are noticeably longer. The sun's rays fall straighter, and provide real warmth at midday. The white shroud of snow shows darker bands, and the roads show through as dark ribbons. In the streets lie pools of water. As March turns to April, the passionate hunter, such as I was in my youth—and who, I believe, will never be extinct in Russia—experiences a period of tense anticipation. If spring is not late in coming, the spring migrants gradually begin to appear. The rooks, the ruination of parks and gardens, and of old, tall trees, arrive first and reclaim their summer quarters in the best birch and aspen groves close to human habitation—the better to have access to grain. They soon begin to repair their old nests with new material, using their strong, whitish beaks to break off twigs from the upper branches. Their loud, monotonous cawing carries far and wide toward evening, when, after their day's labor, they gather in council, always perching in pairs, as if to discuss plans for the morrow.

This is the time to begin daily morning and afternoon rounds of the threshing floors, drying sheds, and millponds strewn with yellow chaff where the water is just beginning to flow. There you are likely to find stock doves, at first in very small numbers: two or three at the most. They may occur in flocks of jackdaws or feral pigeons, foraging for grain along the tracks to threshing floors. At first glance they are not easy to distinguish from feral pigeons, the so-called Russian doves. The difference is that the stock dove is a little smaller and daintier, and dove-gray all over, with pale flesh-colored—not red—legs. It will hardly be necessary to explain that the name "Russian dove" signifies that it is common and tame. But if you see some pigeons from afar, perched on a fence or tree above a threshing floor, you may be sure that they are stock doves; on drawing closer you will be able to confirm this. On their arrival, pigeons, like all other birds, look clean, sleek, and plump. It is difficult to explain why this should be since migratory birds have covered long distances, and food is scarce. Later in the year the stock dove is of less interest to the hunter, but if you can shoot one in midwinter it is a rare prize.

But the air becomes warmer and carries more moisture as April comes into its own, with puddles and rivulets of turbid water on every hand. The snow cover is darkened by patches of thawing ground like stains on a white tablecloth. The springs have thawed, along with the manure heaps and the millpond dam, where manure is spread. By the springs you should look out for redwings and fieldfares, and round the millponds, lapwings (peewits), larks, hoopoes, and starlings. The open water of the river, which even in winter rarely freezes above the millpond, now reaches to the furthest banks of reeds. The deep water is a cold unfriendly blue, but it is time to turn attention to the river, as goldeneye and grebes will soon appear there.[4] In a little while, all this will be set at nought and then forgotten, but at first everything is fresh and precious. . . . But such is the nature of man, and not only a man armed with a shotgun!

At last the completion of the thaw is upon us: a warm sou'westerly breeze devours the snow, now saturated by rain. The ground has mostly thawed, especially on high ground exposed to the midday sun. A different picture presents itself: here and there on the black tapestry of the fields white spots and the ribbons of snowdrifts can be seen, and the winter road, much traveled and firmly packed down, stands out with its dark ridge of dung. The gullies, having first filled with raging blue water, are now still. Their waters have swelled the river, which has forced up the ice in the millpond, burst its banks, and flooded the low-lying areas. This is the season of spring floods. Steam rises from the ground. The earth is "recovering," as the peasants say. The sky is gray and the air dank and misty. It is precisely at this melancholy time that full-scale migration begins, and not only during twilight and darkness, but throughout the day. Until now geese and swans have appeared mostly in pairs, flying high in the gray clouds; now they pass over in great skeins. The cranes come later, sailing in the heavens in broad, extended wedges, like warships in battle formation. Flocks of every species of duck pass over continually, one after another in the daytime; on very fine days they fly high, but on misty and rainy days, and in twilight, they fly low, and at night, when they pass unseen, many species of duck can be identified by the whistle of their wings. Goldeneye, tufted duck, and wigeon have the fastest wingbeats and slice through the air fastest; the sound of their wings merges into a single piercing whistle. Next in speed come shoveler, teal, pintail, and others; and last come mallard and gadwall, whose flight is fairly unhurried, although swift and powerful.

Flocks of curlew (or whaup), black-tailed godwit, ruffs and reeves, and all the other species of small waders, each with its own distinctive flight, its own cry and whistle, fill the air with a variety of sounds, often indistinct and sometimes barely audible. It should be noted that birds on passage do not produce their usual calls, while those arriving and occupying their breeding grounds, even if only temporarily, immediately give the typical calls of the species. Passage migrants are in a hurry, hastening urgently onward, never looking back, to that promised land where they must set to work building their nests and raising their young. Birds that have already reached their destination fly lower, with less haste, looking out for suitable sites, and seeming to converse among themselves in their own tongue, then suddenly alighting as if by common consent. This is the time of what fowlers term "falls"—a word laden with meaning and used exclusively to signify the sudden appearance in numbers of the most prized game birds: woodcock, great snipe, common snipe, and jack snipe. One day you may have taken a good dog and tramped over a marsh, or along the sodden bank of a millpond, or over the puddles of last year's rye- and wheatfields, treading with difficulty through the heavy black earth, and seeing nothing. And early the next morning the marshes, puddles, and flooded fields hold snipe, great snipe, and jack snipe, and the wet fields may sometimes hold a wide variety of all species of game—steppe birds, marshland birds, waterfowl, and even woodland game. The word "fall" expresses all of this.

At this time, in the thawed cereal fields, and on fallow and steppe land, great and little bustards make their appearance, along with sociable plovers. Golden plovers, or "whistlers," begin to whirl in vast flocks beneath the clouds, so high that the naked eye cannot always discern them, but you can clearly hear their constant call, consisting of two short notes—the first high, the second lower. The sheer number of birds makes the calls seem uninterrupted, blending into a single, even tune, soothing to the hunter's ear. When they tire of gamboling and pirouetting in the sun on high, they descend noisily onto the winter crops, and run about nimbly in search of food.

Curlew join the grassland birds a little later, and in smaller parties than when gathering to depart. They wade in the mud beside puddles of water on plowed land, sometimes sinking to the belly despite their long legs, thrusting their long, curved bills to the hilt into the soft ground to extract grains and all kinds of grubs and insects.

The woodcock have already been here some time. Nobody saw when, how, or in what numbers they arrived, but as soon as the ground first begins to thaw, in open woodland, on the forest fringe, in parks and gardens, among raspberry, gooseberry, and other bushes, especially in marshy scrub, beside springs, woodcock appear, sometimes singly, sometimes in sudden large falls.

In places where marshes are few, or where they are completely awash with water and resemble large lakes, snipe, great snipe, and jack snipe like to stick together in large flocks where spring torrents, streaming down from the hills, spread out over valley slopes or gentle declivities, and make their way slowly through grassland, soaking it thoroughly and making it marshy. This happens a little later than the first appearance of these three noble game species and lasts no more than four or five days. Falls vanish as suddenly as they appear. I have sometimes come upon such flocks when almost out of ammunition. After hastening home to rearm, I returned a few hours later to find nothing! Not one bird! Not a feather, as hunters say.

At last the floodwaters abate, the fields and meadows dry out, the rivers subside, and number of birds declines. Large flocks are no longer to be found: the passage migrants have passed through, and the summer visitors have paired and cling close to the sites they have chosen for their nests. Only a few unpaired birds roam about aimlessly. The common and great snipe occupy their former marshland territory, and sometimes new marshes as well, and immediately begin their courtship. The snipe begin to drum, twisting and turning in the blue spring heavens, plummeting from on high in a steep arc, and soaring sharply up again. . . .[5] The time of shooting at newly arrived birds is over.

I must turn to history to throw a broader light on spring migration in Orenburg province in the past, which now seems fabulous. Birds were so numerous that all the marshes, water meadows, pond fringes, plowed fields, valleys, and gullies with their spring freshets were covered with them. "The air groaned" (as the peasants say) with their varied calls, cries, whistles, and the rush of their wings slicing the air in every direction. Even at night with the windows closed, the ardent hunter would be prevented from sleeping. There were birds everywhere: in the garden, among the vegetables, on threshing floors, in the street. . . . That seems hard to believe, but I can assure you that often on going out shooting early in the morning I would find wild duck and pigeons beside puddles in the middle of the street. When you drew near a marsh or a place where a river had overflowed you would be completely at a loss: different species of plovers and sandpipers would be standing there or running about. Flocks of motley ruffs would be darting to and fro among them. Ducks, with their brightly colored drakes, from the sturdy mallard to the nimble little teal, would be exploring the mud, swimming on the water or perched on tussocks. Common snipe would spring up at furious speed from under your very feet while great snipe and jack snipe also took wing. At the same time, apart from those on the ground, new, mixed flocks of many representatives of the avian kingdom wheeled and soared overhead, rising, descending, and flying from one spot to another, every movement accompanied by a special joyful cry. The young fowler would be in a serious quandary: which birds should he choose? Which should he shoot at? And the very superabundance could turn into slim pickings . . .

But those who remember such scenes in Orenburg province are now few. Everything has changed. In the whole of our bountiful province there is now not so much as a tenth of the former abundance of game. For what reasons I know not. But, lest any reader should think that this is the fond memory of an old man who thinks that in his youth everything was bigger and better, I can say that unfortunately this is a generally known fact. I do not share the view that the terrible decline is due to a rapid increase in the human population or an increase in the number of fowlers. I shall not attempt to justify myself or my fellow hunters of that period. In our youth it is true we went in less for hunting than for massacre; but why should there be less and less game with every passing year in areas where nobody shoots at all? And in any case the number of fowlers was always insignificant in proportion to the size of the region. It is clear that there must be other reasons unknown to us. A gradual decline in the number of birds in the province of Orenburg set in long ago, at a time when there was plenty of room for beast, bird, and man. And indeed there is still plenty of room even today.

THE CLASSIFICATION OF GAME BIRDS

I have mentioned the word "game" several times without yet providing a definition. In its strict sense, the word refers to wild birds and animals that can be used as food and that can be trapped or killed in various ways, but mostly by shooting. We are dealing here only with birds. The word "wild" (Russian, *dikii*, meaning "free, untamed") is usually applied to those species that have not been domesticated, or tamed, by man.[6] The domesticated species are few: geese, ducks, pigeons, chickens, and turkeys. To distinguish the first three from their wild cousins, they are popularly given the name "Russian geese," "Russian pigeons," and so forth.

All game birds may be divided into four classes according to their usual haunts, although these change with the seasons and the birds' food requirements: (I) marshland game, (II) waterfowl, (III) steppe and grassland game, and (IV) woodland game. Hunters will gladly shoot game of all categories, giving preference to one bird or another according to its rarity, to their particular needs, and the time of year, but most will prefer marshland birds to all others, so I begin my notes with these. It will suffice to say that they include snipe, great snipe, and jack snipe. This is the aristocracy among game, to which, among woodland birds, only the woodcock belongs.

Here then is my classification of game birds:

Category I: Marshland Game

1. Common snipe
2. Great snipe
3. Jack snipe
4. Black-tailed godwit
5. Spotted redshank
6. Oystercatcher
7. Greenshank
8. Redshank
9. Marsh sandpiper
10. Green sandpiper
11. Wood sandpiper
12. Red-necked phalarope
13. Dunlin
14. Terek sandpiper
15. Common sandpiper
16. Little ringed plover
17. Little stint
18. Ruff
19. Moorhen
20. Spotted crake
21. Lapwing or Peewit

Category II: Waterfowl

1. Swan
2. Gray-lag goose
3. Duck
   (a) Mallard
   (b) Pintail
   (c) Gadwall
   (d) Wigeon
   (e) Shoveler
   (f) Teal
   (g) Goldeneye
   (h) Tufted duck
   (i) Great crested grebe
   (j) Merganser
4. Coot

Category III: Steppe and Grassland Game

1. Great bustard
2. Common crane
3. Little bustard
4. Curlew
5. Sociable plover
6. Gray or Field partridge
7. Golden or Whistling plover
8. Black-winged pratincole
9. Corncrake
10. Quail

Category IV: Woodland Game

1. Capercaillie or Wood grouse
2. Black grouse
3. Hazel grouse
4. Willow grouse
5. Pigeons
   (a) Wood pigeon or Ring dove
   (b) Stock dove
   (c) Turtledove
6. The Thrush family
7. Woodcock
8. Hares
9. Small birds

Strictly speaking, this cannot be considered a fully exact classification, as we cannot define exactly the basis on which a bird is termed "waterfowl" or a "marshland," "grassland," or "woodland" species, for some contradictory features hamper a fully accurate division. Sometimes the same species can be found in the steppe, and in the forest, and sometimes in marshes. If, for example, we say that "marshland birds" are those that breed in marshes, then all species of ducks, geese, and swans must be termed "marshland birds." If we define "marshland birds" as those that not only breed there but live there permanently, then, besides moorhens, water-rails, snipe, great snipe, jack snipe, all the other numerous waders do not *live* in marshes, but only rear their young there. Some of them even nest on the dry banks of rivers and streams. By the same token the black grouse, a forest bird, lives for six months of the year in the open, and even frequents places completely clear of trees. The woodcock, also a woodland bird, in spring and especially in autumn favors bushes in wet marshland, and is found in woodland only at other seasons, while the corncrake, which I have classed with the grassland game, is equally at home in the steppe, amid grain crops, wet pastures, and at the edges of forests. Similar contradictions will be encountered in trying to categorize other game birds. We must then abandon any claim to total accuracy: it will be sufficient if the classification is approximate and has some sound basis.

CATEGORY I

Marshland Game

FOREWORD TO A DESCRIPTION OF MARSHLAND GAME

In embarking upon this account it seems to me best to begin with the best of game, to wit, with marshland game, among which the snipe, or more precisely, all three species of this noble family, stand out sharply and must take pride of place. We are dealing here with the common snipe, great snipe, and jack snipe, three species that resemble one another in plumage, build, appearance, and habits, and in their distinctive manner of feeding. The woodcock is another outstanding member of the family, but this bird will be described under "Woodland Game." What a pity it is that we have no Russian names for these species, but use instead one French name and three German names![1] Among the common people the snipe is known as the "wild sheep," as I mentioned earlier, and the woodcock as the "forest sandpiper" or "red sandpiper." In books the woodcock is also known as *sluka*, and it is said that this is an ancient name still in use in popular speech in southern Russia. I do not know, but I can state with confidence that the word *sluka* is not known in central or eastern regions. The great snipe and jack snipe have no popular names, being known simply as "little gray sandpipers that live in tussocks in the marshes." Some forty years ago I read in a book on hunting that in Russian the great snipe is called *lezhanka;* in a later book, that the great snipe is called *stuchik* and the jack snipe *lezhanka*, but none of this is correct. Among the people, *lezhanka* refers to a mythical kind of quail with red legs, reputed to be so fat that it is unable to fly. Its fat is alleged to possess a curious property: it provokes aching and slight cramps in the arms and legs, and indeed the whole body, of one who consumes it with gusto. It has been my experience to hunt down thousands of quail with falcons, to examine countless killed and netted birds, and to shoot many more, but never have I come across the fabled red-legged *lezhanka.* It is true that in autumn, quail are sometimes so well covered with fat that they rise only with difficulty, and I have picked up many caught by the hawk before they could take wing. The fresh fat of such birds, when used immediately in food, does indeed produce an aching sensation. I know this from my own experience, and that of others, but the fact is that these were common quail, even if they were uncommonly fat. When they have lain for a day or two in the cellar, or when salted, they may be eaten with no ill effects.

This same old book calls the jack snipe the "hairy sandpiper" but this is a translation of a German name that is unknown in Russia. It is not difficult to surmise why the Russian peasant has given no special name to the great snipe and jack snipe, while having his own special names for the snipe and woodcock. The former species lie concealed in marshes where the peasant does not venture without good reason. Snipe, on the other hand, could not fail to attract attention, and thus receive a name, when several at a time wheel in the sky at any time of day over the marshes where they nest, producing with their wings their sharp, far-carrying sound.[2] The woodcock, flying over the forest in the morning and evening in the season of roding, or spring courtship flight, producing its characteristic grunting and snoring cries, often rising in a flurry from under the feet of the peasant gathering firewood, was also noticed for its size and distinctive ruddy coloring, and given a name.

MARSHES

In speaking of marshland game, I shall often have occasion to mention the habitat itself, and will speak of it using various terms: "open," "wet," and "dry" marshes, and others—terms that, to people unfamiliar with such terrain, may convey little. I shall therefore say a little here about the characteristics of marshland habitat, which may be very varied.

Marshes may be "open pastureland." This term denotes ground that is wet only in spring and autumn, or in prolonged periods of rain, free of tussocks, partly covered with false hellebore and scattered bushes. With their thick, succulent grass, they provide abundant hay harvests, so can be called meadows. They may form the fringes of true marshland, and are almost always associated with watercourses in humus-rich black soil, especially in lowland, floodplain country.

"Dry marshland" is the name given to land that bears all the hallmarks of having earlier been fenland: tussocks, sometimes of enormous size, traces of dried-up springs, and various species of marsh grass, now interspersed with meadow species. For the most part, such land becomes overgrown with bushes, being unsuitable for hay-making. It is quite usual for wet marshes and swamps to turn into dry marshland, as springs dry up along with the sources of streamlets, but I have sometimes witnessed the reverse process: dry marshes, which for decades have been a sorry sight to behold, reverting to swamp and fen. This occurs mostly when a long, wet autumn so saturates the ground that it can absorb no more moisture, and sudden frosts ensue, followed by very heavy snowfalls, followed by a wet spring. Then the long-dry springs reopen, the whole area is soaked by the rising groundwater, and a dead marsh is returned to life; the meadow grasses are gone within a year, and in a few years the bushes and trees die too. In such wet years not only do dried-up springs flow again, but sometimes new springs underground appear and morasses form where previously there had been none.

Wet and tussock-covered marshes, invariably fed by underground springs, permanently waterlogged and seldom overgrown with willow scrub, do not give good cuts of hay because the abundant growth of marsh grasses and excessive moisture inhibit the growth of meadow grasses. The predominance of false hellebore, chamomile, and trefoil is visible everywhere. The soft surface of the ground gives slightly underfoot, but to no great depth, as a firmer layer lies immediately below it. On foot the going is not heavy, as the soil does not cling, and the ground has enough resistance. These marshes are the most widespread, and also the best for shooting. Often they are criss-crossed by streams flowing from springs, rather than dotted with spring-fed ponds.

The characteristics of a morass, with mud, standing water,

and permanently flowing springs, are quite different: there are no meadow grasses, and marshland vegetation is also sparse. In places, round patches, or long strips of liquid mud can be seen, with quite large puddles, sometimes reddish in color. Where this is the case, the morass is termed "rusty," or "rust-beds." The reddish tint in the water and mud unfailingly betrays the presence of iron ore. Tussocks here are few, and hardly any grass grows on the mud and rust-beds. Instead there is often much surrounding growth of dense and fine reed, horsetails, and uncommonly tall sedge. The surface of the water on the rust-covered pools is covered with a thin film that reflects a steely blue color in the sunlight. Water spiders race to and fro over it on their long, arc-like legs. The water in the spring pools, which are sometimes quite deep, although with no visible flow, remains fresh and cool even in summer, especially if drawn from the depths. The hunter seeking relief from the heat may brush aside with his cap the debris that collects on the surface, quench his thirst, and cool his head. . . . He will suffer no harm. He can go on his way across the marshes and soon be sweltering in the heat again. But the going is very heavy, especially near springs and patches of mud, where you can sometimes sink to the waist and not easily reach firmer ground. The reason for the presence of these quagmire patches and springs lies in the fact that a fine trickle of groundwater seeps imperceptibly through the silt and the upper layer of the soil. This seepage is so gradual that no flow can be seen: it merely forms little puddles of turbid, sometimes reddish water, which, however, is enough to saturate the marshland vegetation. The peat is exposed and turns into deep, treacherous mire. It dries out from the top, and at times of great heat and drought it even cracks, forming a deceptive trap for the unwary fowler: should he jump onto it from a tussock, delighted to find a dry spot, he will not easily extricate himself.

Although reeds and rushes sometimes grow in ordinary wet marshland, and even in the firmer parts of muddy swamps, there are also rush- and reed-marshes, which resemble wet marshland only in their soil type. They are covered in small tussocks and tufts of reeds that grow on or around them. In these marshes there is little grass. They may be muddy, but not treacherously so, and smaller livestock may wander without difficulty and without risk of sinking in, as may happen in swampland.

In most marshland, various species of moss can be found, but there are specifically mossy marshes (known as "blind" marshes), invariably overgrown with trees, mostly conifers. In the black-earth belt, these marshes are rare, hence their scarcity in the province of Orenburg; the Moscow region, on the other hand, excluding its southern fringe, has them in abundance. The ground is soft and uneven, without being treacherous. In rainy periods they are very wet, while during times of drought the clearings and lightly timbered areas may be completely dry, as they have no springs of any kind to feed them. These wooded marshes owe their origins to the proximity of clay soil, which does not absorb rainwater: the water collects on it as in a clay bowl, and the topsoil above the clay, constantly soaked and swelling with moisture, shielded from the sun by the branches above, gives rise to moss. Sometimes cranberries and whortleberries grow here in profusion. The beautiful green foliage of the latter is well known and its berries provide tasty and nourishing food not only for humans but also for some species of woodland animals and birds.

Lastly, there are peat bogs, not quite accurately known by the folk name "quaking marshes," as the ground does not so much quake as ripple underfoot. In the peasant expression, "the ground dances." These are nothing less than lakes—in the main shallow lakes, though some may be quite deep—covered by a dense and very strong layer of interwoven roots of marshland plants, bushes, and trees that grow on peat. In the middle of such marshes the deepest parts of the covered lake may remain open. Here nature does its work slowly, as I have had occasion to observe: the first basis is provided by aquatic vegetation, which, as is known, will grow at any depth and spread its leaves and flowers over the surface of the water; with every year's decay, these turn into a kind of jelly—the beginnings of peat, which is eventually compacted in thick layers. Of course, this process can take place only in standing water, and most easily where there is shelter from the wind. Duckweed, known by various names in Moscow and the province of Orenburg, covering standing water every summer, combines with the rotting aquatic vegetation, leaves, and pine needles, to form a dense mass floating on the water. (Duckweed appears on rivers too, but it is swept away by the stronger currents.) Spotted crakes and even moorhens run over this mass without falling through, leaving a web of interlacing tracks on the green carpet. When the wind drives this clinging mass to the bank, it adheres to it and becomes seeded by marshland grasses that readily take hold and whose long roots quickly lend it cohesion. Year by year this floating soil mass grows thicker and firmer, the grass cover gains strength, and its annual decay produces the peat soil. At length willows and osiers and even alders and birches begin to grow. The roots of these firmly anchor the soil, which is soon outwardly indistinguishable from the firm bank, of which it seems to be an extension. Eventually even tussocks appear. Sometimes large islets detach themselves and float aimlessly about the lake, with all their vegetation, trees, and birdlife, driven by the wind to one bank, then another, and sometimes becoming attached. This happens only on large, deep lakes; on small and medium-sized bodies of water the process of vegetation growth usually leads to an unbroken layer covering the surface completely from one side to the other, and within a few years the lake has the appearance of a flat marsh like any other, but appearances are deceptive. . . . The moment you are a few paces from the real edge, the surface does indeed begin to ripple, rising and falling not only under your feet but for some distance around, with all the vegetation—grass, flowers, shrubs, tussocks, and even trees. This may cause giddiness in the unwary, and walking on this surface will seem frightening, although it is not dangerous as long as the marsh has no "windows," that is, patches without a firm mat of roots. These patches are aptly called "suction holes," or "sinkholes," by the peasants. Large, clear "windows"—pools of liquid silt or water—can easily be seen, and nobody could fall into them. But smaller ones may be concealed, filled with greenish jelly-like slime, with old, dry grass in its upper layers and a covering of fresh, young shoots of fine grass. "Windows" of this type are extremely dangerous. Hunters, careless in the heat of the chase, often fall into them in their haste to catch a winged bird, as they fix their eyes on the spot where the bird has alighted or fallen, and do not look at the ground ahead. There have been occasions where such carelessness has cost a hunter his life. The liquid, silty, viscous mass, beneath which lies water, will suck a man in if he cannot manage to catch hold of something. It is a mistake to venture alone into marshes of this type. I can say with assurance that morasses sometimes turn into ordinary marshland: probably because the upper layer, growing thicker and heavier year by year, finally reaches the firm bottom and the water seeps to the surface and evaporates.

Such are the types of marsh that I am familiar with. The best of them is the open marsh—meadowland with scattered bushes and trees, which floods in spring. How wonderful this can be on a warm spring morning! When the water level has fallen, leaving wet patches and little crests of black soil deposited from the fields, vegetation thrives as nowhere else. The sun heats the moist, heavy soil, and seems to draw grass and flowers out of it: you can almost see them growing! The bushes and trees are coming out, and their leaves are coated with a scented sheen. Every bush, every tree is wrapped in its own envelope of fragrant air . . .

I pass on to a description of marshland game.

1. COMMON SNIPE

Bekas; Gallinago gallinago

I begin with the common snipe as it surpasses the great snipe and jack snipe in speed and is thus more difficult to bring down. Any true sportsman will grant its superiority here. In the body the snipe is a small bird, about the size of a three-day-old chick, but with a very long bill and legs. The back, wings, and short tail are covered in mottled feathers of a dark brown or a grayish color that is hard to define. The belly and lower breast are white; its dark, slightly bulging eyes are quite large, with a hint of merriment; its legs darkish, almost black. The three forward-pointing toes are equipped with quite long, sharp claws. The underwing is grayish or ashy blue with beautiful gray mottling under the shoulders; on the back the feathers are browner and longer. Each feather is bordered on one side with light yellow. The tip of the bill is slightly flattened, and both mandibles are criss-crossed by notches, rather like a nail file. On the whole the snipe, which does not stand out by having bright-colored plumage, has a handsome and lively appearance. Its bill is disproportionately long in relation to the body: in a large old bird it may be as much as two and a half inches; it uses it to probe the soft, marshland soil, or any other soil that is sufficiently moist, and pull up the whitish rootlets of grass and other vegetation that form its staple diet. Some attribute the delicate flavor of the bird's flesh to this diet. Wet marshes are its permanent haunts. With rare exceptions, it remains well concealed among the tussocks. When danger threatens it will immediately stretch out flat on the ground. It is rare to see one on the ground, and even rarer to shoot a sitting bird.

Snipe usually arrive in early April, always before great snipe and jack snipe, and are found early in the season on thawing marshland and beside spring melt-pools.[3] They may appear at once in large numbers, or gradually, in small parties. Sometimes frosts set in again after their arrival, there are fresh snowfalls, and the pools and marshes freeze over. The snipe then seek springs and the banks of streams, and even manure heaps—any place where the ground is soft. If the water level in the marshes is too high, or in terrain where there is little marshland, snipe resort to pools in fields of stubble and to spring streamlets on pastureland, as I have already mentioned. On arrival, snipe are wary and rise at a distance, not permitting either hunter or dog to come within range. This may be because the marshes and riverbanks are quite bare of cover, and the birds can find no refuge. On wet pasture, however, where last year's growth is thicker and taller, they are much more at ease. I have seldom met fowlers who have seen snipe on passage, but just once I myself saw a flock of snipe passing over very high, early one spring morning. Perhaps they fly at night, like many other migratory species. The fact that snipe can often be found in the morning in places where there were none the previous evening seems to confirm this. Snipe-shooting in spring is incomparably harder than in autumn, and I actually prefer it, although bags are smaller. I prefer it because, in the first place, in spring you appreciate any game, and snipe above all, and second, because the greater the difficulty, the greater the skill required and the more precious the bag. However, if he makes the effort, any skilled fowler can bring down snipe in numbers. Fine-grade shot, known as snipe-shot, Number Nine or sometimes Ten, is used, but on their first arrival a larger shot such as Number Eight is needed.

In spring, snipe are not so fat as in autumn, merely well rounded. They spring up at a distance, calling as they dart this way and that. Rising fast at a steep angle, twisting to right and left with their white underparts flashing, the bird is out of range within seconds. A true aim, swiftly taken, is the only way to be sure your shot will catch this fast-flying bird. There is no time for a long, carefully drawn aim, particularly because a newly arrived bird rises unexpectedly, allowing a dog no time to point or a hunter to prepare to fire. In autumn things are very different. Furthermore, in spring there are no young, tame, summer birds, which fly slower and straighter. They are all a year old or more, and masters of their wonderfully fast flight. Only a skilled hunter and a good gun can overcome this.

Snipe incubate their eggs in May in nests of dry grass, on marshland hummocks amid bushes. The hen bird usually lays four eggs about the size of pigeon's eggs, greenish in color with dark brown speckles. The eggs, like those of all the wader family, are distinctive in coming to a sharp point at the lower end, while the largest diameter is not at the waist, but close to the broad end. I cannot be sure, but I believe the cock shares the sitting with the hen and helps rear the young; he is, at least, always present, frolicking in the air close by. I have never come across social display grounds, and have never heard talk of such, so I suppose that snipe pair like related species.[4] It is true that snipe are said to display [Russian, *tokovat'*], but this is because, after a period of energetic cavorting beneath the clouds, the male usually descends to the ground with a cry of "tokoo-tokoo, tokoo-tokoo."[5] With this cry he sometimes scurries about on the ground, but he usually gives this call while perched on a dead branch or high tree-stump, or even on a bush; the latter perch, however, is very rare. I also know that some commercial hunters lure courting males by mimicking the call of the female, and shoot them on the ground. But all this is by the way. Alas, my observations have gone no further; although I have found many nests of snipe, have paid them particular attention, and watched them from cover, I have never managed to see anything that might shed light on this question.

At the end of May the eggs hatch, and at first the birds keep to dense marshland cover, in young reeds, swamps, and coverts. As soon as the young have grown a little, the female leads them into pasture areas of the marsh, where the ground is drier and the grass thick and tall. There she will stay with them until they are full-grown. By the end of June (sometimes by mid-June, and occasionally even earlier in the month) the young birds begin to fly—straight, slowly, and not very far; on the ground they sit tight and allow a dog to point at close range. I have sometimes killed a brace of old birds at this time, which leads me to conclude that the males also stay with the young. The hen does not display the same determination in protecting her young as a duck and gray-hen: she does not try to lure predators away and does not put her own life at risk. Until the beginning of August it is really hardly worth shooting young snipe: it is too easy and their flesh is too soft, somehow slippery, and lacking in flavor. But, like all zealous hunters, in my youth I did not abstain!

When the female birds begin to incubate, the males stay close to them, and the unpaired birds disperse over hummocky marshland. This is the beginning of the summer snipe season, when bags are small. In July they hide away in inaccessible places and molt. The molt, however, is gradual, and does not prevent them flying fast. But at this season they are hard to find, and it is very difficult to shoot snipe rising among thickets. At the end of July they reappear in open marshes, and remain there until the autumn migration, but they never gather in large flocks as they do on arrival in spring. The best period for snipe-shooting is between early August and mid-September. The later autumn comes on, the fatter the birds, but I have never known common snipe to grow as fat as great snipe and jack snipe sometimes do. In extensive marshes that are not too soft, or at least, not soft everywhere, but firm underfoot, covered with low tussocks and bushes not tall enough to hamper shooting, whole shooting parties may hunt together: each man should have his own well-trained dog and they should walk in line abreast at a fixed distance one from another. If the party is not too large, and all members are true hunters, such shooting can be most agreeable and successful. If, however, there is even one inexpert, inexperienced, or overzealous hunter in the party, and worse still, if he has a half-trained and eager dog, the day's sport will be ruined. I must confess that I have never been fond of shooting in large groups but have preferred to hunt alone or in pairs, at most in a threesome, for as soon as you have a large group with numerous dogs it becomes impossible to observe the conditions that make for successful and agreeable sport.

Nowhere have I found such extensive or splendid shooting marshes as in the provinces of Simbirsk and Penza, particularly those on the border between these two, along the River Inza. Expert fowlers would gather here and the shoots were fabulously productive. In one field a single double-barreled gun in the hands of the best shots could bring down up to sixty snipe, great snipe, and woodcock, which in autumn flock in from the forests and frequent the thickets and marshy levels that flank the river. Jack snipe were scarcer, since they prefer different types of marshes.

Snipe begin to disappear at varying times in different years: sometimes in early September, sometimes mid-September, and sometimes they remain in small numbers until mid-October. I am unable to explain the reason for this wide variation but, whatever some sportsmen may think, the closeness of winter plays no part. On the whole it is possible to say that if water levels are maintained by moderate rain and the autumn is mild, then marshland birds will stay longer; drought, on the other hand, encourages them to leave. Snipe do not, incidentally, always leave at once. It often happens that many will depart while others remain until the hard frosts set in and the marshes begin to freeze. It is my supposition that those birds that hatched last, or the weaker, sickly birds, stay longest. The fact that it is rare to shoot a fat bird late in the season seems to confirm this. The latest date at which I have shot a snipe, and a plump one at that, is 18 October. This was in the steppe, beside a small autumn pool, when the ground already had a light covering of snow. The earliest was on 23 March, when the blinding white snow was still untouched by the thaw and the only signs of melting were in the village streets. I was following the course of the Buguruslan River (in Orenburg province) on skis. The river had long been free of ice as it had little ice even in the harshest frosts. I was after some pochard that had flown upstream from the vicinity of the pool. All of a sudden a snipe sprang up with a cry from under the overhanging bank, where a small spring flowed into the river. I was so surprised that my heart skipped a beat, and I almost let the prized quarry fly out of range, but I recovered and fired. . . . My gun was loaded with grouse-shot. One pellet injured the right wing at the carpal, where the last two pinions are rooted. The snipe descended more than two hundred paces off, on the far bank of the river, and started running quickly along the ice cover, hopping and flapping its wings. . . . My dog was unwilling to plunge from the steep, high, snow-covered bank into the water, and I did not know what to do, but the clever animal ran to a bridge half a kilometer away, caught the bird, and brought it to me without crushing a single feather. . . . I was delighted with it.

I have more than once used the expression "out of range," whose meaning will be plain to all, but how does one determine whether a snipe or other fast-flying bird is within range? I have heard experienced hunters say that if you cannot make out the mottling of a snipe's plumage you should not fire because the bird is out of range. But this rule is worthless since a short-sighted hunter cannot make out the mottling at even fifteen paces, so he should never fire at a snipe, yet such a hunter can often bring down snipe just as well as a keen-sighted one. As a rough guide, it can be said with some assurance that forty paces is the best range and fifty the outside limit for successful snipe-shooting. The hunter learns to judge this distance by eye. Of course there can be lucky shots, but these should be discounted. Occasionally you can hit a snipe at sixty paces, or even seventy, but these are shots fired on the off chance, in near certainty of missing.

To my mind the very best of snipe-shooting occurs when the bird is gamboling on high, unaware of the hunter's presence. As soon as it sees you it swiftly rises to a great height where snipe-shot is unlikely to reach. These were my favorite shots, for which I successfully used Number Seven shot, as it carries a little further, and strikes harder, being slightly bigger. The range is always more than sixty paces. You can fire only when the bird is directly overhead, which means that you have to hold your weapon absolutely vertical. This is a most uncomfortable position, and since the charge is traveling vertically upward it loses momentum that much faster. Many shots have sailed harmlessly into the blue, to fall back, like a shower of rain, round the hunter. If your aim is true the bird tumbles slowly, in a spiral, from the sky. Fowlers will know the beauty of that spiral, and the keen sense of triumph with which they follow it.

Two singular occurrences have taken place when I have been shooting snipe. Once I hit a snipe overhead and it fell in gentle circles to the ground some ten paces off, landing spread-eagled on a large tussock. I could see it clearly and I took my time, reloading as I approached to pick it up. But as I reached out to take it it sprang up and flew away, as if unharmed, before I could collect myself. At that time snipe were scarce, and my aim had been faultless, so I was sorry to lose the bird.

On another occasion my dog brought me a winged snipe. I took it, thinking it had been killed outright, and tossed it down beside me while I reloaded. The bird lay for a minute or so then flew off with a cry (a wounded bird is silent). In order to prevent such annoying losses I made it a rule to finish off any bird that is injured but still alive, and I would advise all hunters to do the same, and be sure to pierce the head properly, since a bird carelessly pierced, so that the point misses the brain, can still fly away, as has happened to me more than once, particularly when hunting blackcock in autumn.

2. GREAT SNIPE

Dupel'shnep; Gallinago media

This bird is generally known in Russian as *dupel'* and I myself follow this practice. Although incorrect, this form is shorter and easier to pronounce. I have given pride of place to the common snipe, but not all hunters would share my opinion. Most prefer the great snipe, which, as its German name (*Doppel*) indicates, is almost twice as big—no trifle this, to a sportsman.[6] It carries much more fat than the snipe and therefore has more flavor. It permits both hunter and dog to come closer, is more tolerant of pointers, and flies slower and straighter. This is why most hunters place it first among marshland game. While not disputing these persuasive arguments, I repeat that I prefer the common snipe for the speed of its flight, and because it is incomparably harder to bring down. The great snipe is so similar to the common snipe in plumage and build that at first they are difficult to tell apart, until you observe the difference in size and the belly, which is not white in the great snipe, but mottled gray. On close inspection it will be seen that the neck and legs are shorter and the bill shorter and thicker. The legs are slightly greener and the underwing much more heavily mottled. The tip of the great snipe's beak, however, has the same tiny notches as that of the snipe.

Great snipe arrive or appear in wet areas sometimes one week, sometimes two, later than snipe, when the weather is a little warmer, as can be seen from my detailed records, spanning twelve years of observations of migration in Orenburg province. They choose habitat less wet and exposed than snipe, preferring less swampy ground among tussocks. They also appear on flooded pastures and fallow plowland overgrown with tall weeds or wormwood, and even in fields with tall stubble standing from the previous year's cereals.

On rising, the great snipe's wings produce a rush of air that the trained ear will distinguish at once from the snipe, even if the sound comes from behind. Once airborne it flies silently, without producing its muffled grunting note, and it alights much sooner than a snipe would. When the period of spring "falls" is past—a time when all three prime species of game are found together, snipe, great snipe, and jack snipe, about whose superiority I have already said enough—great snipe occupy their breeding grounds, in marshes with tussocks, small bushes, sometimes large bushes (not too wet) and begin to gather at their display sites, where they remain all night, so that in early morning they can always be found there, at their chosen sites. Courtship display takes place at night, and so, despite all my best efforts, I have been unable to observe it and form a clear, detailed impression of it. I only know that as soon as the sun begins to set, great snipe congregate at a known site, always fairly dry, level, and usually in an open space overgrown with false hellebore, surrounded by large bushes, where not one bird can be found during the day. It is possible that females join these gatherings, although they continue long after the females have started sitting, and even when the eggs have begun to hatch. I have watched great snipe at twilight chasing after one another, hopping up and down with wings drooping and short tails cocked and spread, like courting blackcock or turkey-cocks. The white undertail coverts, of fine down, often flash in the darkness, but it is impossible to see them clearly. One may only presume, with some assurance, that during this time mating takes place and that the males hotly contest the females among themselves: the crushed grass and plucked feathers that litter the ground lend weight to this supposition. Courtship gatherings last from early May until mid-June. Of course, all the dates I have given may vary by several days, depending on the weather. When the shooting at spring "falls" is over, wildfowlers take advantage of these courtship gatherings and use dogs to flush the birds, at eventide until almost all light is gone, and from first light until sunrise; in the morning, however, gunfire quickly disperses great snipe, and they scatter to secure areas of the marsh, sometimes far off, and remain there until evening. By about an hour and a half before sunset there are already some great snipe close to the display ground, and by sunset they are flocking in from all sides. At this time, if you flush a great snipe and miss it, allowing it to fly out of sight, you need not worry: a few minutes later, provided it is not injured, it will return. A determined hunter can sit all night, hidden in a bush a short distance from the display ground, and shoot great snipe by taking aim at the flashing white patches under their spread tails. In any case, at this time of year the nights are very short; dusk merges into an early dawn, with hardly any true darkness in between. The males continue their dueling throughout the night, and almost until sunrise, when they calm down and disperse, running off in all directions. At this time they can be shot, using a dog to put them up. I sat through one night at a display ground and shot several great snipe, but I did not develop a taste for this kind of shooting, although it has the attraction of taxing a sportsman's skill and agility. The prerequisite, however, is good eyesight, and mine has never been very keen. Moreover, one injures more birds than one kills outright, and often it is difficult to find even the dead birds, because you cannot leave your hiding-place to collect your game until the shooting is over. Clearly, you do not need a dog while you are shooting, but in the morning a dog is essential to seek out the dead and injured birds, and the injured ones often have the strength to get quite a long way away. In conclusion I have to say that I felt a little ashamed of killing birds in this distracted state, in the frenzied grip of the immutable law of nature, blind to everything and deaf to gunshots.

At numerous display grounds where great snipe gather in hundreds, and where no fowler has ever trod—no great rarity in the vastness of Orenburg province—village people, Russians, Mordvins, Chuvash, or even Tartars, catch a lot of great snipe (and blackcock) by using snares. These are placed at intervals of about a foot and woven into a long, fine cord, tied to a number of stakes driven firmly into the ground. When one bird is trapped it starts fluttering and struggling, and other birds rush in and attack it, only to be snared themselves. Most of them are throttled by the cord.

At the end of the courtship season the emaciated males seek the cover of the most impenetrable marshes, overgrown with trees and bushes, and begin to molt. At this time, however, like common snipe, they do not lose the ability to fly. Meanwhile, at the end of May, that is, during the first half of the display period, the hen birds build their nests, mostly on tussocks in order to be protected from damp, in marshland that is not excessively wet but always well covered with bushes, and lay four eggs, identical in shape and color to snipe eggs, but slightly larger. Their behavior during hatching, their concealment of the young, first in inaccessible parts of the marsh, later in open meadows, and finally on open marshland for the duration of the autumn, is exactly like that of the snipe. The only difference is that I have never come across two adult great snipe with a brood. After the molt, especially if the marshes are very wet after heavy rain, which great snipe do not like, they sometimes move onto fallow farmland lying close by, or to meadows overgrown with pea-shrub and wild peach. This, in my view, is where great snipe shooting is at its best, in late July and August, when the birds are so fat that, without seeing them, one can scarcely believe the size of them. They fly very heavily and soon alight again. Occasionally, when I have shot birds of this weight, they have hit the ground like heavy lumps of clay and the skin of the belly has burst. But they do not appear often or stay long in these haunts, least of all in fallow fields, where the young grass, despite strong growth in the Orenburg black soil, remains short, and therefore provides little cover. I have only once found large numbers of great snipe on fallow land: they were extraordinarily fat, and at first quite tame, but later became wary, though they lingered for about a fortnight. Perhaps they liked the soil loosened by the plow, and the succulent grass roots. Even when sowing began the birds remained close by for a few days, on meadows of feather-grass. At that time I shot more than a hundred splendid birds.

By mid-August the great snipe return to open marshland, where they remain, with common snipe, until their departure, which, incidentally, may be as much as two weeks earlier than that of the snipe. This is the season of the great shooting parties of which I have spoken.

Great snipe are usually shot with the same shot as is used for common snipe, that is, Number Nine, but it is better to use Number Eight. However, for birds at their display grounds, to which they return after having been scattered by shots, and where they become so wary that they will rise when you are fifty paces off or more, I have successfully used Number Seven. At sixty paces snipe-shot will not kill a great snipe outright, nor will Number Eight, or only rarely, though it may wing the bird, which will carry the shot for a long distance. If it does not die soon it will hide, slowly sickening, in the least accessible areas of the marsh. I have sometimes found and killed such birds in late autumn when all other great snipe have long departed. I have found wounds on them that have healed, and even old shot that has grown into the flesh—always easy to tell from fresh shot, which is much bigger to the touch.

Plump great snipe that are not yet wary of hunters, and that will still allow a dog to come close, may be caught by trained sparrowhawks. If a great snipe rises at six or seven paces, the hawk will catch it. But, of course, no shooting man will want to use a hawk to catch great snipe if he has the chance to shoot them.

3. JACK SNIPE

Garshnep; Lymnocryptes minimus

There is no doubting the fact that this small wader is a member of the noble family of snipe. The Germans call it *Haarschnepfe,* which is to say "hairy snipe," on account of the long hackles of its upper neck and back. These, however, bear no resemblance to hair and might more accurately be termed plumes, but since we have no other name for this bird but the Germanic *garshnep* it will have to keep it. Inappropriate it may be, but it is the name everybody knows. I have already spoken of the name *lezhanka* given to this species in *The Sportsman's Manual* of 1813, published in Moscow—a name that nobody in Russia knows.

The jack snipe is half the size of the common snipe. Its speckled belly and the proportions of its build, legs, and beak are exactly like those of the great snipe, while its plumage is that of both the common and great snipe, except that the speckles on its back are a shade darker and ruddier, with a grayish-green, almost metallic sheen. The skin of the neck is plump and fleshy, allowing those long plumes to grow from it. The jack snipe's exclusive haunt is wet marshland, preferably with clumps of reeds. Its usual diet consists of the roots of marshland grasses, especially the sweet roots of young reeds (whose first shoots also have a very sweet taste), and various grubs and insects.

In spring the jack snipe appears at the same time as the great snipe, in the very first "falls" of the latter, but it departs much later, even later than the common snipe. As soon as the brief, busy period of spring arrivals is over, the jack snipe seeks a home in wet marshes of reeds and mud. The reed marsh is its element, as was once forcefully brought home to me. One spring, when the spring migrants had all arrived and jack snipe were present in suitable localities, a large pond on my land dried up. It had become almost completely overgrown with reeds, which in winter had been mown for various purposes. Jack snipe had disappeared not only from the wet surrounds, but also from some places further away. Snipe and great snipe remained around the fringes, but not a single jack snipe could be found. I went on shooting as before, surprised only at the absence of jack snipe. Then I heard that some peasants who had been fishing in the remaining shallow puddles among the reeds had put up a lot of jack snipe. I hurried to the spot, and what should I find? All the jack snipe in the district had gathered on the muddy bed of this dried-out pond, now densely covered with the roots of reeds. The mud was so wet and deep that the birds could only perch on the exposed roots. Wading through it was infernally difficult: the mud was up to my knees and in places higher; my dog sank to its belly, and could not keep up, but in any case I did not need it, as the birds rose with no prompting. For three days I waded through that impenetrable bog, making the sort of superhuman effort that only an ardent young hunter is capable of. I shot eighty-three jack snipe, which, of course, I could not have done in ordinary marshland, or on their spring arrival; compared to common and great snipe, the jack snipe is very much rarer in Orenburg province, and it is unusual to shoot more than a dozen in one field.[7] I would have shot many more, as their number was increasing every day, but a weir was put in place and the pond began to fill, driving out the jack snipe, which dispersed and reappeared in their previous haunts, only in far smaller numbers.

The jack snipe is usually very tame. It will fly up soundlessly from right under your feet, or under the nose of a dog that has been pointing for some time, and fly quite straight, without the sharp zigzags of the common snipe. But its flight is somehow uncertain and uneven, rather like the floating of a butterfly, which, together with its small size, makes it much more difficult to shoot than a great snipe, especially in windy weather. On rising it will immediately launch itself into the wind, but, lacking the strength to fight it for long, will suddenly veer to left or right with a sideways motion, before heading directly into the wind again. The trick is to catch the bird at the moment it turns into the wind again after being carried to one side. At such moments the wind resistance and the efforts of the bird combine to make it stand still in the air—a fact known to experienced sportsmen, who will rarely miss a jack snipe. When the wind carries them to one side, particularly if it catches them from behind, the long hackles are ruffled and the bird presents a peculiar unbirdlike appearance, more like an airborne ball of flax or wool.

In early June, jack snipe disappear, and until mid-August they are nowhere to be found: at least, I myself have never found any, and nor have I heard of other sportsmen doing so. I am not persuaded by the theory that they hide in impenetrable marshland, overgrown with bushes, trees, and tall reeds, to rear their young to independence, and then return to their usual marshes. It is odd that a fowler as indefatigable and ardent as myself, tramping the length and breadth of the most difficult marshland in the summer heat, should never have found a single nest or brood, or have flushed a single jack snipe. As far as I know, others have also failed to find either nests or broods of young.[8] This leads me to suppose that jack snipe fly far off to rear their young, into truly impenetrable wet forest, where humans cannot follow until the ground freezes again. Whatever the facts of the matter, it will be seen that I know nothing of the breeding sites of the jack snipe, and can say nothing on this subject.

In late August, toward autumn, jack snipe begin to reappear here and there. By now the young are difficult to distinguish from their parents. Only the slightly larger bulk of the adults, and the fact that they put on flesh earlier, gives them away. If you shoot a full-fleshed jack snipe at this time of year, it will certainly be an adult, as you will be able to verify by the coarse flight feathers. In young birds these are not only soft but lightly veined with blood, as in all young birds. By late autumn these distinctions are hardly apparent.

I have never found jack snipe in large numbers in a single marsh (I am speaking here of autumn shooting), never so much as a brace, but I have heard that in other provinces, in Simbirsk and Penza, they are very numerous in autumn, and that it is common for a dog to put up two or three at once, and sometimes two may be killed with one shot. However, they sit so tight and so well hidden that even the best dog sometimes walks straight past them. Left to itself a jack snipe will rise only when you virtually step on it. They are best shot with

Number Ten shot, since you do not have to shoot at long range, and fine shot travels in a broad, sieve-like pattern, and a rising bird will be brought down even if only the edge of the pattern catches it.

The more autumn advances, the fatter the jack snipe grows, until it is fully enveloped in fat. The great snipe are all gone, then the common snipe follow—but the jack snipe still linger. . . . The weather turns colder, the marshes begin to freeze, a thin, glassy layer of ice covers the water between the tussocks, trapping white bubbles of air; there is nowhere for a jack snipe, small though he is, to find cover, and no patch of mud left—yet still the jack snipe lingers, now hastening to seek unfrozen springs. Here he finds refuge and will not leave it until the bitter end, until the hard frosts leave no water unfrozen. Even at times of frost, when the first fluffy snow was falling, I have been surprised to discover jack snipe, pressed against the frozen ground at the head of a spring, and been amazed at my dog's firm set on bare, open ground where there seemed to be nowhere for anything to hide. After my repeated, and eventually angry "Take!" the dog lunged forward—and up sprang a jack snipe.[9] I have not always managed to shoot them, because my gun was loaded with large shot, but when I did succeed I was delighted. Hunters may imagine how, having long since seen the last of the best game species for six tedious months, I treasured these last, belated specimens.

I must mention one singular feature of all three snipe, and especially of the woodcock: they never stand erect on their feet and do not extend their necks in the manner of other wading birds. Their legs and necks always seem somehow bent and bowed, which lends them their peculiar attitude. It is very difficult to distinguish the male from the female by the plumage.

ON THE FLESH OF THE SNIPE FAMILY AND ITS PREPARATION

The three species I have described, the common snipe, great snipe, and jack snipe, together with the woodcock, are well known to all gourmets for their unusually delicate flavor. So widespread and well established is their fame that there is no need to dwell on it, although, truth to tell, when the birds are lean and tough, their flesh differs little from that of other waders. Aware of their reputation, many people will eat them and commend the taste. And indeed, when they are fat there is no doubt that they are superior in flavor to all other waders, however fat the latter might be.

It is argued that since these birds feed exclusively on vegetable roots they may be cooked whole—an honor accorded to no other game except thrushes, out of respect for the diet of berries that feeds the latter at certain seasons. With regret, I must refute this view: the woodcock, common snipe, great snipe, and jack snipe do not feed only on roots, particularly the woodcock and great snipe, which do not always frequent wet marshes and cannot always obtain roots in sufficient quantity. They eat grubs, various insects, flies, and midges or gnats.

As for cooking birds ungutted, I would advise treating all varieties of wader this way. My experience has convinced me that they will be much the tastier for it. For the squeamish or fastidious I propose a special way of cooking not only the snipe family, but all other game species without exception. There is no doubt whatever that when we discard the innards of a bird, we discard the fattest and most tasty parts. The innards should therefore be carefully extracted, cleaned of all waste matter, lightly rinsed in cold water, and replaced in the body, the incision sewn up, and the bird then cooked in whatever manner you prefer. According to taste, you may even mince the guts and mix them with finely roasted breadcrumbs, with vegetables, or spices. I shall make so bold as to suggest that the flesh of these birds owes much of its fame to the fact that they are always stewed whole, always in saucepans, enveloped in bacon fat, or in paper soaked in it. Common snipe are tenderer than woodcock and great snipe, and jack snipe are tenderer than snipe, and hence tastier. In places where these splendid birds are plentiful, they may be put into storage by marinating them in jelly with vinegar, lightly salted and basted in fresh, melted butter, like quail. The dish should be placed on ice, then, once the frosts set in, it may easily be moved about.

I recently learned from the esteemed hunter P.V.B., that he keeps common and great snipe—as well as other game, no doubt—perfectly fresh until the spring, even when shot as early as July. The bird is placed in a large mold of the type used for ice cream, turned and frozen hard. Then the mold is cut into ice, and since the ice will not melt in an icebox, the bird is kept as fresh as if it had only just been shot.

4. BLACK-TAILED GODWIT

bolotnyi kulik; modern Russian, *veretennik; Limosa limosa*

This bird is best known by the name of "marsh snipe" [*bolotnyi kulik*], but sportsmen often call it *ulitka* or *nettigel'.* I do not know the origin of either of these names, the Russian or the German.

The peasants of Orenburg province call this bird *veretennik,* from the call that so often rings out across the marshes where they are common, sounding like "vereten, vereten." The similarity, though, is not close, and besides, the bird has a wide range of different calls: short and shrill when it is driving off a predatory or otherwise unwelcome bird from its home, a magpie or crow, for example. It will fly at these like a hawk to chase them away, or stoop, falconlike, from a height. The call is pure and long drawn out when the bird is cruising at high altitude, and can become a hoarse groan when a hunter or dog approaches its nest or young.

In the body the black-tailed godwit is no larger than a feral pigeon, but has very long legs and a long neck and bill, which make it seem quite a big bird. The upper mandible is slightly oval and bulbous at the tip. Its plumage is a ruddy buff color. The male is smaller than the female, with lighter plumage, but its neck is much redder.

Black-tailed godwits arrive in about mid-April. Although I have seen them passing through on passage in huge flocks, they are usually found in ones and twos in marshland, beside ponds and on wet fields, and only rarely in small parties. When they first arrive they are quite well nourished, but later grow very lean and remain so until they depart. From the time of their arrival, when they are found in all wet places, hunters shoot them on the ground, riding or walking up close, since they soon become quite tame.

As soon as the spring floodwaters have subsided, the black-tailed godwit takes up its habitual residence in the marshes where it breeds every year, unless compelled by some particular circumstances to move to a new site. The reasons for this may be several: sometimes a marsh dries out when the springs that feed it fail or are blocked by trampling cattle, or the marsh is drained for hay-making or tillage. Black-tailed godwits are not fastidious, however: they are at home in marshes of all kinds, be they swampy, peat-bog, hummocked, wet or dry, as well as in the open feather-grass steppe, near wet lowland hollows overgrown with bushes, as long as there is little human disturbance.

On taking up their territories the godwits form pairs at once. The male helps the female build a nest on a tussock or dry spot. The female lays four fairly large eggs, slightly smaller than hen's eggs, similar to great snipe eggs in coloration and in shape the same as those of all birds of the wader family. The male shares all domestic chores with the female; he is a good father to his children; he sits on the nest when the female leaves it, and when she is sitting he flies nearby to keep any intruders at bay. Alas, he is often the ruin of himself and all his offspring by his vigilance, as his patrolling flight and calls reveal the nest site to the merciless fowler.

After three weeks' incubation the young are hatched, covered in yellowish-gray down. They are able to run and seek their own food almost at once, and a day later the nest is empty. As with all waders except the snipe family, their diet consists of various insects. At first the parents stay with them in the marsh, then take them to drier ground on meadows and cornfields, where they begin to fly as soon as they attain full size.

I recall with sadness the massacre of birds that I, like all other fowlers, was responsible for in the vast marshes of Orenburg, teeming with all manner of game, chiefly godwits, which stand out among waders by their unusual determination in the defense of their young. These ravages are all the more devastating when the birds are incubating. In this way whole generations are exterminated. If the young have hatched and been out of the nest for just a few days, they will survive, as they can feed without their parents. As soon as a hunter comes anywhere near a nesting colony, one or two birds will fly out to meet the intruder, sometimes as far as two furlongs away. We used to jokingly call them "messengers." Blind instinct does not distinguish dangerous intrusions from harmless ones, so the black-tailed godwit will fly to head off a man, a dog, and even a horse or cow. It will hurl itself straight at a hunter, flying right up to him and hanging in the air above his head with legs extended forward, as if to perch there in the air. It will repeatedly alight and run away, trying to lure the hunter away from its nest. With a dog this ruse may work, but the hunter will have seen where the bird flew from. He will kill the messenger, and head straight toward its home. The closer he comes to the marsh the more godwits fly out to meet him. When a shot is fired close to the nesting ground, the whole avian population of the marsh seems to rise and circle the fowler, filling the air with varied cries and the rush of wings. Only those males or females incubating eggs remain on their nests until the danger is acute. This population consists chiefly of black-tailed godwits, with smaller numbers of lapwings or peewits, and redshanks and marsh sandpipers. As the fowler strikes out onto the marsh, and if he happens to approach a nest site or some fledglings hiding in the grass, the parents fly closer and closer to him, with pitiful cries, whirling over his head, mobbing him, so close as to almost touch the muzzle of his gun. But an experienced sportsman, and a good shot, will not have to endure this for long. Only a novice of little shooting experience loses his head, with the result that his hands and feet tremble, and he will repeatedly miss, hampered by the short range, as the shot does not have time to spread out. Shooting black-tailed godwits in flight at this time, once you have the knack and can remain calm, is easier than shooting sitting birds: you let them fly off a certain distance and avoid firing when they are turning sharply. This situation will usually result in a marsh that hours before teemed with noisy bird life and rang with their bright calls being turned into a still and lifeless place. Only slightly injured godwits, and those that were scared off in time, sit silently watching from afar, waiting for the destroyer to leave, so that they can hurry back to their nests. . . . But no such thoughts enter the fowler's head: he cheerfully gathers his booty, counts the bodies, and heads for the next marsh.

But not all marshes frequented by sportsmen always suffer such ravages. This happens only on new, previously untouched hunting grounds. If the black-tailed godwits are not wiped out the first time, owing to a hunter's lack of skill or his excessive hot-headedness, by the second time the birds will be far warier: only at first will they fly in close, but then they will stand off at such a height that even duck-shot will not reach them. And only a few birds will fly over the hunter, while the others will sit at a safe distance. From time to time the flying and sitting godwits will exchange roles. It is very difficult to shoot these "trained" godwits (as fowlers call them), and larger shot is needed, even as large as Number Six. Usually Number Seven or Eight is used.

While the parent godwits are tending their young in tall grass or rising cereals a dog may be used to flush and shoot the young, just like great snipe, as they do not rise high, and settle only a short distance away to hide in the grass again, where they let a pointer come close and even withstand the set. The time for this is the end of June and the very beginning of July. In mid-July they appear in family parties on the sloping banks of pools and lakes. A little later they gather for departure in large flocks along the great rivers and large steppeland lakes, and in early August they are gone, at least from those parts of the province where I have lived and hunted. Perhaps further to the south they stay longer.

Black-tailed godwits, the unfortunate victims of all fowlers and so pitilessly annihilated by them, are not highly prized game, no doubt because they are numerous everywhere and while they are sitting and hatching their young only the laziest hunter does not shoot them. Even the poorest shot, who cannot hit a flying bird, may shoot sitting birds. But on their spring arrival, or just before they depart, no hunter will pass them by. The taste of their flesh is exactly like that of all the wader family: dry and tough when the birds are lean and wiry; and very tender and succulent when they are fat. Young birds, even with little fat on them, have a superb flavor. In the province of Orenburg they depart so early that they have no time to put on much fat, but occasionally I have killed an old, belated godwit, probably a passage migrant, and found it well covered in fat.

5. SPOTTED REDSHANK

Krasnonozhka, shchegol'; Tringa erythropus

There is good reason for both of this bird's Russian names: *krasnonozhka* [redshank] on account of its long red legs, as if dipped in bright vermilion; and *shchegol'* [dandy] on account of its clean, handsome lines and plumage. It is rather smaller than the black-tailed godwit in the body, but its legs and neck, in proportion to its size, are very long, and at first glance the bird appears larger than it actually is. Its bill, however, is much shorter than the godwit's. The plumage is speckled all over, dark gray, almost a smoky or ashy color. The whitish belly and neck are covered with fine streaks and striations of exactly the same color, in very straight lines. The tail is short, like that of most waders. In my view, the spotted redshank is the most beautiful of all.

In the province of Orenburg the spotted redshank is a bird of passage: it does not nest or rear young here. I state this with assurance since neither I myself, nor any other fowlers have ever seen young birds in these parts. Spotted redshanks appear only in spring and autumn, from mid-August until late September. They are almost always encountered singly, occasionally in pairs, usually with other small waders and with ruffs, which gather in small flocks prior to departure.

The spotted redshank has an agreeable ringing or whistling call. By its cry alone you can tell from afar that one is present on the bank of a pond, lake, or river. Its clean, sleek plumage is explained, no doubt, by the fact that it is always well fed at the times when it is shot, and in September even fairly fat. For the same reason its flesh has more flavor than that of its congeners. Being an uncommon and handsome visitor that does not stay long, it attracts much attention from the fowler. Speaking for myself, I have always prized it most highly and pursued it tirelessly to the kill, or until losing sight of it, ignoring all other related species that keep company with it. It is not particularly tame or easily killed, perhaps because, when stealing toward it, you always put up other sandpipers with which it feeds on the sloping banks of ponds, constantly probing the mud with its bill. It feeds on the same fare as other waders; that is, grubs, insects, rootlets, the seeds of marshland grasses, and even silt and ooze, which is always present in the crop of all marshland and water fowl.

6. OYSTERCATCHER

Kulik-soroka, morskaia soroka; Haematopus ostralegus

This wader is known by many names. It is called the "Volga sandpiper," because, evidently, it is found in large numbers along the Volga. But it also occurs in numbers on the sandy banks of other large rivers. It is also called the "stallion" [*zherebets*], and I recall a hunting book that used the name "sea-pie."[10] I can explain neither of the last two names, but the name "magpie" [*soroka*] is fitting, as its markings, and even its build are somewhat similar to those of the common magpie, although it has a shorter tail and much longer legs, neck, and beak. It is much larger in the body and meatier than the black-tailed godwit. The oystercatcher is a tough, robust bird, not easily killed. Its bill, nearly two inches in length, is fairly stout, and bright crimson in color; its legs a pale raspberry color, shortish and sturdy, similar to those of ducks but without the webbed toes. It has a thin red eye-ring and the eyes themselves are also red, except for the black pupil. The head, neck, and throat, like the mantle and tip of the tail, are a brownish-black, with the faintest suggestion of a greenish-blue sheen. The breast, belly, underwing and undertail coverts are of the purest snow-white, and a white band runs along the trailing edge of the wing.

In the places where I used to shoot, that is around the rivers Buguruslan, Bol'shaia Savrusha, Bokla, and Nasagai, or Mochegai (the latter name is favored by the local people), the oystercatcher does not nest or rear young, but by the Bol'shoi Kinel' and the Dema I have found birds with young, and, albeit half-heartedly, they did attack me and my dog. It is probable that they would have shown more determination had they had nests with eggs. I have occasionally come across them by my own pond and by others nearby, in spring, in late April, and in August, but never in large numbers. Their call is also quite distinctive and far-carrying. Perhaps the oystercatcher should not be classed with marshland game as it does not rear its young in marshes but on the bare, sandy banks of rivers; but still less can it be classed with other categories. Strictly speaking one might create a separate category of "riverside birds," but this would consist of only three wading birds so there is little need to separate them.

Oystercatchers are held in little regard by hunters; I myself have never pursued them and in all my life have killed no more than twenty. Their flesh is dry and tough when they are thin, but on arrival and before departure they are very fat and quite succulent, though at these times, especially in spring, the fat has a slightly fishy flavor, presumably because they catch and eat small fish as they run along the shores of rivers in flood.

The oystercatcher has one other notable characteristic: the red coloration seen in the eye, beak, and legs, also shows in the skin, the flesh, and above all in the fat. When the bird is roasted the fat is a bright orange color. The taste is disagreeable even when the birds are fat. The appearance of the oystercatcher is somewhat ungainly and awkward. In shape it is halfway between the graceful form of the sandpiper family and the build of a magpie or jackdaw, and the piebald plumage, in spite of the bright colors and red bill, eyes, and legs, is thoroughly unsightly and unpleasant. At least, this is the impression the oystercatcher has always made upon me.

7. GREENSHANK

Rechnoi kulik, Bol'shoi ulit; Tringa nebularia

This sandpiper is slightly smaller than the spotted redshank but proportionately a little fatter. Its plumage does not stand out by bright colors: it is neither pied nor mottled, but a grayish white with some indistinct shading, gentle and agreeable to the eye. The belly, gorget and undertail coverts are white; the bill a plain flesh color, and the legs a light greenish hue. It stands a little shorter and more heavily than the spotted redshank, but at the same time it is quite slender and handsome. The Russian name of "river sandpiper" is just: you will not find it by brooks or even small creeks, but only along rivers of medium to large size, usually with sandy banks. It may also occur on lakes. Of course, it can sometimes appear by small ponds and streams, but such occurrences are exceptional. Its pleasant ringing call carries a great distance. In spring it arrives fairly late, much later than many other sandpipers. I have never found it in flocks but only in pairs in spring, and in July and August with broods of young. It does not breed in open marshland—at least, I have never found a nest—but it is probable that it rears its young not far away, in wet and flooded woodland along medium-sized rivers or even smaller ones, as I have come across birds with young at places where dams have formed ponds on just such rivers.[11]

Greenshanks remain in the Orenburg area until early September, at which time they are quite plump. On their arrival, like other birds in spring, they are by no means lean. Their flesh is tastier than that of other sandpipers and in this respect they are the equal of the spotted redshank, but since they are shot much more frequently they are somewhat less highly prized than the rare and beautiful spotted redshank. But all hunters prefer the greenshank to most other sandpipers, which it resembles closely in diet and all other characteristics.

You will never shoot greenshanks in great numbers, first,

because they are scarce, and second, because they are quite wary, especially the older birds. I have always had great respect for them, and have fairly often had occasion to shoot them in flight: it was my good fortune that they often happened to fly straight toward me.

8. REDSHANK

Travnik; Tringa totanus

I do not know why the bird should bear the Russian name of "grass-bird" [*travnik*]. If it is because it prefers to rear its young in the grass that grows on the banks of ponds and rivers, it is by no means alone in this. Nor does its diet consist exclusively of the young shoots of short riverbank grasses; its food is the same as that of all other sandpipers. At first glance the bird is like the spotted redshank: it also has mottled gray plumage, though a shade lighter, and also has a red bill and legs, but it is far smaller than the other bird, especially in the body. Its legs are a pinkish-red; its speckles less bright and well defined, and it is altogether less robust, well built, and handsome. The redshank is a very common bird and is often met with.

Here is a description drawn from life of a young redshank; older birds have much lighter plumage. From the tip of its bill to the tip of its tail it is eleven inches. The bill is just under two inches long. The first half of the bill from its base is reddish with some black on the upper mandible, and the tips of both mandibles are blackish. The head, neck, and back are grayish-brown, the same color as the wings. The primaries are dark chestnut. The tail is of medium length, whitish with brown barring. The belly is whitish but streaked with brown. The legs are four inches long and reddish in color. I should add that in older birds the chestnut color is not apparent.

The redshank's spring arrival is in mid-April. Before this, birds fly over on passage in quite large flocks at high altitude, without landing in our province. Then, when the weather is a little warmer, they appear in pairs along the banks of flooded rivers, ponds, and meres. They are quite tame and at this time may be approached and shot. They reclaim their breeding sites in the marshes at the same time as black-tailed godwits and are usually found close to them. I have only rarely come across them in marshes where there are no godwits, and the reverse is also true. In their habits too they are very similar: they also nest on tussocks; the female lays four eggs and the male shares the incubation and care of the young, in the protection of which they are no less zealous. They differ in the following respects: redshank eggs are half the size of godwit eggs and much lighter and greener in color; the speckling on them is not dark brown but greenish to dark gray; they do not take their young out into thick meadow grass or standing corn but keep them in the marshes, sedge, and grass on the fringes of ponds. I should also point out that young redshanks are fledged about two weeks before young godwits, that is, earlier than any other waders except common snipe: in my notes I have recorded that in 1815 the first redshank young started flying on 8 June![12] This, however, was a unique occurrence, not repeated once in a dozen years. Usually young redshank are fledged around 20 June. There may be three reasons for this consistently early fledging: (1) the parents begin nesting early; (2) they incubate for less than three weeks; (3) the feathers, particularly the flight feathers, develop quickly in the young. I am in no position to confirm or refute any one of these possible reasons. The third of these seems most likely and my own evidence tends to dismiss the second, since my observations show that all species of this family begin sitting at the same time. When the young are fully grown, by the end of July, the parents stay with them on the bare, open banks of pools, lakes, and rivers. They are happy to frequent muddy areas. Their call is fairly loud and at the same time musical. When they fly up the call is like the tinkle of a little silver bell.

They depart at the same time as black-tailed godwits. All that I have said about the slaughter of the latter while they are rearing their young also applies to redshanks. Being zealous in the defense of their young, or, as fowlers crudely—even cynically—put it, "stupid," they boldly fly right up to the hunter, ceaselessly giving their short, ringing call, and perish, owing to their habit of hovering motionless in the air with legs extended over the head of a dog or hunter.

The flesh of redshanks is usually dry as they are always lean, but it is not tough. On their spring arrival and before departure in autumn, they are a little meatier, but they are never fat. It follows that they are not much prized as game, though held in higher regard than marsh sandpipers and others of the family. I am not of this view: I have always preferred some of the small sandpipers to redshanks and other medium-sized species.

9. MARSH SANDPIPER

Porucheinik, Tringa stagnatilis

The Russian name *porucheinik* clearly suggests a preference for streams [*ruch'i*], but is not fully apt. In reality no sandpipers regularly frequent streams except for the common sandpiper, unless the small rivers on whose banks it may sometimes be found be termed streams. The marsh sandpiper is much smaller than the redshank and of much slighter build, although it stands tall and has equally long legs. It seems skinny, puny, and fragile. It is speckled gray in color but much lighter than the redshank. The belly and undertail coverts are white and the legs greenish. It also arrives in mid-April and departs at the beginning of August. In its habits and way of life it is close to the redshank, with which it keeps company in the marshes, but it is far less numerous. It too is determined in the defense of its young and will attack a fowler with a call very like a groan or sob. But fowlers are not eager to shoot them. Only after killing godwits and redshanks in great numbers will they bother to shoot marsh sandpipers, which, as a result, do not suffer the same depredations. Their eggs are a little smaller than redshank eggs and less green, similar in color to the plumage of the birds themselves, that is, speckled gray. The call is brief and not resonant. The bird is always lean, even on arrival and before departure, so the meat is always rather dry, but not tough or coarse. Of all the medium-sized sandpipers the marsh sandpiper is considered the poorest game. I have never seen these birds in any numbers.

10. GREEN SANDPIPER

Chernysh; Tringa ochropus

The names *chernysh* and *chernyi kulichok*, or "black sandpiper" are purely local, being used only by Orenburg fowlers.[13] I have been unable to discover what this bird is called in other provinces. Ordinary folk do not always distinguish them from other small sandpipers of the same family. The green sandpiper, properly speaking, is one of the medium-sized waders, rather than the small ones. The body is even a little fleshier than the marsh sandpiper's, although it is shorter in the leg. It is a very lively, agile bird, roundish and well proportioned. From lower breast to tail the underparts are pure white, the neck speckled gray, and the mantle to the tail a dark color with fine white speckling. The wings are even darker, with no speckling at all toward the tips. The speckles, however, are nowhere very visible at a distance and the bird appears almost black when seen flying past or running along the shoreline. The tailfeathers are very white but have dark spots at the tip, giving the impression of a band or fringe. The bill is black, as are the eyes, while the legs are greenish.

Although all waders run very nimbly the green sandpiper is the most energetic, except for the common sandpiper. When flushed, and in its fast flight, it gives a pleasing, resonant call, sounding like "tilly, tilly."

It is less tame than some of its relatives, or perhaps this only seems so, as it will not stay in one place but keeps running along or flying very fast. It is quite difficult to shoot when flying away or when flying straight toward you. It is much easier to hit by firing across its path if it happens to fly in your direction, because it flies much faster than any other wader with the exception of the common snipe. It may quite often be shot as it runs along the ground.

In spring it arrives at the same time as the other medium-sized sandpipers, or even a little earlier. The birds are almost always found in pairs or singly, but I have never come across even small flocks. When all other birds are sitting on their nests, green sandpipers can still be seen, though in smaller numbers, and some can always be met with throughout the summer, from which we may conclude either that the males do not share in incubation and care of the young or that many individuals always remain unpaired. I do not know where they breed but in July they appear with broods of young, which proves that they nest somewhere close by.[14] On arrival and before departure the birds are fairly fleshy but I have never had occasion to kill a fat one. Sometimes they can be found along the banks of lakes, ponds, rivers, and creeks until the end of August. By then, of course, they are fatter and much tastier, although at all seasons their meat is good to eat.

11. WOOD SANDPIPER

Fifi; Tringa glareola

This small, chestnut and gray speckled sandpiper is known to sportsmen by the name "fi-fi," in imitation of its repetitive call. This is also a local name, in this case, one I have borrowed from Saint Petersburg fowlers. From afar it looks similar to the marsh sandpiper, but is more of a greenish-gray color, shorter in the leg and smaller overall, but neater and better proportioned. Its light-green legs are actually too long for the body but this in no way detracts from its appearance; the belly and upper breast are very white; the upper parts are speckled, gray to chestnut and greenish at the same time; the eyes are small and black, the same color as the bill, which is just over an inch long. The tail is short, with dark slanting bars across the white feathers forming chevron shapes, and the underwing is a smoky gray.

The wood sandpiper appears in Orenburg province only in late April and early August, and is gone by midmonth. It is always found in small flocks, although before departure the flocks may be quite large. In Orenburg province it is solely a passage migrant. It frequents the sloping, muddy edges of ponds and lakes, especially where there is silt or ooze uncovered by receding water, and meadows on which there are puddles. Local fowlers have not come across any nests, but it is well known that on the autumn passage (that is, in August) wood sandpipers appear in vastly greater numbers than in spring: on the return passage they are accompanied by their young. It is sometimes possible to shoot several of them at once. Their flesh is tender and tasty, although they are never fat. They depart so early that they have no time to put on weight.

12. RED-NECKED PHALAROPE

Poplavok; modern Russian, *kruglonosyi plavunchik; Phalaropus lobatus*

This bird is one of the category of small waders. Although longer in the leg and neck than the green sandpiper, it is much smaller in the body. The name *poplavok* [swimmer, float] refers to one of its distinguishing features: its three forward-pointing toes are joined by fine webbing, and it swims on water like a duck, and even dives. One might suppose that it is able to catch small fish, but the birds never smell of fish, and in all my anatomical investigations I have not once found any trace of fish in the crop.

The red-necked phalarope is a fairly graceful and well-proportioned bird. Its legs are of a light flesh color; the belly and throat are whitish; the rest of its plumage is bluish-gray, but the crown of the head is dark, and there is a darkish spot under each eye.

In the Orenburg region this is a bird of passage, and, as far as I know, it does not breed anywhere in these parts. In spring I have come across these birds very late in the season, and always in small parties. They reappear in August, evidently on the return passage, again in small numbers. I am therefore unable to say with certainty whether the August passage includes young birds, or if these are nonbreeding parties. The former seems to me more probable. In any case they are very uncommon in the province of Orenburg, though I have heard that they are seen in large flocks in more southerly regions.

The webbed toes do not prevent the phalarope from running with great agility along the edges of pools. When it swims it is not with the serene ease of a duck, but with jerky and hurried movements. On the water the birds stay close to one another, and I have had occasion to kill three or four phalaropes with one shot. Their flesh is tasty and succulent, although they are never fat.

In speaking of small and medium-sized sandpipers I have not mentioned which shot should be used, so I will state here, so as not to repeat it, that at short range snipe-shot Number Nine, is best; Number Ten for the smallest stints. At longer range I prefer Number Eight. One should bear in mind that small and medium-sized sandpipers have little resistance to shot.

13. DUNLIN

Chernozobik, krasnozobik; Calidris alpina

This bird may owe its Russian names *chernozobik* [black-throat], and *krasnozobik* [red-throat] to the black or reddish speckling of its upper breast. For two weeks during the spring passage vast flocks of dunlin cover the shores and islands of the Gulf of Finland. There the bird is known by these names, which are in use in Orenburg thanks to fowlers who have shot them in the region of Saint Petersburg. Here they have a more general name: *seryi kulichok* [gray sandpiper].

The dunlin is a sandpiper of medium size, well rounded, fleshy, and handsome. Its legs and neck are not particularly long; its bill is short and straight.[15] It is entirely speckled with dark yellowish spots, rather like those of the fieldfare. On the upper breast the plumage is either black or clay colored.

In Orenburg, dunlin occur only on their spring passage, from mid- to late April.[16] In summer, or even autumn, I have never seen them, but I have heard that in Penza province they appear for short periods in August, evidently on the return passage, so it is possible that this also happens in some districts of Orenburg province. In spring, dunlin regularly appear in quite large parties, which scatter along the edges of ponds, lakes, and flooded rivers. They are quite tame. I have sometimes killed up to eight with a single shot. They are always very fleshy, and their meat is tasty and succulent.

The dunlin is a very handsome and pleasing wader, from a distance resembling a ruff, although much smaller. Since it appears only once a year, and that for a short period, I have always pursued them eagerly. I recall some years in which none appeared at all, though I searched for them at all the sites they usually favored—to no avail.

I have heard that near Saint Petersburg dunlin pass through in fabulous numbers (like black-tailed godwits), and that one fowler managed to kill eighty-five of them with one shot. Although I heard this from the most reliable sources, I confess that I cannot imagine how it is possible to kill so many with one shot. In our province many fowlers do not know the dunlin at all.

14. TEREK SANDPIPER

Morskoi kulichok; Terekia cinerea[17]

This little sandpiper is even more of a rarity and is known even less than the dunlin in our province. It has happened that years have passed without my seeing one. The name *morskoi kulichok* [sea sandpiper] is known only to expert fowlers: ordinary hunters (and ordinary folk) do not know it. I believe that this name too has come to us with fowlers who have shot it in coastal areas, where it occurs on spring passage in huge numbers.[18]

The Terek sandpiper is much smaller than the dunlin, and short in the leg, but still it is a plump and handsome wader. It has no distinctive markings on the breast but the bird as a whole is covered with fine, light-brown speckling, making it rather like a small ruff at a distance. It has one remarkable feature: its bill, which is quite long in proportion to its body, is upturned, and slightly flattened from the midpoint to the tip. This bill is a pale flesh color, but the flattened part is whitish.

The Terek sandpiper is also distinguished by its characteristic whistle or peep, which is difficult to convey. The bird occurs for very short periods at the end of April, in small parties, sometimes with small ruffs or dunlin, on the banks of ponds, flooded rivers and small pools. Its flesh is tasty and succulent. Its diet is the same as that of its relatives.

15. COMMON SANDPIPER

Zuek, perevoshchik; modern Russian, *perevozchik;*
Tringa hypoleucos

This is the smallest of all the sandpipers except for the little stint. The body is slightly larger than that of a house sparrow, but looks more robust. All its parts are in good proportion and it shares the build and lines of other sandpipers. The back, upper wings, tail, neck, and head are grayish-brown, with indistinct speckling and patterns. The plumage of the belly, undertail coverts and underwing are pure white. The eyes are dark and the bill and legs of light flesh color. As it stands in one spot it ceaselessly bobs its tail. It may owe its Russian name *zuek* to its nimble darting movements, or perhaps to the call with which it so often flies over the water, which might be compared to a hurried "zuyee, zuyee." Its other name, "ferryman," it owes to fowlers, because of its frequent flights from one bank to the other over rivers, creeks, ponds, and lakes. If two sportsmen are combing opposite banks and flush a common sandpiper, it will repeat this maneuver—flying from one side to the other, with its habitual cry—as many as a hundred times, like a ferryboat shuttling to and fro. It can also swim very well, and even dive to a certain depth when wounded in the wing, though it has no webbing on its toes. The common sandpiper arrives earlier than all other sandpipers, and always appears in pairs. It runs about tirelessly and, on seeing a hunter approaching, starts running so fast that you cannot catch up. It nests not in marshland but on creek and riverbanks and ground that is completely dry and may even be quite elevated. The male helps incubate the eggs, of which there are always four, and is inseparable from the young when they hatch. The eggs are small, though larger than sparrow eggs, and very beautiful, of a mottled greenish color. Unlike other sandpipers they do not mob fowlers or their dogs when they have eggs or young, because they do not fly high, but always skim low over the ground or the water. Nonetheless, though still flying low, they will circle round a hunter or a dog uttering their call, often perching on some rock or stump protruding from the water, or at the very edge of the water, and running ceaselessly to and fro with the special cry, resonant, and long drawn out, that you never hear from a common sandpiper in flight, but only from one running along the ground or at moments when it is standing still. When the young are partly grown the parents stay with them on the banks of small rivers, especially in places where there are shoals or sandbars. I have often rounded a sharp bend and seen a whole brood with father and mother running along the sand. At the first hint of danger the young seek cover wherever they can, while the parents begin to fly or run back and forth, trying to decoy a fowler in the opposite direction; truth to tell, however, I must say that parent common sandpipers show less determination in the defense of their young than do black-tailed godwits, redshanks, or marsh sandpipers.

Later, when the young are full-grown and beginning to fly easily, which happens in about mid-July, they move to the open banks of ponds, and in August they depart. I have never seen them in flocks; even broods of young disperse, but other hunters have reported seeing them in small parties.

Although this sandpiper, by virtue of its small size and the difficulty of shooting it, attracts little attention from fowlers, I have always loved to pursue it and shoot it both sitting and flying. By walking along the top of a riverbank beneath which they were running, I could overtake them, then look over the top and make them fly up. I used Number Ten shot. The flight of the common sandpiper is distinctive in being very erratic and jerky: in between bursts of speed it seems to slow right down. Shooting it is not easy and the number bagged will not be great, but to my mind it makes for enjoyable sport. I have never shot more than five brace in one field, and that only after pursuing them for several hours. Their flesh is very tender and tasty, though it is a pity that there is so little of it. It is best in a pâté or sauce.

16. LITTLE RINGED PLOVER

Pesochnik / peschanik; malyi zuek, malyi galstuchnik;
Charadrius dubius

It is not difficult to see why this bird bears the name of "sand-bird" [*pesochnik, peschanik*], though harder to understand why it should also be called the "sand kinglet" [*peschanyi korolek*]. Strictly speaking, it should not be called a sandpiper, as it lacks the long legs, neck, and bill of that family. Its lines, and particularly its bill, are very like those of the lapwing and the golden plover, of which more will be said in the chapter on grassland or steppe birds. But the little ringed plover inhabits only sandy lakeshores, pond edges, and the banks of medium-sized and large rivers; here it rears its young on the bare sand and stays with them until it is time to depart. So it would be hard to count it as a grassland bird. The body is slightly larger than a sparrow's; the legs are not very long; the head is large in proportion to the body, with prominent cheeks, and the head seems all the bigger for the feathers on the crown of the head, which project to form something resembling a small crest; the belly is white, the breast and head dark brown and the neck white. It looks as if it is wearing a bowtie, which is why many hunters call it the "cravat bird" [*galstuchnik*]. All in all, it is more skewbald than mottled, having a yellow ring round its eye, to which it owes another name, "yellow-eye" [*zheltoglazka*].

The little ringed plover arrives quite late in the spring. I have never found its nest but have been told that it lays its eggs on bare sand, scraping out a small hollow for the purpose. Like the common sandpiper it flies low and never defends its young by going for a fowler's head. Instead it circles round him or flits from one spot to another, but most often it will run along the ground, trying to lure a man or dog away. It has its own low and rather mournful call. Sometimes when you hear the call you will look for the bird and pick it out with difficulty, standing on a sandy rise and ceaselessly bobbing its head. Its flesh is tender and tasty although the bird is never fat. It departs fairly early, at the beginning of August.

Fowlers rarely bother to shoot at little ringed plovers, chiefly because they never gather in even small flocks, and to fire at a single bird seems a waste of a cartridge.

This bird has a relative that is twice its size, with large black eyes and no yellow eye-ring, but I have seen so few that I am unable to say anything more about it.[19]

17. LITTLE STINT

Kulichok-vorobei; Calidris minuta

This is indisputably the tiniest of the sandpiper family, and although known in Russian as the "sparrow-stint" [*kulichok-vorobei*] owing to a certain similarity in size and plumage color, it is actually smaller than the ordinary house sparrow. Miniature though it is, it has all the features of a sandpiper, and is so well proportioned, and its feathers so beautiful—just like those of a smaller ruff in autumn coloring—that I know of no prettier bird. I once supposed that the little stint could be considered the third and smallest variety of ruff (which I have still to discuss) since its lines and coloration are so very similar, and also because in autumn they so often occur in the same flocks. But, persuasive though these reasons seem, I am unable to call the little stint a third ruff because it lacks the principal distinguishing mark of that species: the male little stint has no plumes in spring and does not change its plumage in autumn. At least, neither I nor any other fowlers have witnessed anything of the kind.

Little stints arrive fairly late, in the latter half of April, and occur mainly on the bare, flat muddy banks of ponds, free of grass, although they are sometimes met with in spring along the edges of meadows. They always appear in small parties, darting about in a tight group. They stay no longer than two weeks and then disappear until late July or early August. They return in larger numbers in autumn, very likely with their young, but where or how they rear them I cannot say. In late August or early September they disappear with the ruffs. In Orenburg province they are evidently passage migrants. They are very tame and easy to shoot; the smallest shot, Number Ten or even Eleven, should be used. On arrival in spring they are always plump, and are well covered before their departure. The flesh is exceptionally tasty but there is little of it. It is used in sauces and pâtés.

I have always been so fond of these tiny stints that sometimes it has seemed a pity to shoot them. When I have had the opportunity to steal up on a flock unobserved and watch them running about without a care, finding food in the mud and sometimes stopping to rest, I have observed them in admiration for long periods, and occasionally even stolen away again without firing a shot. . . . And these birds are keenly sought by the passionate hunter!

When a flock of little stints fly with their swift, soundless flight from one spot to another, a short, faint note can be heard, rather hoarse, but at the same time melodic and pleasing to the ear. I have tried to keep little stints with minor wing injuries in a large cage over a small muddy puddle. I supplied a plentiful variety of insects and seed but to no avail. The birds soon died.

18. RUFF

Bolotnyi kurakhtan, modern Russian, *Turukhtan;*
Philomachus pugnax

The name *kurakhtan*, or *kurukhtan*, or even sometimes *turukhtan* belongs, as it should, to a bird with some outward resemblance to a chicken [Russian, *kuritsa*]. Some grassland birds are fully entitled to this but there is also a variety of sandpiper bearing this name, with which I am dealing here, and so named because, for all its sandpiper features, the males have long plumes that in spring can be raised or lowered, or project mane-like from their thick necks. In brief, at this season they resemble farmyard cockerels. It seems advisable to treat the ruffs as two varieties: the marsh ruff and the grassland ruff, as they never mix and are found in very different surroundings. The marsh ruff itself can be divided into two types differing only in size, the greater ruff being twice the size of the lesser, about the size of a young pigeon. Its long legs are a pale flesh color in the male and pale greenish in the female, or reeve. The long neck and bill, which, however, is shorter than that of other sandpipers, show its connection with the other members of the family. The ruff is very slender and beautiful: the greater ruff is similar in size and elegance to the greenshank while the lesser resembles it only in elegance, being of much smaller size.[20]

The males of both forms arrive in mid-April. Their plumage is spotted with bright colors in large blotches and patches and they have long manes and the slightest of crests. Ruffs have one characteristic that sets them apart from all other birds: the males in spring are mostly different from one another in both the coloration of their plumage and the shape of the patches. I offer here a detailed description of a single male specimen. Although this bird was far less beautiful than some others, the whiteness of its mane was quite unusual. Its bill was just under an inch long and of plain horn color. The eyes were small and dark, the head a speckled yellowish-gray. The mane, which starts from the back of the head, is of long, white plumes, fairly firm at the base and lying along the sides of the neck and throat reaching as far down as the belly. On the nape of the neck, projecting two fingers' breadth from the head, are some short feathers of plain gray color. The belly is flecked with large black blotches and spots on a light-yellow background. The back is all gray with dark brown streaks, the upper wings dark, and the underwing edged with white but ash-gray at the axillaries. In the short tail there are feathers in a variety of colors: some white with little dark spots, others gray and light brown. The legs are a pale flesh color.

About three weeks after their appearance in large flocks, ruffs move on with all the other birds of passage, and in autumn, that is, in August, the returning males are ash-gray, maneless, and crestless, hardly distinguishable from the females, which have the same appearance and color in spring and autumn, the lower breast and belly always white. The change in the males is a feature of this species, distinct from the eclipse of drakes, which I shall treat separately. However, even in their autumn hues, ruffs are still beautiful, shapely, well-built sandpipers, although they do not stand out by variety in their plumage.

In spring they appear in large, sometimes very large flocks along the margins of wetland pools, lake shores, flooded rivers, and ponds far from human habitation. They often make a cheery sight as they scurry nimbly about in meadows just beginning to turn green, their brilliant plumes with tints of gold glinting in the sun. It is as if a broad rainbow band were spread upon the ground and was running along it in rippling waves. At this season it is best to shoot them from a *drozhki*, or four-wheeled open carriage. Although they are not fearful or wary it is difficult to kill great numbers, as they do not stand still, but run ceaselessly and scatter, like streams of water, in all directions. When you see hundreds of these beautiful birds in front of you, greed dissuades you from firing at a single bird, but only rarely are they close packed, so it is easy to miss the ideal moment. Naturally, one always hopes to bag a male with a mane. I have occasionally, however, shot as many as ten with one discharge, but only in flight, when a whole flock happened to fly toward me in tight group. Greater and lesser ruffs are always found in mixed flocks, both in spring and autumn. In Orenburg province they do not stay long in spring, only about three weeks. Where they move on to, and where they rear their young I cannot say. Three times in my life I have shot females of the lesser race, in different marshes. They behaved as if close to nests with eggs or young, but I have never found their nests anywhere. These instances, quite untypical of the bird's normal breeding habits, remain an unresolved riddle to me. There is one other singular phenomenon: in early August, always on mown, short-grassed, or well-trodden marshland, I have occasionally come across greater and lesser ruffs hiding singly in the grass. After withstanding the set they eventually rose before a dog, like great snipe. These birds disappeared very quickly. How and whence they appeared for short periods in this fashion is another riddle to me, but many fowlers have noted these curious occurrences. Later, in the usual manner of passage migrants, they appeared with their young, but always in small parties of the greater and lesser forms, along the banks of ponds and river shallows. This is also strange, since most other sandpipers on their autumn passage appear in much greater numbers than on the spring passage.

In autumn the ruff is distinguished from the reeve by its thicker neck and darker, more variegated breast. In addition, the male is always much larger. In autumn the birds linger for more than a month and by their departure time are very plump. In spring too they are fatter than other birds of passage.

I have always had a particular fondness for ruffs, not only for the handsome spring male, but also for the little gray birds of autumn, and have pursued them at every opportunity. Their flesh is always tasty and succulent. At the season of spring passage, it is unsurpassed. Besides this attraction, I must admit that their beautiful and endlessly varied plumage, the irregularity of the patterns of the spring males, with their splendid manes of yellow, reddish, cherry, and most commonly green, catching the sunlight and shot with gleaming gold, has always drawn me to them, exciting curiosity and the hope of finding one quite different from any I have seen before. And often my curiosity has been satisfied.

These are all the waders known to me, with the exception of the curlew and the woodcock, which I shall treat in the chapters on grassland and woodland game. Just once in the province of Orenburg I saw a pair of waders the size of black-tailed godwits and similarly proportioned but almost all white. My companion, then a young man, fired a shot at them but unfortunately missed. Whether this was a different species, or a mutant form (a freak, as these are popularly known) of black-tailed godwit, I cannot say.[21]

On another occasion I killed a medium-sized sandpiper similar to a green sandpiper in build. It was all white, with pale greenish legs, and a beak tilted not downward, but upward, like that of the Terek sandpiper. The latter feature points to a distinct species, as the conjunction in one and the same bird of an abnormality in coloration with a rare abnormality in the bill seems most improbable. As for mutants, or "freaks," this term is generally applied to a bird with white plumage instead of its usual coloring. For example, one comes across albino, or pale jackdaws, hooded crows, starlings, sparrows, and blackcock, and even woodcock and jack snipe, although I have never seen albino specimens of the last two. Perhaps there are such mutant forms among all species; among the first five species I have mentioned I have not only seen, but shot albino specimens.

19. MOORHEN

Bolotnaia kuritsa; modern Russian, usually *kamyshnitsa; Gallinula chloropus*

The moorhen is about the size of a young feral pigeon. It fully deserves the name of "hen," being very similar to one in shape, especially its beak. Its plumage is all dark green, shot with very beautiful steel-blue tints and with fine white speckling, especially on the lower neck, chest, and belly. The upper parts are much darker and the underparts lighter. The male is uncommonly handsome: while his plumage is exactly the same as the hen's, he has on his head a fleshy shield of bright scarlet and bands of the same color on his legs, a finger wide, right at the bend of the knee; the rest of the leg is greenish. The shield and the bands show only in spring; by autumn the male cannot be distinguished from the female. A wildfowler (N. T. Aksakov) who kept a pair of moorhens for two years in a specially designed pen with a muddy floor fed them on flies, grubs, and cockroaches. In autumn the male lost his shield and red leg bands. Even without these, however, and with plain, uniform plumage, the female is a very pretty and appealing bird.

In very small numbers this beautiful bird frequents the wettest of marshland, preferably close to pools or lakes well grown with reeds, flags, and sedge, and covered in summer with duckweed. Moorhens like running about on this green carpet when it is thick enough to support them. They run so lightly and nimbly that they leave behind them only the patterns of their feet on the soft surface; on water lilies, however, they skid as if on a polished floor. They are also able to swim well, although they lack webbing between the toes. If the duckweed is thin, they are perfectly comfortable swimming in it, ceaselessly foraging with their bills and swallowing aquatic insects that can always be found nesting in decaying duckweed, which they also eat readily when it is still young and green. They dart with extraordinary agility among dense reeds that may be one-fourth or more under water.

Of the time of the moorhen's spring arrival I know nothing, and even doubt whether, with their low and ponderous flight, they could withstand a long journey. They appear late in the spring, when the marshes and ponds already have a lush growth of vegetation. Nor can I say anything definite about the manner, time, or place of their breeding. It is probable that they nest in ordinary marshland not far away, but difficult of access, and safe by virtue of being very wet, for although I have never found their nests I have seen young birds, always singly, not in broods. Moreover I have come across mature hen birds throughout the summer and have even shot them occasionally. This leads me to conclude that moorhens, unlike some sandpiper species, rear their young in places not far removed from their usual haunts. I have been confirmed in this opinion by the same reliable hunter, N. T. Aksakov: in his village in the province of Simbirsk, moorhens reared young several years running beside the same small lakes, surrounded by reed-beds and with heavy growth of burdock and cow lilies.

Moorhens are a rare and most desirable prize! They are very difficult to shoot as they almost always cling to places the fowler cannot reach and where a dog cannot find the fallen game. A dog will not merely be up to its neck in water—it will have to swim. If you happen to come upon a moorhen on open ground it will immediately seek cover in an inaccessible place. It is rare indeed to shoot one flushed by a dog, as one might a corncrake or great snipe. More often it may be shot when you happen to see one swimming out of the reeds or sedge and making for the far side of a fenland pool or pond. It may sometimes be encouraged to do this by a dog, while you wait with your gun for it to cross. But for this you need to know exactly where the bird is hiding.

I can say nothing definite about its calls either. Once, as I sat fishing from a boat among some reeds, I heard a whistle, like the clipped call of the spotted crake, but less pure and slightly hoarse. A moment later a moorhen swam into view out of the sedge and I thought that this bird was the source of the call. Several years later I heard exactly the same hoarse call in the reeds round a small lake. I sent my dog toward it, sure that there was a moorhen there, but the dog flushed out a spotted crake, which I shot. This incident caused me to think that perhaps on that earlier occasion I had also heard a spotted crake but a moorhen that happened to be in the sedge at the same time swam into view, for there is nothing to prevent them sharing the same haunts.

Toward autumn moorhens become very fat and tasty. They are usually quite plump and their flesh is tender and succulent. They disappear in early September. At least, I have never seen one later than mid-September.

In all my life I have shot no more than ten moorhens, and that only after going to much trouble to seek them out. Many fowlers have not only never shot one—they have never even seen one! Of the ten I have killed three were swimming on the water, two running across thick duckweed, one was perched on a wooden platform lying in the water, and four were put up by my dog, including two in somewhat unusual circumstances. In late May I was returning home along the bank of a pool, finding no birds at which I might discharge my gun and thinking of firing into the air as the barrel needed cleaning. Suddenly my dog, which was splashing through the thin reeds and sedge, startled two birds from an isolated clump of reeds some way off. They were at least two yards apart and my gun was loaded with fine duck-shot. I thought the birds were a brace of teal and fired an unaimed shot at one of them. The discharge came only after a pause, which meant the shot could not be true, but both birds fell.[22] My dog rushed to them and brought back a moorhen. Delighted, I sent it for the other bird, and it brought me a cock bird with full red shield and leg bands. Of course, only a fowler who appreciates the range, the distance between the rising birds, the incorrect pellet size, the wild shot, the improbably fortunate scatter of the pellets and the rarity of the quarry, can imagine my joy. May all passionate hunters on their homeward path be as fortunate as I was in this chance to discharge my gun!

20. SPOTTED CRAKE

Bolotnyi korostel', korostelek; pogonysh; Porzana porzana

This bird also bears the names "the drover" [*pogonysh*] and "the shepherd" [*pastukh*]. Both these names are singularly fitting: its frequent, clear whistle, short and clipped, is very like that of a shepherd mustering his flock. The bird closely resembles the moorhen, or, to be more precise, it is nothing other than a miniature moorhen, one-third or one-quarter of its size, but as the male spotted crake lacks the scarlet shield and leg bands it is difficult to tell the cock from the hen. With its miniature size the spotted crake seems even more graceful, better proportioned, and more pleasing to the eye than the moorhen. The name "marsh crake" [*bolotnyi korostel'*] is also apposite: its call is just as quick and frequent as the hoarse, croaking cry of the corncrake. Although the spotted crake lives and rears its young in fairly wet marshland, where it clings to beds of reeds and sedge along the fringes of pools, meres, and the millponds, its usual haunts are far more accessible to the fowler and his dog than those of the moorhen. It may quite often occur in ordinary marshland. Only in late autumn will it tolerate the set of a dog, perhaps because it is then unusually fat and tires easily from fast running. At any other season it will run without stopping, just like the moorhen and the corncrake, and often retire into places where no dog can find it or flush it. Here it should be mentioned that all these three species, moorhen, spotted crake, and especially the corncrake, have damaging effects on a pointer's ability to seek and retrieve, as the scent of these birds is so strong. The excited dog sees that after each set the quarry is further off, rushes on in pursuit, loses the scent, becomes confused, and develops the worst of habits.

I have never found a spotted crake with young but once my dog caught one sitting on its nest and brought it to me unharmed. I even kept it alive for a week or two. Seeing that it was eating little and losing weight I released it in the same marsh. There were sixteen eggs in the nest, each about half as big again as a sparrow's egg, of an indeterminate yet beautiful faint greenish color, with fine pale-yellow stippling. If I had not myself taken the bird from its nest I would never have believed that such a slight little bird could carry so many eggs or incubate them. The eggs all lay in a circle, as they always do and as they must; they could not possibly all fit under the hen's narrow belly so they seemed to form a wall surrounding her flanks, breast, and tail. To this day it is beyond my understanding how they could all receive the warmth needed to hatch them, yet all the eggs of this bird did.

Like the moorhen, the spotted crake feeds on various insects, duckweed, and grass seeds. It also flies just as slowly, low, straight, and heavily as the moorhen, and sometimes just as far. It develops just as much fat in autumn, if not more, but lingers later, disappearing in late September when the frosts begin to bite. When peasants are mowing sedge beside ponds and marshland lakes their scythes often catch young spotted crakes and even adult birds. I have seen young birds almost fully feathered but with traces of completely dark down still clinging to them. There is no doubt that the chicks on hatching are just as black as those of corncrakes.

Spotted crakes are incomparably more numerous than moorhens; they can be heard whistling in all marshes, but shooting them is difficult and many find it tedious. I have, however, shot as many as thirty in a summer. Once, on 29 April 1815, I killed a crake that was not dark green but a dark coffee color and very beautiful. Unfortunately, the page in my notes on which I described it in detail has been torn out and lost and

I do not recall all its characteristics. My surviving records say, "shot a crake of an unusual kind not known to me," with a reference to the page that is missing. No doubt this was an aberrant form, as I have seen nothing like it before or since.[23]

The pure, melodic whistle of the spotted crake, together with the drumming of the snipe and the urgent call of the corncrake, which often lives in nearby flood-meadows, imparts to a May night a breath of life much easier to feel than to convey.

The moorhen and the spotted crake, like the corncrake, have a quite distinctive mode of flight: slow, labored, and awkward. Their hindquarters unbalance the body, so that they seem to walk through the air in a perpendicular attitude or fly as if winged by gunshot.

21. LAPWING OR PEEWIT

Chibis, pigolitsa; Vanellus vanellus

A Russian saying has it that the peewit is "the wheel that made the carriage lame, the lowest form of marshland game." Why should this be? I really do not know. Its flesh tastes no worse than that of any other wading bird, and it has prettier plumage than many others. Nor can it be said that it is particularly abundant, yet hunters look on it with disdain, perhaps because it can be found in many places and it is tamer than all other game birds.

The lapwing stands somewhere between a godwit and a ruff, which it resembles in size and build; its legs and neck are quite long, but by no means as long as those of the true waders. The dark-colored bill, though shaped differently from that of a chicken, is only half the length of that of a wader of comparable size: no more than half an inch. The bird is twelve inches from billtip to tail. On each side of the head below the eye is a white band, and between these on the throat a dark bib reaches down the breast, while the belly is white. Its legs are five and a half inches long and of a reddish hue. The head and back are greenish with a bronze to golden sheen. The wings are dark brown, almost black above, and white underneath as far as the wrist joint. The tips of the primaries are white. The tail is quite long. Almost the last two inches of the tail are dark brown and the two inches above that are white, covered at the very top by a number of downy reddish rump feathers. Both sexes have crests consisting of four dark green plumes.

The lapwing has distinctive rounded wings and flies with occasional slow wingbeats, producing an unusual, muffled sound. It tilts from side to side in flight and sometimes rolls right over in the air. This flight is peculiar to the lapwing. In spring they arrive very early, appearing before all other game at the first sign of thawing snow and trickling water. What a joy it is to see the first lapwing at this time of year and to try and shoot the first bird of spring—at a time when it is warier than usual! In Little Russia the bird is known as the *lugovka* [meadowbird] because of its preference for hayfields. (It also has the name *chaika.*)[24] The names *chibis* and *pigalitsa* are probably due to its call, which both these words represent well, and which, of course, is known to everybody. The peasants say that the lapwing cries, "Who are you? Who are you?"

In spring lapwing usually appear singly or in very small parties of up to ten, whereas in autumn, before their departure, they gather in vast flocks. When warm weather has set in they form pairs and occupy their nesting grounds earlier than the black-tailed godwit in marshland, flooded fields, and water meadows. For the most part they share their breeding grounds with godwits, redshanks, and marsh sandpipers, but sometimes they remain apart from them. They are found in all provinces and even close to Moscow, where no other marshland birds, no other waders, are known to breed. The lapwing fashions its nest from last year's grass on a tussock or raised dry spot, and lays four eggs, the same shape as those of other waders and in color, speckling, and size like those of the great snipe but somewhat darker. The male and female take turns at incubation and jointly care for their young, which, like godwits, they soon lead into the meadows and then into cereal crops. In July they appear in broods on the banks of ponds and rivers and often in mown meadows. In August they gather in large flocks along large rivers and lakes before disappearing in early September. Their diet is identical with that of all other wading birds. The adult birds are devoted to their young, no less so than black-tailed godwits. They too rush to head off danger, drive off unwelcome birds, and just as boldly attack a hunter and his dog, but they are less prone to perish doing this as fowlers rarely shoot them. Only occasionally, returning homeward from an unsuccessful shoot, with a near-empty game bag, might one shoot a brace or two of lapwings to raise the score and fill the bag. In spring the first lapwings are quite plump and tasty, but later, right up to their departure, they are scrawny, tough, and dry (like most larger waders), although the pleasing flavor remains permanently. The flesh of young birds before their departure, once they have begun to put on a little weight, is tender, succulent, and very agreeable to the taste. Adult birds with plenty of meat on them are difficult to shoot because, when they gather in large flocks before departure, they become very wary and soon move off to the great rivers. Fowlers seldom pursue them, although this is the season at which the birds are fattest. I did once manage, using large shot, to bring down a lapwing quite late in the season—in mid-September, I believe—from a flock flying high overhead, probably on their migration flight. When roasted and basted in fat its flavor was surpassed only by that of the snipe family.

Once in August I shot a lapwing with absolutely snow-white wings. It was in the middle of a large flock and it cost me much effort to shoot precisely that bird. It was extremely handsome.

CATEGORY II

Waterfowl

FOREWORD TO A DESCRIPTION OF WATERFOWL

Waterfowl are the closest neighbors of marshland birds; since they rear their young in marshy places, if not in marshland proper, I pass on to them directly, although, on their merits as game, waterfowl should occupy the last place. The elongated oval of the boat-shaped body, the configuration of the limbs, the abundance of down and finely lacquered feathers impermeable to moisture clearly indicate that birds of this family are designed not for occasional swimming on water, but for a life spent constantly upon it. Their gait on land is slow, labored, clumsy, and ugly: swans, geese, and ducks tread gingerly on land, slipping as they waddle, and lurching from side to side, while the fish-eaters are hardly able to walk at all; water is their element. On water they are quite at home. Without any apparent bodily movement, without any effort, smoothly, soundlessly, they cut easily through the surface of the water in all directions, turning at will, paddling invisibly with their webbed feet. Here they are agile and beautiful to see. Man has observed and imitated them to create the small boats from which today's large vessels have developed.

We must first consider the kinds of watercourses and bodies of water that will be referred to in this chapter.

Everything in nature is beautiful but water is its crowning glory. It is alive and flowing, its surface ruffled by the breeze; as it moves it gives life and movement to everything that surrounds it. It appears in different guises, and the laws governing its variety are beyond understanding. From the summit of a high, primordial peak of dark shale, a clear, cold stream falls in leaps over the mountain ledges and, depending on the gradient, forms either a series of small cascades or one or two large falls. If the channel is bounded by rocky banks the water flows in a narrow stream; if it runs over a broad rock surface it falls in a wide sheet; if the surface is neither rocky nor steep the water will gouge out a permanent shallow channel, and its surrounds will be vibrant with bright, green life. Grasses, flowers, bushes, and trees not usually found in mountainous terrain will flourish inexplicably: forget-me-nots, wild daffodils, spotted orchids, willow, and birch. There will be no others anywhere near; but the wind evidently disperses all kinds of seeds that do not all find ground where they can grow.

Sometimes the people of Orenburg province will construct simple watermills on mountain streams with a long drop. These structures will be picturesquely attached to a steep cliff, like a swallow's nest on a stone wall. The stream is channeled into a makeshift pipe, the hollowed-out trunk of a stout tree, firmly attached to the cliff face. The water falls straight onto a waterwheel and there you have a functioning mill, without any dam, millpond or millrace . . . , and it will turn and turn, milling day and night. When there is no milling to be done the pipe is moved aside, and the stream will again tumble down the mountainside, its steady roar now uninterrupted. The mill-shed is sometimes perched high up on a long, awkward frame, or on crooked struts of uneven length, looking shaky, precarious, and barely clinging to the mountainside. There is nothing to show a skilled human hand, no regularity that might conflict with nature. On the contrary, these structures complement nature. But what possible machinery can draw the seams of water right up to the mountaintops when water, by its very nature, tends to the lowest position on the earth's surface? No satisfactory explanation of this phenomenon has been presented, not even by modern science. Sometimes springs flow from a point halfway up a mountain side, but mostly they rise at the foot of the slope. Some springs, however, of a quite different nature, rise from the ground at low, marshy points, forming pits, or pools around them varying in size according to their position, and small streamlets flow from these. If the basin is deep the surging outlet can be seen only at the bottom: the water flows from the openings, carrying sand and soil particles with it. Whirling and tossing, but without rising anywhere near the surface, these particles sink and form a smooth, even covering on the bed of the pool. If the basin is shallow and the flow of the spring strong enough, then all the water, with sand, soil, and even small pebbles, will seethe in noisy agitation, like a kettle on a stove, from the bed to the surface. Both mountain springs and those that rise in lowland marshes flow in streamlets. These may flow out of sight, disappearing into the ground or concealed by vegetation. Sometimes you hear the babble of a brook but cannot find any water. Hot and thirsty, you approach and part the shrubs or thick grass, and the clean scent of moisture reaches you, and at last in the dank gloom you find a trickle of clear, cold water. How precious this can be to a weary hunter on a hot summer's day! Sometimes the stream may flow over open ground, on sand or fine gravel, meandering over a level meadow or open valley floor. Here the water is less clear and transparent, as the wind deposits dust and debris on the surface. Nor is it so cold, as the sun's rays penetrate the shallows. It may happen, however, that a brook of this kind will disappear into the ground to reemerge on the surface half a mile away or even more, and the water, now filtered and cooled by the earth, will again be clear and cold, though not for long.

Streams such as these unite to form small rivers, some of which flow through deep forest ravines, filling hollows and depressions as they flow and forming small pools. In places the flow is cut by the driftwood of the spring flood, which forms a kind of weir, behind which the water rises, forming a small pond, until it finds an outlet at the side or until it can flow without hindrance over a stout tree trunk, breaking the silence of the empty forest with its low murmur. Various birds frequent the watercourse and hunters say that hazel grouse are fond of dozing in the trees to the murmur of the river. The water holds salmon and speckled trout, which at twilight rise to the surface to catch the midges and moths that teem over it. I have sometimes wandered into remote forest gullies such as these and often lingered there: higher up the heat is still intense; the summer sun is tending to the west; the trees are still half in the sun and the breeze rustles their leaves, but down here the shadows are deep and all is still and cool.

Other small rivers flow along even valley bottoms or across broad meadows. In some places the winding banks are densely grown with willow-bush and alder; in others, there is only sedge and other grasses. The bed is smooth and even and the depth varies little. Depending on the terrain and the soil, there may be extensive marshland nearby, fed by springs and well grown with reeds, willow scrub, and small trees. On rivers of this kind, where the banks are higher, simple watermills can sometimes be built to operate one pair of millstones, rarely more. Their small millponds serve to spread the retained water, not simply maintaining existing marshes, but creating new ones, with new havens for all sorts of game. I shall have more to say further on about millponds.

There is one particular class of river that, if judged by the volume of flow, might be considered merely streams, although at first sight they appear much larger. These are the rivers of the steppe. They consist of a series of pools or small, deep, and unusually clear lakes linked by shoals, or shallow streams, sometimes little more than trickle. These rivers are always fringed by a particular type of soft reed and cow lily, which grow and flower at any depth. The water flows quite fast over the shoals, but in the pools there is hardly any visible current. Occasionally there is a thin growth of shrubs on the banks. If you can look down upon such a river, winding across the steppe, from a height, which is an uncommon occurrence, you see an unusual spectacle: an endless, winding thread, capriciously tangled, with blue sapphires, set in green, threaded on it, interspersed with tubular silver beads. The flowing water gleams like silver, and the sapphires are the still pools between the green banks.

A number of streams, big and small, eventually merge into one, and the stream with the greatest volume, by rights—or the one with the greatest good fortune, with no obvious right—retains its original name, swallowing the names of all the others, and flows on its way as a mighty river, usually lined with dense, mixed woodland.

Depending on the altitude and terrain, the adjoining land may be dry or marshy. In the latter case endless reed-beds interspersed with bushes, woodland, and lakes of greater or lesser depth, offer to all game, but particularly waterfowl, the safest and most extensive fastnesses in which to breed and conceal their young.

Sometimes a river will flow for a long distance through vast, empty forests, acquiring the character of untamed isolation, at once somber and solemn. Its banks lie untouched and untrodden; only occasionally will a hunter venture here, but without leaving any lasting imprint—the vigorous vegetation fed by the heavy moisture quickly revives the crushed grass and flowers. The banks have a lush and irresistible growth of broad- and narrow-leaved sedge, flags, reed-mace and large forget-me-nots; and in the stiller waters, dark green lilies of unusual size float on their long stems, carried evenly by the current. Waterfowl seem to fear the loneliness and duck do not frequent rivers that run too deep into remote forests. The waters are left to the fish and amphibious animals. The powerful currents run free in the silence and gloom of the wilderness and only the branches of ancient trees that lean over them, or that have fallen into the water, resist the current, endlessly producing a steady but muted rumble. A large pike will break the surface with a splash; a mink will swim across the river; or a desman will plunge in—nothing more, but even these faint sounds are soon absorbed into the surrounding silence. The mixed deciduous forest merely gazes at its reflection in the water: linden, aspen, birch, and oak, casting their shadows, straight or slanting, to right or to left, according to the position of the sun, upon the surface of the river.

When many rivers of this size converge they form second-magnitude large rivers such as the Oka, the Belaia in Orenburg province, and many others, and these later join with others to form first-magnitude rivers such as the Volga and the Kama, of which the second is slightly smaller than the first, whose name triumphs over that of the lesser river. Despite a great variety in volume and current, both types of rivers are really one: their channels are always sandy and always carved deep; as the level falls in summer, the water exposes the shore on the flat meadowland side and the river rolls its waves over broad yellow sands, broken by shoals of variegated shingle: for this reason these shores seem to me bare and barren, devoid of anything that might delight the human eye. It is true, of course, that the hilly side—almost always the right bank—may offer picturesque, majestic views, but these are best seen from afar, or on paper or canvas. We all have our own tastes and mine does not favor large rivers—neither the towering cliffs on the one side nor the dreary sandbars facing them on the other. I even find it frightening to look upon a vast expanse of water that so imperiously cuts me off from the far side and cannot always be crossed without danger. The Volga or the Kama during a storm present a fearsome spectacle. I have often seen them while a thunderstorm rages. The white-crested yellow and brown billows and the boats rent like matchwood stand out in my memory. But I shall not argue with the admirers of awe-inspiring images and shall readily agree that I am not receptive to visions of grandeur.

As for field sports, the great rivers are decidedly unpromising: the spring floodwater lies so long, submerging vast areas on the meadow side, that before it begins to subside all the birds are on their nests. In spring there may be duck and sandpipers but only along the edges of the floodwater, and in autumn migratory flocks gathering for their departure may appear on the open banks of the great rivers, but only for very short periods. For wildfowling this is most unsuitable. And at the time of the spring passage the Volga and the Kama are still locked in ice, already blue, cracked, and with some open patches, but still holding fast.

I should now move on to speak of lakes. Lakes have no flowing water but are none the worse for that. They may be of one of four types: (1) floodwater pools, or simply small hollows along the courses of rivers, which in spring fill and overflow with water; when the waters recede during the summer heat, they may dry out completely; (2) larger lakes, also formed by floodwaters, or receiving floodwater via some watercourse, but additionally fed by springs opening into the lakebed or banks; from lakes such as these surplus water may flow in a stream or form extended areas of boggy ground. These lakes always hold clear, fresh, though not always cold water. Of course the droughts and heat of summer cause some water loss, but they do not suffer degradation except for the usual summer algal blooms that affect all rivers without exception, being apparent in some degree even in the fastest flowing cold springs. As they spread moisture and vegetation around themselves the green shores of such lakes may form a fringe of willow and alder, and reed-beds may also develop; (3) woodland lakes, of gloomy aspect and dark hues when the banks are dry and not marshy and when dense forest reaches right down to the water's edge on all sides; sometimes they may be surrounded by a broad expanse of boggy or even turfed marshland with a sparse growth of trees, and will have water of almost normal color. The dark-colored water of forest lakes, besides being partly due to the reflection of tall dark trees, is caused mainly by the fact that the lakebed is composed of rotting leaves that from time immemorial have covered it every autumn and turn into coal-black humus, which settles on the bottom. It is widely believed that the leaves give the water its dark color as they become saturated and decompose in it. Lastly (4), there are steppeland lakes: these are always of substantial size and the purest, most limpid and beautiful of all lakes. They are no doubt fed by strong springs hidden on the bottom, which make good the water loss caused by evaporation during the heat and drought of summer, a loss that is often barely perceptible. The fact that the water is much colder in certain places and at certain depths is further evidence of the presence of springs. In the province of Orenburg there are many such lakes: the ones I know best are two delightful lakes a short distance apart in the Belebei district, called Lakes Kandry and Karatabyn'. Each has a circumference of many miles. Steppeland lakes are distinguished by their extraordinarily clear water, even cleaner than that of the pools formed in the rivers of the steppes. In the latter the water is sometimes so clear that a depth of nine to twelve feet appears no deeper than five; but in Lakes Kandry and Karabatyn' a depth of three fathoms looks no more than eight or nine feet; further out, the depths of the water look dark blue, the bottom cannot be seen, and at depths of six or seven fathoms the water seems terribly dark. The refraction of light in the waters of these lakes is so deceptive that as you wade out from the shore to bathe you think you are walking uphill, and lift your feet higher at ever step. Lake Kandry is ringed by lovely meadowland that is enlivened by the proximity of a large body of water. The side that is ten fathoms deep lies close to the hillier side. In the middle of the lake a small green, wooded islet seems to rear out of the water to form a haven and a breeding ground for a variety of gulls in great numbers. On two opposite sides lie level plains, and the fourth side is of reed-beds, with signs that there was once a stream (an extended marshy strip lying along a small hollow). Bashkirs have told me that their old folk remember a time when this stream linked Lakes Kandry and Karabatyn'. Nowadays they are not joined even in spring. The Bashkirs even have a legend about a future union of these lakes, but I have been unable to track it down. In any case in steppeland lakes the rise in levels in spring is insignificant. They are not rich in marshland birds or waterfowl; only in late autumn do departing birds visit them in large flocks, for short periods, as if to bid them farewell. On the other hand these steppe lakes teem with many kinds of fish (though none of the sturgeon family) and these have uncommonly fine flavor.

I cannot leave aside man-made ponds and reservoirs, to which I have referred only in passing but shall often mention in my account of waterfowl. They may be of two types according to whether they are formed by damming or by excavation. The former are found on rivers and streams, while the latter are usually dug in damp lowland ground. Near Moscow, however, where the soil is predominantly clay, a pond may be cut in the ground almost anywhere, even on a hillside, and rain and meltwater will remain in it, as in a china cup, the whole year round. Ponds may be so constructed as to trap floodwater carried by gullies and hollows in spring, even if these are absolutely dry in summer: during the summer the gully is dug deeper if necessary, and a strong weir built with a firmly set overflow sluice, or sometimes without one. In spring the floodwater fills the gully and the excess is diverted or flows over the top, or into traps built in the spillway. The outlet may be completely sealed off when the flood begins to subside. Ponds of this type may be very deep. They are not truly pools of standing water, with no outlet: the water is changed, if only once a year. But as to their bird life, they are hardly worth mentioning.

On the other hand, millponds, several versts long, with broad reedy margins and aquatic grasses and flowers in the shallows, with flowing water, on sizable rivers feeding watermills of four to eight stages, provide a true haven for all kinds of waterfowl, which will flock in from all sides. Broods of duck of every kind, as well as young moorhens and coots, are safe and well fed in the reeds. No duckling will be seized by a pike in the reeds and no chick taken by a kite or osprey, which is also called the fish eagle on account of its preferred diet. Birds of prey need light and open spaces, and the reed-beds are dense and dark. In vain do ospreys, saker falcons, kites and buzzards endlessly describe wide circles in the sky or hover motionless over the water. They can hear the peeping calls of the young, the quacking of the parent ducks, hear the rustle of the reeds and even see the tops stirring as the ducklings below move through them, but they cannot touch them: "many a slip twixt cup and lip!" Raptors will not plunge into tall grass or bushes to capture prey. This may be due to an instinctive fear of colliding with something hard or sharp, or of damaging their flight feathers. But if some unschooled chick or duckling should become separated from the rest of the brood, or, hearing its mother's call, strike out across open water, then death lurks both above and below: in the water the wide gape of the pike or sheat-fish lies in wait, and above it the long talons of the birds of prey.

Such is the variety of bodies of water, of which I have described but a few, and without going into detail. On these our waterfowl swim, dive, and spend their lives, and to them I now turn.

1. SWAN[1]

By virtue of its size, strength, grace, and stately bearing the swan has long been justly called the king of all waterfowl. As white as snow, with small, bright, clear eyes, black bill and feet, and its beautiful, long, supple neck, it is indescribably handsome as it calmly sails through the green reeds, over the smooth, dark-blue surface of the water. Its every motion is imbued with charm: when it begins to drink, scooping up water in its bill then raising his head and stretching out its neck; when it bathes, dipping and splashing its powerful wings, sending drops of water flying and rolling off its downy body; when it preens after this, arching its snow-white neck easily and gracefully backward to straighten and clean any crushed or soiled feathers on its back, flanks, or tail; and when it extends one wing into the air like a long, slanting sail, and begins working through every quill with its beak, airing it and drying it in the sun—everything about it is regal and picturesque.

Swans almost always arrive in pairs. They appear quite early in spring, in early April, when there is usually still snow lying. I have never seen herds of swans: in those parts of the province where I have hunted regularly, swans appear only on passage and are not breeding residents. It was rare for me to see one outside the time of spring or autumn passage. Only occasionally did one or two unpaired birds take a liking to some suitable place in my neighborhood and remain for two weeks or more if not frightened off.

I recall a strange episode in my youth: in the middle of a hot summer a party of seven swans would fly down every evening on our large, reedy pond. They usually arrived at sunset, spent the night there, and early the next morning, as soon as the village people awoke and began to move about on the dam and along the road that ran past the pond, the swans would fly away. Where they came from and where they flew off to I do not know. This went on for about two weeks. Finally an old fowler took his decrepit fowling piece bound up with pieces of string, loaded it with bits of scrap iron (for want of any lead shot), waded into the reeds up to his waist, waited for the swans to fly in and swim up to within a few yards, and let fly, killing one swan outright. Of course the others flew off at once but the next day they reappeared at the usual time, settled in the middle of the pond and swam about, keeping well clear of the dangerous reeds. They cackled softly among themselves, gathered in a huddle, took wing and flew away, never to return.

I have never noticed the autumn passage of swans. Many fowlers have told me that swans are not merely resident but also rear their young in various districts of the province and especially on the Volga lakes between Tsaritsyn and Astrakhan'; that they build their nests amid dense reeds, that both cob and pen care for the young, that they lay only two eggs (though others maintain that they have three or four in each clutch), and that vast herds of them inhabit the arms of the delta where the Volga flows into the Caspian. I cannot attest to any of this: I am merely retailing what I have heard. Personally I only saw a few swans every year, usually flying overhead well out of range. I also saw them swimming on lakes, but I always came upon them when least expecting them and at such great distance that not even buckshot could reach them, let alone goose-shot. Occasionally I did fire a shot, but it was more in the nature of a salute than one with serious hostile intent.

Just once in my life, while I was wading knee-deep in the floodwater of the Buguruslan River among dense bushes, a swan flew toward me and came quite close. I hit it with ordinary duck-shot: it shuddered, lost height, and flew off. The next day a Mordvin from a neighboring village found it dead, half a mile from the place where I had shot it. Its flesh was so tough that it was difficult to chew even after it had been soaked for two days. The taste resembled that of a wild goose but goose is much tenderer and more succulent, with more flavor. Its crop contained no fish, and hardly any other food. I cannot say what swans feed on but it is probable that their diet is the same as that of all other waterfowl.

I do not understand why in times past our grand dukes and even emperors considered swan a special delicacy. It is possible they had some way of making the flesh tenderer, while the idea that the bird served merely to decorate the table may well be false. The swan figures in our ancient folk songs, that is, those that apparently originated in southern Russia, and it still figures in popular sayings, although this could not happen in the lands that are now the Russian heartland as the bird is so little known. In the south, in Kiev, it has found a place in folk song and on the royal table. It used to be carved by no less a personage than the grand duchess herself, which shows that it was eaten. Perhaps from here, according to legend and ancient tradition, it made its way to the tables of the Muscovite grand dukes and emperors, and into popular speech, in which the words *lebedka* and *lebedushka* (derived from *lebed'*, "swan"), are firmly established terms of endearment.

Miraculous tales are told of the strength of the swan: it is said to be able to kill a dog with a blow of its wing if the dog approaches a slightly injured bird or attacks its young. I have even heard of a fowler whose arm was broken in this way by a swan. To judge by the bird's size, muscular strength, and its stout, tough bones and feathers, these stories can well be believed. Of course nobody has heard a "swan-song," but its loud call and muted cackle, very different from that of a goose, is known to all hunters, including me. From all I have said about the swan's strength, it will be clear that they are resistant to gunshot. In places where they are resident, buckshot is used to shoot them, and only at short range. Swans are shot not for their meat, but for their down, whose prime qualities are well known.

Swans are easily domesticated. For many years running I have seen some that spend the summer on a pond and the winter in a warm hut. But I cannot be sure whether they were caught as cygnets or as full-grown birds. I have heard that tame swans will breed like farmyard geese, in huts and pens, but to start the process it is first necessary to obtain some fresh swan's eggs and place them under a goose for incubation. When the cygnets hatch and grow up in a flock of geese (with their wings clipped in their first year), they become completely tame and behave like farmyard geese.

2. GRAY-LAG GOOSE

Seryi gus'; Anser anser

In ancient Russian songs this bird is rightly termed the "gray goose" [*seryi gus'*]. The gander of the wild variety is indeed gray and distinguished from the female only by its darker back and the blackish speckles on its breast. The gander is slightly smaller than the goose. Farmyard geese, though mostly white or skewbald, occasionally have exactly the same plumage coloration as the wild birds, that is, as their former selves. The only differences are that farmyard geese have reddish beaks and legs and are a little stouter and heavier; the wild birds are better-proportioned, neater, daintier, with yellowish to greenish beaks and legs.

On the spring passage geese appear very early. Often, when there is still snow lying everywhere and the ponds have not begun to thaw, skeins of geese can be seen flying high overhead, following the rivers, directly toward the north. The skeins always fly very high, but pairs or single birds fly much lower. On my daily rounds of the pond, and along the bank of a river that was always clear of ice by a very early date, I always had one barrel loaded with goose shot and several times I succeeded in downing one of these spring visitors. Later, when the weather was warmer, the fields had thawed out, and the spring floodwaters had spread, the skeins would fly much lower and land in open spaces to rest, feed, and swim on the water. Their diet consists mainly of fine young grass shoots, seeds, and cereal grain. Geese are insatiable eaters. When food is plentiful they will eat so much that they can hardly walk; a full belly overbalances the whole body so that it even becomes difficult for them to fly.

In spring geese are very wary and will rarely admit a fowler within range, whether he be in a carriage or, worse, on foot. It is necessary to find some suitable locality where it is possible to steal up close to them unobserved. This may be in woodland, among bushes, or using the concealment afforded by a hillock, a gully, a high river bank, or unmown reeds on ponds and lakes. Obviously, the very largest shot must be used, and it is no bad thing to have a number of cartridges loaded with buckshot in reserve, to fire at a flock of geese when a close approach is out of the question. It is most satisfying to pick off a clean-feathered, well-fed, spring goose at the limit of your range!

When they have explored the cereal fields, where some of last autumn's spilt grain can still be found, and the flooded rivers, lakes, and ponds, the geese form pairs and begin to busy themselves with their nests, which they always build in the most impenetrable reed-beds and marshland with a dense growth of young alder and birch, usually lying beside largish rivers. Here I am thinking of the rivers of the black-earth belt. I have often found nests and always in places so difficult to access that I sometimes wondered how I myself had got there. The nest is usually on a dry spot, or a high tussock. It is broad and round, fashioned from dry grass and lined with feathers and down, plucked by the female from her own breast. Hunters say that up to a dozen eggs are laid but I have never seen more than nine. The eggs are identical to those of farmyard geese, except perhaps a tiny bit smaller and less pure white, more an indistinct off-white. During incubation the gander shares the work: I have myself at times flushed a male bird from its nest and often found both parents minding a brood of goslings. As with all birds that breed but once a year, the incubation cycle of wild geese ends in late May or early June. Any exceptions are the result of some accident, causing the loss of the first clutch of eggs. In suitable open areas, that is, in river valleys with broad, reedy lakes, even at this season substantial flocks of unpaired geese may be found. As a rule they will spend the day on one lake and the night on another. The experienced wildfowler will know this, or ought to know it, and will always be able to creep up on them as they swim on the water, feed on green shoots in a meadow, or settle down to roost along a river bank. He may instead lie in wait for them as they fly from one lake to another at a set time of day.

When the eggs first hatch the goslings are covered in yellowish-gray down. They are soon able to swim and dive so the parents move their brood at an early stage to a quiet area of water—a lake or stretch of river with good cover in the form of tall grass, bushes, and reeds, so as to be able to hide if necessary. Many people have told me that the mother will carry the goslings one by one by the scruff of the neck, if the water is far from the nest or the terrain too rough for the young to make their way through it. I do not question this, but I must say that even the youngest goslings are extremely spry and nimble, and I have often lost sight of them in places where some strength is needed to run or even find a path through the tall grass and young bushes. I stress that this movement takes place as soon as the eggs have hatched, when the young must still be very weak. When they have grown to half-size or more and are almost fully feathered, but cannot yet fly, that is, in late June or early July, wildfowlers begin to hunt both young birds and old, which are then molting.[2] I have never cared much for this kind of shooting as at this time you can hunt the geese down even without a gun, using dogs specially trained for the purpose. The fowler can shoot only those young and old geese that the dogs flush onto a lake or river, which is not many, as a molting bird and the young goslings sit tight in the grass, bushes, and reeds, where they retreat at the slightest sound and the least sign of danger. Only extreme danger, such as a dog's gaping jaws right above them, can compel a molting bird or a young bird whose pinions are not fully developed to spring out onto open water. What a splashing commotion they create with their clumsy, stubby wings, made heavy by an onrush of blood, and how awkward their movements are! Even when dabbling they look absurd, with their tail-ends still exposed on the surface. At such times, of course, they are easily shot, and you do not even need large pellets. The birds are very weak, and Number Five shot will be most suitable. However, well-trained dogs, even mongrels, are able to bring in plenty of geese without a shot being fired. At this, the molting season, the parent birds are in poor condition and often skinny, so their flesh is dry and unappetizing, but that of the young is very tender, and although they are not yet fat, their flavor appeals to many.

At last the goslings grow into full-fledged young geese; the parents' molt is over, many broods have joined together to form flocks, and their nightly, or rather morning and evening sorties to ravage the cereal fields, where winter rye and spring crops are rising, begin. An hour before sunset, skeins of young geese rise from the water and fly to the fields, led by the older birds. First they circle over a wide area to see where best to land, at a safe distance from busy roads and from people working in the fields, and where the grain will be most plentiful. Having chosen their spot, they descend. Given the choice, geese will eat awn-free grains and pulses, such as buckwheat, oats, and peas, but when there is no choice they will eat any kind. Their leisurely repast will continue until the darkness is almost complete, but as soon as the loud, commanding cackle of the parent birds rings out, the young, who have dispersed widely as they greedily feed, hurry to reassemble, lurching forward, unbalanced by their full crops, calling to one another, until the whole gaggle heavily takes wing with shrill calls, flying slowly, low over the ground, always taking the same direction, to the lake, the river bank, or the remotest corner of the isolated pond they have chosen to spend the night. On reaching this site, the geese descend noisily onto the water, throwing up a bow-wave as their breasts push through it, hurriedly quench their thirst and at once settle down to roost, selecting for this purpose a stretch of flat, level bank, with no growth of bushes or reeds to provide cover in which danger might lurk. When a large gaggle has roosted for several nights at one site the grass on the bank will be crushed and trampled and their warm droppings will have turned it red and dry. The birds tuck their heads under one wing, settle down on their bellies and go to sleep. But the parent birds mount guard and take turns to stay awake, or sleep so lightly that no sound escapes their keen hearing. At the slightest rustle the lookout sounds the alarm and all the others reply, rising, shaking themselves, and stretching their necks in readiness for flight; but the hubbub subsides, the lookout gives a quite different call, on a low, soothing note, and the whole flock replies with similar notes as they settle down to roost again. This may happen several times a night, especially in September, when the nights are already quite long. If it is not a false alarm, if some man or beast really approaches the flock, the parent birds quickly take wing and the young rush headlong after them, their sonorous calls so piercing over the marshy shores and the water sleeping in the mist that they can be heard half a mile away and more. . . . And all this panic may be caused by a stoat or weasel brazen enough to attack the roosting geese. If the night passes peacefully, at the first light of dawn in the east the lookout wakes the flock with a ringing cackle, and all fly off, the parent birds in the lead, to their favored fields, and settle down to an early breakfast that they espied not long ago over a late supper. Again they fill their empty crops and again, on a signal from the older birds, the gaggle assembles, now in the bright light of day, and flies to another lake or stretch of river, or to a large pond where they will spend the day.[3]

Woe betide the farmer who belatedly discovers that geese are visiting his fields! They will eat all his grain, lay his standing crops flat, and trample them down as if a small herd of cattle had grazed on them. If he discovers them early he can take various steps to scare off his uninvited guests.

I have shot geese at different times: hidden in standing corn waiting for them when they flight to or from the fields; lying in wait at the roost, when it is too dark for them to make out a fowler lying flat on the ground; and lastly, approaching the roosting flock in a boat, as a boat can move so silently that not even the lookout can hear it in the gloom of night. Of course, in all these circumstances it is not possible to kill large numbers. One is almost always shooting at birds in flight, but well-aimed shots with both barrels may bring down three or four from a flock. One may also approach them in a cart, or, depending on the terrain, creep up on them, using the available cover, as they graze on mown meadows and cereal fields after harvest, when the peas and buckwheat have already been threshed. At this time the geese are reduced to foraging for such grain as is left, and to picking at winter seed grain and young aftergrowth. It is also possible to hunt them at midday if you know in advance where to find them. At midday geese sleep again, sitting by the waterside, and are less vigilant than at night. Moreover, the sounds of the daytime activity of other living creatures make it difficult for the lookout to hear the approach of a wildfowler. If possible, they are best approached by boat.

Throughout the autumn game season geese should be shot with the largest pellets. An autumn goose is very different from one during the molt, very strong, and resistant to gunshot. It uses its wings to fight doggedly, and I have witnessed one with a broken wing using its good wing to hit a dog so hard that it squealed in pain for some time, and thereafter was in no hurry to pick up a live goose.

By the end of September, by the time they depart, geese grow very fat, especially the older birds, but, as wildfowlers have observed, their flesh reaches its best only when "the frost has nipped it," which is common enough by late September in our part of the world. By this date the morning frosts are freezing the puddles and forming an icy fringe round the shallow edges of ponds and lakes. Be it from frost or from some other cause, it is a fact that the later the season, the finer the flavor of the goose. This is beyond question, yet it should be noted that by this time food is already scarce.

To tell the truth, one shoots wild geese less for the sport of it than for the table, and the fowler whose sport is the noble marshland wader can have little time for them. Geese must usually be stalked; sometimes you have to crawl on the ground to get near them, or lie in wait for them to fly over. None of this is to the liking of the true sportsman: it is not so much skill with the gun that is required, but rather much patience and stamina. I went in for this only in my youth, when I was guided by older hands who could not hit a snipe, which they in any case spurned on account of its size, as they judged their game by weight. True sportsmen do not go after geese, although they will, of course, shoot them with pleasure when the chance presents itself.

I have mentioned that geese flight to and from cereal fields by the same route, that is to say, always over the same stands of trees, always following the same valleys, and so on. This has led to the invention of net traps, in which the birds can be caught in large numbers. These traps are nothing more than huge square nets of stout cord, with a mesh large enough to permit the bird to be held in it, but not pass through. The net is suspended between two long poles in the path usually followed by a gaggle of geese in the late evening, virtually at night, as they return from the fields to their roost. Steel rings are attached to the tips of the poles, with cords running through them. The cords are tied to the upper corners of the net, which can thus be raised to the full height of the poles.

The cords lead to a hide, or bush, in which the trapper waits. The net is not drawn tight. It simply hangs, and the lower ends are loosely tied to the poles. When the birds fly into the net, pulling it tight, the trapper lets go of the ends, and the net falls to the ground with the trapped geese inside it. Duck may also be caught in this way. It is worth noting that geese that only brush against the net, without getting caught in it, fall to the ground in such alarm that they honk and flap their wings, unable to fly off again. No doubt the darkness of night contributes to their state of shock. Sometimes two or three such traps are set side by side a short distance apart, so that the flock will still be caught even if there is a deviation from the route.

There is a special variety of goose known as the brant goose [*kazarka*].[4] It is much smaller than the common wild goose and has a short beak, with pointed patches on the sides of it. The plumage is almost black. In some southern districts of Orenburg province they occur frequently on passage and are even shot. I, however, have never managed to see one. I have always been very puzzled by its name, which is so close to the name of the Khazar people.

3. DUCK

Species of duck are many and varied. I shall deal only with those that I am fairly familiar with. By virtue of its geographical position and large size the province of Orenburg encompasses extremes of climate and natural habitat, bordering to the north on the provinces of Viatka and Perm', where the mercury freezes in winter, and to the south on the Caspian Sea and the province of Astrakhan', where, as is well known, the tenderest varieties of grapes are grown in the open air. These factors permit a wide variety of all forms of life, including a range of species of duck, especially during the spring passage. I do not intend to discuss those duck that are only passage migrants in the province: that would lead me to digress too far and leave the reader with an incomplete picture of the subject. The passage of duck here is very different from that of the sandpipers, which stay a week or two in spring and one month or two in autumn. The duck species on passage can only be seen in spring, never in autumn, and never remain in one place for as much as one day. Only rarely do they fall prey to a wildfowler, so it seems superfluous to speak of rarities that I have seen only fleetingly and of other sportsmen's tales.

I shall tell only of a remarkable duck which I shot as a very young man. Some ten years later a friend of mine shot an identical bird and I was able to examine it closely. It was a little larger than the biggest farmyard duck. Its plumage was light brown with fine, dark speckling; its eyes and feet were vermilion and the upper mandible was edged with a narrow band of the same color; a grayish-blue stripe ran across the flight feathers; its down was pink, like that of a bustard, and the flesh and skin an orange color. The flavor of the meat was superb and quite different from that of ordinary duck. The tail was long and straight, like the tail of a drake pintail, but this bird was a duck, not a drake.

Before embarking on a description of the duck family, I feel I should mention a singular feature that separates duck from other birds and that applies equally to all duck species.

It will be apparent that, when copulation takes place at display grounds, at communal gatherings, neither the males nor the females can be joined by any special feeling for each other. One day the male mates with one female, the next day with another, depending whom he happens to meet. The behavior of the female is exactly the same. From this it follows that they never form pairs and that the female alone, unaided by any mate, has to take responsibility for building a nest, incubating the eggs, and rearing the young. Where there is no marriage there is no father.

By contrast, in all species that form pairs, both cock and hen, like husband and wife, share in the rearing of the young and display equal zeal in protecting them. This law is unswervingly observed by all birds that pair. The only clear exception is the duck family. All duck form pairs earlier in the season than other birds; the drake constantly gives proof of a jealous, passionate, and utterly selfless devotion to the duck, and at the same time—implacable hostility and anger toward her nest, eggs, and young! The female is obliged to discharge all her maternal duties without his knowledge. If he should find her nest with eggs or newly hatched ducklings he will tear the nest apart and (it is said) eat the eggs, or at least crush them and kill all the young. I myself have never witnessed such outrages, but others have. I have seen with my own eyes how the duck tries to hide from the drake, and how he seeks her out and pursues her, angrily punishing her for fleeing from him, for not wanting to fly with him to some other place, or for refusing copulation. And I have seen the ruined nests, broken eggs, and dead ducklings. This is quite enough to persuade me of the truth of the stories told by others. In my view the explanation for the unnatural behavior of the drake lies in his quite extraordinary concupiscence, which leads him to hate everything that distracts the female from himself. In all birds that live in pairs the male is attentive to the female, and male pigeons show tenderness and devotion, but no other birds display the mad passion of the drake. However, both sexes are equally devoted to their young.

There are fowlers who suspect blackcock, which work themselves into a frenzy at the display ground, of demolishing the nests of their females, but I have never observed any such thing.

Male great snipe are also frantic during display, but nobody suspects them of similar outrages. It is my opinion that such suspicions are idle because blackcock do not form pairs, and therefore the male has no motive for destroying the nest; the gray-hen is not his life's companion and will not be induced to return to him.

The drake, however, having laid waste the nest, regains complete control of the duck. She will not part with him for a moment until she has built a new nest and begun incubation again—out of his sight. We may even suppose that some females do not succeed in rearing any young throughout the summer. This is why all fowlers sometimes come across duck in pairs as late as June and even early July, when the birds enter the eclipse season.

3A. MALLARD

Kriakovnaia utka; kriakva; Anas platyrhynchos

The name of this duck is usually pronounced *krikovnaia utka*, which is most fitting, as it suggests *krik* [shout], and the mallard has the loudest voice of all the duck family. It is also called *kriakva* and *kriakusha*. All three names stem from the word *kriakat'* [to quack], which imitates its call so well. The Ukrainian word for a duck is *kachka* [from *kachat'*, "to sway," "to waddle"], another highly expressive word: when a duck walks, it sways constantly from side to side, and when it is on the water in a breeze, it rocks on the waves like a boat. A close resemblance in build and some resemblance even in plumage indicates that farmyard or domestic duck are descended from the mallard. In all flocks of farmyard duck, brindled, variegated, and white, a few can always be found with plumage very like that of the wild mallard duck, or even drake, while others with only slightly greater differences are common. The resemblance in size and plumage between farmyard duck and other wild species is not nearly so close. This is a curious fact: there is no obvious reason why other members of the duck family should not be domesticated.

The mallard is the largest of the wild duck. The drake is exceptionally handsome: the head and half of the neck seem to be of green velvet with a golden sheen; round the neck is a narrow white band below which the throat and breast are dark purple. The belly is grayish-white with very beautiful decorative hues. The lower feathers of the tail are white, short, and stiff, while the upper feathers are greenish and curl up in ringlets. The feet are pale orange and the bill a greenish yellow. On the dark wing is a bluish to cherry-colored iridescent patch. The back is darkish, tending to reddish. On the lower rump is a tuft of short, soft, dark green feathers. The female is speckled all over with elongated dark striations on a light brown background. A shiny green speculum shows in the wing. There are no curly feathers in the tail. The feet are the same orange color as the drake's and the bill is of the usual flesh color.

In spring, mallard arrive in flocks at the end of March, earlier than the other duck except for goldeneye. At first they fly in huge flocks in powerful, direct flight high above the ground, which is still covered in deep snow, not yet properly thawing. Later, when spring gathers momentum and in the space of a week changes the sad picture of winter into a jolly spring scene, when the streams begin to flow, pools and lakes form, and rivers burst their banks, the flocks of mallard fly lower and settle on suitable land. At this season they are difficult to shoot as they are very wary and will not permit close approach, whether on foot or on horseback. They are then most easily shot in flight, especially in the late evening, when they fly much lower, or when they flight from one pool to another. This kind of sport is known as "position shooting," referring to fixed positions over which the duck always fly. But this does not last long, as the birds soon divide into smaller parties, and begin to feel at home, thus becoming tamer. Then they may be cautiously approached in an ordinary cart, or a hunter's *drozhki*, which is no more than a shortened, unsprung peasant carriage with the hood removed. To shoot duck, large duck-shot, Number Two or Three, should be used. For more wary birds, goose-shot may also be used. An approach on foot can be ruled out at this season as the duck remain in large flocks on open ground.

But the spring gets warmer by the hour and the spring floods subside. The duck in small parties finally form pairs and mate, after which the birds are tamer, especially because, once the grass has grown, it provides a place for them to hide in. The drake, the most concupiscent of males, will not move a step away from his duck, will not leave her side for an instant, and will not be induced to take wing before she does. Sometimes the duck will be splashing in a puddle or sifting the ooze with her bill while the drake stands guard over her on the bank or a nearby hummock; when a fowler comes within range and the female does not notice, the drake will become agitated, quacking as he turns this way and that as if to warn her of the danger, but she pays no heed; he will not fly away on his own, so can be killed outright by an accurate shot. The female then flies off, showing not the slightest sympathy for her late partner. The picture is very different if a fowler should shoot the female (although his choice will always fall on the drake). The drake will not only circle the hunter in flight, without, however, coming too close to him, but will even remain for several days near the spot where his mate was taken from him.

At this time of year it is easier to approach the scattered pairs of mallard. Often it is easiest to creep up on them on foot, using the cover provided by, for instance, bushes, riverbanks, or hillocks, for a duck that is ready to nest or start sitting never stays with the male out in the open. She always hides in a hollow, near bushes, reeds, or unmown grass: she must deceive the ever-watchful male and get away from him; she must hide, steal along the ground for as much as a furlong, and then fly up and by herself begin the great work that is the aim of all living creatures. To do this she has to resort to various ploys. When she feels within her the weight of a number of eggs, fertilized at varying times and now formed into minute yolks, some of them already quite sizable and even enveloped in a film of white and contained in a soft, but tough skin, the female fashions a nest in a well-hidden spot and then, when she feels that one of the eggs is already hard and ready to lay, she selects a place from which she can easily escape, usually beside a pool or lake, puts her head under her wing, and pretends to be asleep. The drake will alight beside her and go to sleep, without pretending. The duck, who observes him watchfully from under her wing, at once hides in the grass, sedge, or reeds, then steals away some distance—the distance depending on the lie of the land—takes wing, and flies low and indirectly before alighting and making her way on foot to the nest she has woven out of dry grass in some safe, dry spot, well grown with bushes, in the marsh. She lines her nest with her own feathers and down, lays her first egg, carefully covers it over with grass and feathers, walks away some distance in a different direction, rises, and flies by an indirect route, approaching the spot where she first hid from the other side. There she lands again and steals up to the drake, who will be waiting for her. Only rarely will she find him asleep; he usually awakes during her absence, which may last over an hour. When he wakes he begins anxiously calling his mate, hurriedly looking about him, and jerkily swimming about the pool or lake; then he rushes to look for her round the banks, but without venturing far, and constantly looking back to see if she has returned or if she is swimming toward him over the water . . . which may sometimes happen. Tiring of his vain efforts to find her, the drake stops searching and begins swimming to and fro, looking round constantly and quacking, until at last—heaven knows how or whence—his mate suddenly reappears. He rushes frantically to meet her, seizes her with his beak by the neck, jumps onto her back, and there and then, in the water, begins copulating with her. . . . No sooner has she freed herself from his amorous clutches, shaken down her feathers, and emerged upon the bank, than he is seized by a bout of renewed lust, and he again copulates with his partner. This is repeated several times in the course of an hour. If the drake should espy another drake flying toward them he will immediately fly up to see him off, asserting his prior claim. If an unpaired drake should try to join the pair in flight an aerial duel with the lawful spouse inevitably ensues, accompanied by a special short high-pitched call well known to wildfowlers. The sight is often spectacular: both drakes hang vertically in the air, gripping each other by the neck, flapping with great power and agility to avoid falling to the ground, yet despite all their efforts sinking steadily downward. In all my observations, the lawful husband always emerges victorious.

Sometimes the duck employs a particular form of caress to send the drake to sleep: gently and persistently she tickles his neck and back with her bill. Hence the peasant saying, applied to humans, also used by fowlers, that "the drake likes having his head scratched." Sometimes the female will find a way to get away from him even while he is awake; he has only to start paying serious attention to the matter of food, or be distracted by something else, and she will vanish from sight with astonishing alacrity. But not all her attempts are successful. Sometimes the drake notices, guesses her intention, and flings himself in pursuit just as she is about to disappear in the grass or reeds, catches her, seizes her by the neck, drags her onto the water, shaking and pecking her so long and hard that her feathers fly. The punishment is immediately followed by a bout of conjugal passion. In the meantime nature gradually achieves its end—the duck lays a nestful of eggs, finally gets away from her mate, and settles down to incubate them. The eggs number up to twelve and are just like those of farmyard ducks except for the faintest tinge of yellowish-green. The female sits almost without interruption; only once a day will she leave the nest to find something to eat nearby. During the three-week incubation period she grows extraordinarily thin. At last the ducklings hatch, all covered in grayish-yellow down. If there are many eggs there will almost always be one or two "rattlers" among them. This name denotes an egg in which the young bird has not formed, so that the half-empty shell rattles when it is shaken. Such eggs probably occur because not all eggs can receive equal warmth from the brooding duck when there are so many. "Rattlers" do not occur when only eight or nine eggs are laid. A few hours after hatching there are no young left in the nest: the mother leads them to the still water of a reedy pond or lake. She helps them along by carrying them carefully in her beak over difficult stretches. Many fowlers have witnessed this, including myself.

In the meantime the drakes, abandoned by their partners, stay beside the pools and lakes where they last saw them. Many of them may have been shot by fowlers, which helps promote the unhindered hatching of the young. If you should catch sight of a drake or hear his low quack at this season you are assured a kill: he will either allow you to come within range, without moving, or will fly toward you, circling round the same spot.

At last the drakes reach their eclipse, when they too seek dense cover in the same reedy ponds and lakes, from mid-June until almost the end of July. During this period, the unpaired drakes, which have not begun to molt, only occasionally fall victim to a fowler's gun, and duck-shooting effectively ceases, if you do not count the females killed while brooding or rearing their young. However, at this time many ducklings and molting birds can be caught by trained dogs, which can even drive them into ordinary fishermen's nets.

Duck are the most devoted of mothers. Should a dog or a human scare one from her nest, for which you have to practically step on her, she will feign injury or inability to fly, sitting in one spot, trembling all over and falling down constantly, giving the impression that you need only take a few steps to catch her. Few dogs will not be taken in and fail to run after her. Usually the duck will lure a dog half a mile away or more. Wildfowlers know all about this ploy and yet, often out of unforgivable covetousness, they will forget why the bird is behaving in this way and that with it a whole brood of young will perish, and shoot it anyway, if not hampered by a pursuing dog that the duck is "leading by the nose." However, once the duck has lured the dog away, it will soon return, fly straight at the wildfowler, and be shot.

When the young have hatched, the female displays even more determination in their defense. If a human should come upon one swimming on open water with her brood the ducklings will rise and almost run along the surface with piteous squeals, rushing headlong to seek the cover of the nearest reeds and even diving if space permits. Meanwhile their mother will beat the water with her wings, fill the air with a special cry of alarm, and circle before the intruder to draw his attention and lead him away from her young. If the duck and her brood should seek cover in an isolated patch of reeds or the grass on the bank, and the hunter and dog should come so close that there is no possible escape, the duck will spring out or fly out, depending on the distance, onto the open water and perform the same maneuver. This act of panic will be terminated by a gunshot, killing the bird outright. All fowlers do this without a second thought since the resilient ducklings, however small, will look after themselves and grow up without their mother. Sometimes the orphans will attach themselves to another brood. I have seen a female with twenty ducklings swimming behind her, moreover, of varying age.

Very occasionally the female lays her eggs and hatches them in a hollow tree, or in the abandoned nest of a crow or magpie. It is difficult to say what motivates such an unusual choice, so opposed to the natural order observed by all varieties of duck. Yet I have witnessed such an instance myself, and a hunter whose word I can depend upon has told me of another. I also recall that a mallard or gadwall once laid its eggs on the threshing floor of a granary.

All in all, ducks are the most voracious eaters. They eat from morn till late at night, and eat everything that they can find: they pluck young goose-grass on the banks, and ravenously consume peat moss, or sphagnum, leaves and flowers, hungrily swallow small fry, crayfish, little frogs, and all kinds of flying, floating, and crawling insects. If this does not suffice they fill their crops with silt and mud, doing this several times a day. Farmyard ducks also happily take meat products. Their constant appetite is matched by the speed of their digestion: all foods are broken down in the crop with incredible speed. The duck's digestive juices are evidently very strong. The bird defecates constantly, and its droppings are even more acidic than those of geese.

August comes on. The mallard ducks, including the mothers of young broods, which molt later, have completed their molt, although the eclipse of the drakes is not quite over and will not be completed until September. This does not, however, prevent them flying strongly and for long distances. All broods of ducklings are well grown: the young birds are a little smaller than their parents, lighter in color, all of them are gray, and all look like females. Only on close inspection can the drakes be distinguished. Under the gray feathers on the head the bottle green is beginning to show through, and the deep purple on the throat. The feathers are as soft as velvet. The tailfeathers have partly developed but are still straight and as sharp as daggers, not yet curling upward. By mid-September both young drakes and old can be seen in all their glory, in their true and varied colors.

Throughout August the duck-shooting is at its best and most rewarding: the young birds are still quite tame—"silly," as fowlers say—and will permit a close approach. They can also easily be shot in flight as they rise from the small rivers along whose banks a hunter may walk, taking care to look ahead at every bend in the river to see if any ducks are swimming on it. If any are, he should hide behind bushes or move away from the bank lest they see him and fly up out of range. He must run ahead and wait for them to swim up close. If the river banks are steep and the birds are startled by the sudden appearance of a wildfowler they rise vertically with a flurry of wings, and bringing them down in various picturesque positions is easy and delightful sport. A good dog is essential here, preferably a Newfoundland or a poodle. Then no duck will get away, not even one that is only slightly winged or one that comes down on the far side of the river, perhaps in dense and marshy thickets. In September the sport is even more enjoyable as the birds have put on weight and the drakes have emerged from eclipse. This might seem unimportant, but if you ask any fowler he will tell you that he would far rather shoot a bird in full plumage, "in season," and well fed.

Although mallard are very common and therefore not

much sought after I remember shooting them in autumn with great pleasure. Moreover, it is the first bird you become familiar with when starting to shoot, the bird that first makes the young heart of the passionate hunter beat faster, and our childhood impressions remain with us for life. Duck species are so varied in size and plumage and the drakes of many so beautiful, and in autumn all can be so fleshy, that I continued to seek them with pleasure when not so young, along the meandering Buguruslan River in the early morning, when the frost had chased the flocks from the muddy banks of the pond, and from the shallow pools, and scattered them on the winding river. Often I came home laden with game: fifteen or more ducks so big that I could not fit even three in my game-bag. Fowlers say that a winged duck is cunning and there is much truth in this: an injured bird has extraordinary ability to hide, even on clear and open water. If it has the strength it will immediately dive, swim fifteen or even twenty fathoms under water and surface, or rather, poke up its bill and part of its head, while clinging close to the bank so that it is impossible to see. If the banks are grassy, you have no hope of finding an injured bird without a dog. It will climb out of the water and disappear. In open water, if the banks are bare and steep, it will raise its bill onto the surface to breathe, and swim with the current, with its whole body submerged, so that you cannot pick it out. But a good dog is hard to shake off and will not let the bird crawl to shelter on the bank, and the experienced fowler, knowing where the duck will surface by the alignment of the head, will wait for its bill to appear, take speedy aim and hit the half-submerged head.

Although, as I have said, ducks always eat a great deal, they never eat as much as in August, because after the molt young and old alike are wasted and hungry, like patients recovering from an illness. In August their usual diet is supplemented by a most nourishing and desirable delicacy—grain. If there should be cereal fields near the pond or lake where the young have grown up and where the parents have changed their plumage, they will start visiting the fields, at first on foot, beating a broad path, and later flying to them in flocks. Woe to the farmer who has fields of buckwheat, millet, peas, or oats nearby! Like geese, duck prefer grains without awns, but if these are unobtainable they will eat those with awns, and even pull stooks of rye apart to get them. Once the stooks have been taken to the threshing floor, flocks of duck continue their dawn and dusk visits to the fields, where they forage for spilt grains and ears until their departure, usually in November. At this season, in addition to other methods, it is possible to shoot them as they flight to and from the fields.

In October duck congregate in large flocks and at this time it becomes difficult to shoot them. They spend the day on large bodies of water, in such numbers that the water is literally covered in them. I recall a verse from a letter written by a young wildfowler, who describes the scene fairly accurately:

The ponds and lakes with duck are covered.
A living carpet thus they weave.
They ripple, wave-like on the surface,
As under them the waters heave.[5]

Such a vast flock, on open water, as they always are, or on bare sloping banks, cannot possibly be approached on foot, by stealth, or using horse and carriage. And being in such large numbers, they will not settle on a small river as they did earlier in the season. I therefore resorted, with some success, to the following ploy, even in late October: I would flush the flocks from large ponds with a few shots and dissuade them from settling again, when, after circling a few times, they again descended toward the middle of the pond. They would then fly either up or down the river, but, being attached to their favorite haunts and not wishing to fly too far from them, they were forced to split up into small parties and settle in scattered groups along the river. I would leave my companion by the pond to fire occasionally at returning parties of duck. His shots were harmless, of course, but they forced the birds to keep to the meandering river. Meanwhile I myself set off on foot along the riverbank, making no sound, and showing myself only at points where I knew from the lie of the river that the duck would be sitting. Often I succeeded in bagging up to ten large fat mallard, mostly drakes, since, given the choice, one always aims at a drake. In these conditions I would only recommend keeping cool and not shooting at duck that rise too far off. A flock of duck, once dispersed, will scatter along a river, so the birds that rise do not fly far, but merely alight again with those on the river furthest from the hunter. The shot size needs to be chosen in accordance with the distance at which the duck will rise, from Number Three to Number Five inclusive. The greater the range the larger the shot. I have always used a smaller shot, Number Four. For successful shooting, however, much depends on the locality. First of all, there should be no large ponds or lakes in the vicinity, giving the flock a haven where they can remain together; second, the riverbanks should not be gently sloping or clear of bushes, as without them the fowler can be seen from afar and the duck will not allow him to come within range.

Mallard, particularly drakes, can also be lured by imitating the cry of the female, at the time when the females are hiding from them. On their spring arrival a "trained" farmyard duck with plumage like that of the wild bird may be used as a decoy. For this purpose the farmyard duck is harnessed, tethered by a cord to a stake, and provided with a platform to rest on in the middle of a pool of water, and a hide is set up nearby for the fowler to sit in. The duck will quack ceaselessly at the top of its voice from boredom, and wild drakes and even ducks will alight on the water beside it, right under the muzzle of a gun. This is a form of sport that I have no time for.

Wherever the conditions are right, snares are set to trap drakes, more precisely, snares attached by a cord to stakes close to the decoy female. In the province of Orenburg nets are also employed to catch them in flight, or at least they used to be, as for geese, because they also follow well-established flight paths to the fields. Hawks and falcons are also used to hunt them: with hawks, without great success, if any, but duck-hunting with falcons is the most splendid sport of all, although it now seems to have completely died out in Russia. The Bashkirs of the province still keep falcons, but the birds are poorly trained, in particular, not trained to gain height to a point where the human eye can hardly discern them and stoop with lightning speed upon their prey. Instead the Bashkir falcons are trained to overtake duck in almost level flight.

Mallard flesh is rather dry and tough when they are thin, that is, in June and July, but always nourishing. The flesh of their ducklings is very tender and many people are very partial to it, especially when it is fried with sour cream, but I am not fond of it. Plump autumn mallard, on the other hand, chiefly from the previous year's brood, have wonderful flavor: they are tender, succulent, and have that tang of the wild, with which the fatted farmyard duck can never compare. It must be admitted that all species of duck without exception sometimes smell of fish. This is because of the abundance of small fry in the waters that are their home. They are obliged to eat it sometimes, for want of other food, but mallard flesh hardly ever has a fishy taste.

I have spoken in some detail about the mallard. Henceforward, in describing other ducks, I shall deal only with their distinguishing features. The habits of all dabbling duck, their mode of life, and their diet are so similar in practically all respects that I would otherwise have to repeat myself.

3B. PINTAIL

Shilokhvost'; Anas acuta

This duck is a little smaller than the mallard and its lines and build are unique: the body is slightly slimmer and more elongated, the neck much longer and thinner, as is the tail, especially of the drake. The duck is entirely pale gray and finely speckled; along the flight feathers lies a glossy, greenish-gray band, nothing else. The belly is whitish. The drake is quite handsome: he has a short, almost black, bill; the whole head, down to a finger's breadth below the occipital bone, is coffee-colored; from the head down the upper side of the neck runs a band that is dark at first, then hatched with steely gray, joining the back, which is the same color, above the wing joints. The rest of the neck, throat, and breast are pure white. From the neck, up both cheeks, curving white stripes reach almost to the ears, against the coffee-brown background. The back is light blue-gray or has gray hatching. There are greenish-bronze, gold-tinged stripes on the wings, with buff edging on the upper surfaces and white edging below. Along the back

toward the tail lie long dark feathers with whitish borders; some of these have whitish stripes running along them. The dark and white hues taken together are very beautiful; the upper wing is darkish ash-gray, and the underwing light gray. The upper tailfeathers are the same color. Two of these are somewhat darker and longer by almost a quarter. They lie one above the other and project very stiffly, like an awl or knitting needle, which, no doubt, accounts for the Russian name *shilokhvost'* (awl-tail). The undertail coverts are almost black and the feet dark, but lighter than the beak. In spring, pintail arrive later than mallard and at first appear in large flocks. Their flight is faster than that of the mallard; they have faster wingbeats and produce a whistling sound owing to the shape of the wings, which are narrower, though long. When ducks form pairs in spring, pintail are encountered far less frequently than other species; their nests and broods of young are also harder to find and therefore better appreciated by fowlers than mallard. In autumn I have not seen large flocks of pintail at close range but have sometimes identified them by their distinctive muted call, rather like the low honking of geese, or by their flight and the whistle of their wings; the flocks were always flying very high. Even less frequently have I found individuals scattered along rivers. As a rough guide, I can say that you can expect to shoot ten times fewer pintail than mallard. This is rather strange as during the spring migration they pass over in huge flocks.

In all other respects, apart from the fact that the eggs are slightly longer and narrower than the mallard's, the pintail shares all the characteristics of all other duck species, and so pintail shooting is like shooting any other duck.

Although I have shot relatively few pintail compared to other duck, a singular incident occurred when I was walking along the banks of the Berlia River in the province of Samara, between a small pond and a much larger one about three versts away. My driver and *drozhki* were following a short distance behind me. Seven large pintail came toward me high overhead. I fired both barrels but none of the birds seemed to pay the least attention. A few minutes later my driver called out to me that the same birds were flying back again: something had apparently prevented them landing on the small pond and they were returning to the big one. They were flying so high that it would have been impossible to hit them. I watched them fly over and went on my way. Suddenly the driver called out again that the same seven pintail were coming toward us again, adding that "something must have stopped them landing on the big pond too." We both fixed our eyes on the duck, now flying even higher than before, right above us. All of a sudden, one of them somersaulted in the air, quickly lost height, and fell to the ground not far from me: it was a pintail drake, with the shoulder bone of its right wing broken in two. . . . This seems unbelievable but it was exactly so. With any other wound a bird can fly for some time, but it is simply impossible to fly, let alone for a long time, with a broken wingbone. There was no doubt that these were the same birds I had fired at: my keen-eyed driver had not let them out of his sight. So there is no other explanation but that the shot had struck the bird's carpal bone and caused a slight longitudinal crack. Under the strain of fast flight the bone had then snapped crossways, causing the bird to fall. I realize that many will find this explanation unsatisfactory but I can think of no other. The coincidence is also astonishing: the fracture occurred at the very moment when the duck, having flown several versts back and forth, were flying over me for the third time, so that the bird fell almost at my feet.

3C. GADWALL

Seraia utka; Anas strepera

The Russian name "gray duck" is not very descriptive as the females of all species of duck have gray plumage, or more precisely, speckled gray plumage, and this so-called gray duck is very like the females of all other kinds. But the gadwall nonetheless fully merits this name as it is grayer than all others and particularly because even the drake lacks any distinguishing marks. The Russian song about a "gray duck" no doubt refers to this bird.

The only difference between the sexes is that the drake has somewhat finer, lighter speckles and a narrow reddish-brown border with a brilliant sheen on one side of the white patch that both sexes have on the wing. Gadwall are sometimes known as "graylings" or "half-mallard." The latter name is not fully appropriate, as they are only a little smaller than mallard. There are no striking differences between gadwall and other ducks beyond the fact I have mentioned, that the drake closely resembles the duck and that all other species are more colorful and more beautiful. They are quite common and much more frequently shot than pintail, although I have not seen large flocks of gadwall during the spring passage and fewer still during autumn passage. There is a certain contradiction here that is a little difficult to explain.

In spite of its unsightliness, or rather, its plain plumage, which easily passes unnoticed, gadwall are more highly prized by wildfowlers than all other species except mallard and pintail, being quite large and fleshy, sometimes very fat and only rarely smelling of fish.

Many fowlers have told me that there are two kinds of gadwall, with similar plumage but differing in size. At first I shared this view as I had also noticed great differences in size, but later I decided that this was because of the age of the birds. Some doubt remains, however and I leave this question for the most experienced of fowlers to decide.

3D. WIGEON

Sviiaz'; Anas penelope

The Russian name *sviiaz'* is a wildfowler's term, and I cannot say how it originated.[6] The bird is popularly known as "redhead" [*krasnogolovka*] and "white-belly" [*belobriushka*], because the head of the drake and part of the neck are brick-red and the belly of both sexes brilliant white in the sun. Smaller than the mallard and pintail and even shorter in the body than the gadwall, this duck is roundly and robustly built. Its fast flight, with sharp, rapid wing-beats, shows its strength. The drake is very handsome and colorful; right above his eyes is a white spot; the rest of the head and half of the neck is reddish-brown; then follows a band of rippling gray, quickly fading into the light reddish color that covers the throat and breast. The belly is white and the back covered with beautiful lateral markings. Across the wing from the scapulars lies a long, broad patch of pure white with a black border, beneath which a greenish-gold stripe is visible, itself edged with velvety black. The tail is short, pointed, and fairly stiff. The bill and feet are small and black. The primaries are dark gray to buff.

The duck, on the other hand, is all dark except for her white

belly. At first glance she is very like the tufted duck and it is very difficult to imagine that her mate could be so handsome and so different.

In early spring, wigeon fly in large flocks. They can be told at a height by their fast flight and a distinctive sound, whistle-like with a kind of hiss, which gives the occasional name "hisser." The whistle is produced by their fast flight, blending with their rather hoarse quack. In autumn all three of the foregoing kinds of duck flight to cereal fields in flocks or small parties, but I have never seen wigeon among them. The same applies to the species that follow.[7] I should add that all of them (to say nothing of goldeneye) usually smell of fish. We may suppose that, as they do not eat grain and do not grow so fat as mallard, pintail, and gadwall, they catch the small fish that appear toward autumn in vast shoals, as tiny as barley pearls, and swim in all waters. In any case, even without grain, wigeon, like all other duck, wax very plump in autumn, although in this regard they can never compare with mallard.

The wigeon has no other peculiarities, aside from the fact that, although it arrives in vast spring flocks, throughout the year it is encountered by wildfowlers far less frequently than it should be. Perhaps because of this and because of the beauty of the drake and his rounded, robust, fleshy build, the wigeon is prized by fowlers more highly than some other duck, after the mallard, pintail, and gadwall. I, for one, must confess that I have always been only too glad to be able to put a red-headed drake wigeon in my game-bag.

3E. SHOVELER

Shirokonoska; Anas clypeata

The shoveler [Russian, *shirokonoska*, "broad-bill"] is also known as *plutonos.* The former name is fitting and indisputably right for this duck: its beak is unusually broad at the tip, like a rounded oar-blade; the basis for the latter name is unknown.[8] The bird is richly feathered, but for all that it is smaller than the foregoing species and of still slighter build. All in all it is rather puny, feeble, and skinny: at first sight you would think it much like any other duck, but when you pick it up you find it is all feathers and bone. Although, like all wildfowlers, I have very often killed shovelers, I have never come across a fat one. The duck is speckled all over, covered with quite bold brown speckles on a yellowish background; the pinions have a glossy blue stripe running across them. One ought to be able to say that the drake is very handsome:

skewbald, with a rich-brown belly, a white band on his neck, the back and wings gray-blue, the underparts light gray, but, for all this, he does not look particularly handsome and cannot compare with the drake wigeon.[9] I have not noticed flocks of shoveler either in spring or autumn, but, as I have said, they are quite often met with singly or in pairs, like gadwall, which is a little odd. Fowlers have little time for them.

Duck are not, on the whole, particularly resistant to gunshot, and the shoveler is less so than most. Nevertheless, the following incident once happened to me. There was a pond about ten versts from my home. In the shallows there were all kinds of game birds but wading was difficult, though this did not prevent me from coming here often. Once when I was wading among tall reeds up to my knees in mud, with my game-bag fairly full of small birds, I saw a brace of shoveler flying straight toward me at low level. They were flying straight and level at exactly head height. I let fly with snipe-shot and killed them both outright, duck and drake. As I did not want to crush the common and jack snipe I had in my bag, I tucked the shoveler by the neck under my leather belt, tightening it, so that they should not fall out. I went on walking for more than an hour. Finally I returned to my *drozhki* and emptied my bag into a leather case, tossing the shoveler in first. I made no haste to return home: I did some more shooting on the way and filled the case with a variety of birds. On my return I stood by as the game was lifted out of the *drozhki*. When the servants reached the bottom of the case the drake shoveler suddenly flew out and vanished from sight, apparently completely unharmed! . . . It can sometimes happen that a bird is stunned and concussed by a head wound, appearing to be killed outright, but then comes to and flies away. It is not uncommon, but it is amazing that this drake was not throttled by my tight belt, by which it hung for so long by its neck, and that it was not suffocated under all the other birds in the case.

The obverse of these stunning or concussing wounds is the internal wound, ultimately fatal, but with which a bird sometimes manages to go on flying for some time before suddenly dropping dead. I have known many such cases and will tell of one of them. Having driven my *drozhki* up to a large pond I fired at a pair of teal that were rapidly swimming out from the low bank toward the middle, where a large raft of tufted duck lay out of range. I killed one of the teal and my dog retrieved it for me. The tufted duck, startled by the shot, rose from the water and circled before alighting again in the middle. I reloaded and waited on the bank in case some sandpiper or duck should happen to fly toward me. Suddenly the whole flock took wing again as if something had frightened them and flew away. I looked, and saw one duck struggling on the surface in its death agony. I sent out my dog, which brought me a tufted duck, now dead, covered in blood from a wound level with its heart. This is ample proof that a bird may fly with a fatal wound. But the coincidences here were extraordinary! That duck was wounded at a range of at least ninety or a hundred paces, by a ricochet. My Number Four shot had skimmed up from the surface, for I had fired at the teal half that distance away. The bird had risen with the flock, apparently unhurt, and flown some distance with it; then it had returned, alighted at the previous spot, and died before my eyes. This leads one to wonder how many injured birds might be lost, without the sportsman knowing it.

3F. TEAL

chirok-trestunok; Anas querquedula; garganey (summer teal);
chirok-svistunok; Anas crecca; teal

The Russian name *chirok* may have to do with the bird's call. The teal chirrups, that is, its call sounds like "chirk, chirk." Teal are of two kinds, the summer teal, or garganey, and the common teal. The cry of the former is much thinner and more drawn out, but much more penetrating and far-carrying than that of the common teal. Why it is sometimes called the "teal-crake" [Russian, *chirok-korostelek*] I do not know. If this is by reason of its call, the short, hoarse note of the corncrake or landrail more closely resembles the cry of the common teal.[10]

The two teal are the smallest, nimblest, fleetest fliers, and the most elegantly shaped of all the duck family. The female garganey is entirely light-gray with a light blue-gray bar in

Garganey

Teal

the wing, hard to see unless the wing is extended. In the drake this bar is much wider and blue, almost sky-blue, with a bright gloss; in addition, on each side of his head, up the brick-red neck, run white stripes a little more than two inches in length; the drake is lighter colored than the duck, with a whitish belly.

The common teal is always smaller than the garganey and some individuals are very small. I once shot a female so small that it looked like a mallard duckling: with its miniature proportions it was very pleasing to the eye. Common teal are as gray and as mottled as garganey but their coloration is more yellowish, and darker: the female is mottled gray all over with quite a broad, glossy green wing-bar. In the drake this bar is broader still, and brighter; up the side of the head, from halfway down the neck to the eye, runs a stripe, or rather, an elongated patch, about two inches long, but twice as wide as in the garganey. This patch or stripe is reddish-yellow, like the dappling on a foxhound.

During spring and autumn migration teal appear in large flocks. In spring they always arrive a little later than other duck and in autumn they stay longer than all except the mallard. Throughout the season teal are more often met with singly than other duck. Despite the fact that they are common and that they are the tamest of all duck I have always preferred them to many other medium-sized ducks. They arrive quite plump and are very fat on departure, only slightly less fat than mallard, although I have never noticed them flying to cereal fields. They are very fast and nimble fliers, especially when they congregate in large flocks. As the flock circles over the spot where it intends to land the birds twist and turn, massing in a dark knot, then unraveling into a lighter skein. Several times during late evening shoots in spring and autumn I have been startled by a whistling sound and even a sudden rush of air as a tight-packed party of teal sped right over my head.

I have said nothing about the size of the eggs of the preceding kinds of duck, except the mallard. Being very similar in color and shape, the eggs vary in size according to the size of the birds, but teal eggs are so small, dull-colored, and of such a tender greenish hue, that they must be mentioned separately. It is a strange fact that in the nests of mallard and other large duck I have never found more than nine or ten eggs (although I have found ten times more nests of these duck than of teal), while in teal nests I have found up to twelve, so that even the walls of the nest were lined to quite a height with eggs. I could not help wondering, as I did on finding the nest of the spotted crake, how such a small bird could warm and hatch so many.

From springtime on, throughout the summer, either in pairs or singly, teal may be met with wherever there is water, but they are especially fond of small rivers, lakes and ponds, often even in villages, where they will fly in to join farmyard ducks. In autumn it is sometimes possible to fire a lucky shot into an unexpected tight-packed flock of teal. I once killed nine teal with a single charge loaded with grouse shot. A winged teal is a more agile diver than all other duck, except of course the goldeneye, and the most skilled at hiding in the grass.

I prefer the flesh of a plump, autumn teal even to mallard, if it does not smell of fish—which, unfortunately, is sometimes the case. It has about it more of the taste of the wild. All duck eggs are very palatable but teal eggs are the tastiest.

The above are the best kinds of duck that I know. I shall now speak of those that are less prized, or valued little by wildfowlers, mostly because they all, without exception, always smell strongly of fish.[11] All are fish-eating duck, which are true waterfowl. Water is their true element, on which they live day and night. For them the land hardly seems to exist.

3G. GOLDENEYE[12]

This is a small, but robust, fleshy, and well-formed duck. The name *nyrok* [diver] is fitting, although in the art of diving the grebe is its equal and the mergansers surpass it.

Goldeneye have brindled, or rather pied plumage. Their coloration is plain and somber—black and white. The drake is more colorful and handsome than the duck. Their flight is very swift and the rapid wing-beats produce a special sound, less a pure whistle than a rapid trill, which cannot be conveyed in words. A rather similar sound is produced by a little bustard in flight. Fowlers will be very familiar with it. On seeing a human the goldeneye does not rise immediately from the water: instead, it begins diving with such agility that on a large expanse of water it is well out of range within a minute. If it is on a narrow river and the bird has to swim with the current, it swims under water so fast that a fowler has to run as fast as he can to catch up with it. Finally, when he appears suddenly, too close to the surfacing bird, after cutting it off at a bend in the river, the bird will take wing. At first it picks itself up with difficulty, pattering with its wings along the surface, but it soon gathers momentum, flying very fast and rising high in the air.

Goldeneye appear in spring before all other duck. Sometimes, in late March, the province of Orenburg is still enveloped in deepest winter. There may be no sign of the approach of spring except the dazzling glare of the glassy surface of the snow. . . . And all of a sudden, high in the sky, beneath the clouds, you hear that distinctive sound, so easily recognized: that trilling whistle produced by the rapid flight of vast flocks of goldeneye. Looking up, a sharp eye can make them out, flying high and fast, like a little gray cloud driven by a strong tailwind. It is difficult to convey the sweet feeling produced in the heart of the wildfowler by this distant, as yet indistinct sound, signaling the beginning of the return of bird life, promising the speedy coming of spring, after a long, unbearably tedious winter, whose endlessness would drive him to despair. . . . As an example of how long the Orenburg winter can sometimes be, I recall that on 1 April 1807, before sunrise, the temperature was twenty degrees of frost by the Reamur scale! This fact speaks for itself and nothing needs to be added. There is no question about it, in spite of the late date, 1 April, for I recorded it precisely in my wildfowling notes. I do not know how other hunters feel but I have always been delighted to see the goldeneye arrive, and in gratitude for their early appearance and the joy I experienced at the time, have always felt a certain respect for them and have shot them whenever I have had the chance. . . . "Odd gratitude! Odd respect!" will be the response of readers who are not wildfowlers. But we have our own logic: the more respect you have for a bird, the harder you try to shoot it.

At first, large flocks of goldeneye fly over without landing—there is nowhere for them to land anyway. Later, whenever gaps appear in the ice, on rivers or ponds, pairs of goldeneye can be found. From then until summer they remain on rivers and ponds, singly or in pairs. Throughout the summer you will find few goldeneye, and mainly drakes, but in autumn they again congregate in large flocks before departing. I have never found their nests, but have come across broods of young. I believe I can affirm that goldeneye, unlike all the foregoing species, do not build their nests on dry ground, but, like other diving duck, they contrive to make them in reeds or dense, tall sedge right on the water, or just above it. I have found two such nests and will describe them in due course. The goldeneye is the first of a number of ducks that are almost bereft of the ability to walk on land: their feet are so constructed that they can be used only for swimming or paddling, like oars. The feet are situated very far back, near the tail, and project behind. This is less marked in the goldeneye than in some other species. The goldeneye forms a kind of transition stage. The bill is of normal proportions, blackish, not too slender, and not pale flesh-colored, like that of all the other diving ducks except the tufted duck. Nature has thoughtfully equipped all waterfowl with long, thick down, which prevents any drop of water reaching the skin, but the diving ducks, from the goldeneye to the sawbills (especially the latter), being built for a lifetime on the water, have the thickest down of all. The goldeneye is always on water: from morn till night it catches small fingerlings, though not spurning insects and other small aquatic creatures.

Females with ducklings, which are astonishingly nimble, cling to the reeds and will not be flushed out onto open water. Goldeneye are always quite plump and in autumn can grow very fat. Their flesh would be succulent, tender, and palatable, were it not for the smell of fish. I have met people who are not put off by the smell and who consider goldeneye a delicacy to be savored. If you skin a goldeneye, scrape out the giblets, wash it thoroughly, soak it for an hour or two in salty water and then roast it, very little will remain of the fishy smell and anyone with a healthy appetite can eat it with pleasure. The goldeneye has good resistance to gunshot and needs real duck-shot, nothing smaller than Number Four.

There are other kinds of goldeneye: one kind is no larger than a teal; and the others are big, with red heads, broad, ash-gray beaks, and broad, apricot-colored feet. I have never managed to see either of these at close quarters.[13]

3H. TUFTED DUCK

Chern'; modern Russian, *khokhlataia chernet'*; *Aythya fuligula*

The collective name given to this duck [*chern'*, "mass; blackness"] is fitting: they always appear in vast flocks when spring

is well established. Not only have I never encountered them singly or in pairs, I have never come across small parties. They usually settle on large clear pools or lakes, covering the bright water with a thick black shroud. The water looks literally black, so in this respect too the name is apt. They occur here only on passage, in spring and autumn. On large bodies of water they remain for some time, especially in a fine warm autumn. I do not know where they breed but it is not in those districts where I have lived, so I have never seen them with young.[14]

In size, bill shape, and plumage, the tufted duck is very similar to the goldeneye, that is, the upper parts are black, and the underparts whitish. I have not managed to shoot many. It is difficult, as they always sit in the middle of a lake, so that you can only approach them by boat, which I have sometimes done, but the bird is hardly worth the trouble. I have killed them only when they have chanced to fly straight toward me. I have not noticed any difference between the plumage of the duck and the drake but others have told me that the drake is distinguished by a deeper coffee-colored sheen, its larger size, and its black crest.

This bird's plumage is unattractive but it is robustly built. The bill and feet are of exactly the same color and shape as those of the goldeneye and the flesh does not smell so strongly of fish. If you succeed in paddling out from a reed-bed to within range of a flock of tufted duck it is possible to kill as many as ten with one shot.

31. GREAT CRESTED GREBE[15]

For a long time I thought that the "goosander" [*krokhal'*] was a distinct diving duck from the grebe, as in my youth I killed two of the latter without crests and with much lighter plumage and larger bodies. At that time ordinary fowlers called these *krokhali.* Later I learned that these were one and the same species and that the diving duck I had shot were mature grebes or "goosanders," which are always larger and lighter colored. Subsequently I have often come across birds without crests, so perhaps only the drakes have crests.[16]

From beak to tail, or rather, to toe, as these birds have no tailfeathers, their length is eighteen inches. The beak is two inches long, dark gray, slender, very strong, and sharp at the tip. The head is small and elongated, with a dark brown stripe along its forehead, ending in a crest behind the occiput, right round the neck, two inches high, more like an old-fashioned ruffle than anything else, rust-red in color, but dark brown near the feather roots. The neck is long, dark ash-gray above, and the back ash-brown, seeming to end in the feet that jut out behind. The feet are dark lead-gray above and whitish-yellow below, with irregular dark blotches. The legs, from the feet to the belly, are not rounded, but completely flattened, and the three toes are webbed by a strong, unbroken membrane that is almost lead-gray in color.[17] The toes are also flat, not rounded, as in all other birds. Just above the ankle, where the foot begins, is a fourth toe, shaped like a tiny flat scoop with a claw of the same shape. In proportion to the size of the bird, which is as large as a mallard, the wings are very small and narrow. They are gray-brown in color; both edges of the primaries are white but along the middle of the wings runs a dark brown band, three fingers' breadth across, the same color as three of the pinions. The underparts, from the legs right up to the crest or tippet, is covered with fine, white, silvery feathers, at first sight rather like hairs. Under them lies a splendid, thick, tender down of dark gray color. The underwing is brilliant white.

Great-crested grebes are true fish-eaters and smell so strongly of fish that it is practically impossible to eat them. For this reason fowlers rarely shoot them, unless it be to discharge their guns, or for the down, which is just as good as that of the merganser. The Russian people, however, have long known this bird by the name of *krokhal'* (this is undoubtedly the older term), as it lives on in the popular saying, "He (or she) trembles over her like a *krokhal'*," expressing somebody's love and concern for somebody else. This refers to the drake's deep attachment to the duck, or the duck's particular devotion to her young, which the common people observed.[18]

Unfortunately I am not very familiar with the habits of this bird, remarkable though they undoubtedly must be, as is evidenced by the singularity of their flattened tarsi and the way they build their nests, floating on the water. I once found such a nest, and the grebe that was sitting on it, as on a boat, floating about on a small lake surrounded by vast reed-beds. Seeing me close at hand the bird slipped off the nest into the water and dived. There were nine eggs, in size and shape similar to hens' eggs, of a pale greenish color with speckles.

In the spring migration season I have never noticed grebes in flocks. They turn up somehow unexpectedly, always singly and always in very late spring. Their usual haunts are deep pools with plenty of open water and large lakes with reeds. Their diet consists mainly of small fish and partly of aquatic insects. Grebes are hardly able to walk and can only squat on their feet, and that only in shallow water, which offers support. This gives them a strange posture as they sit leaning backward in a half-standing position, with their sharp beaks pointing upward. In their wings they have very short feathers, which make the wings themselves look narrow and longer than they are. Grebes generally fly with difficulty, especially when they first take wing, until they have picked up speed, and only extreme circumstances will induce them to rise from the water at all. More often they evade danger by persistent diving, at which they are surpassed only by mergansers. Some fowlers, however, have seen large parties in swift, high flight.

There is another kind of small grebe, one-third the size of

the large variety, just like it in its proportions and plumage, but lacking the crest, I believe. Unlike the crested grebe, this kind is always met with in flocks: they are much faster fliers. I cannot account for the name *gagara*.[19]

Grebes are sometimes confused with mergansers, owing to their long, straight necks when extended, but there are a number of marked differences between them, which I shall proceed to tell of.

3J. MERGANSER[20]

The word *gogol'* is commonly used among ordinary folk to describe the peculiarities of people, or their walk, although this bird can hardly walk at all. The comparison is based upon the fact that, like grebes, they hold their long necks very straight and their heads high. For this reason people who for whatever reason have this habit or affectation, lending them an air of cheeriness or even haughtiness, are compared with these ducks. Even without particularly keen sight one can pick out the long necks of grebes and mergansers, held upright, like sticks, among a mass of ducks swimming on a lake. Mergansers stand out most of all, as they submerge their bodies much deeper than other ducks, so that their necks seem to stick up straight out of the water.

The merganser is the last, and the most remarkable of the diving ducks, and its diet consists exclusively of small fish. It is slightly smaller than a grebe, and comparable in size to a medium-sized duck such as the shoveler or wigeon, but its shape is longer and more boatlike. Its plumage is gray, even bluish, with a slight gloss. The feet project straight from the back and are greenish, with unbroken webbing between the toes. The bird is hardly able to walk and rises from the water with even more difficulty and reluctance than a grebe. In all my life I have never ever seen one in flight. Its bill is slender, rounded, and quite different from that of ordinary ducks: the tip of the upper mandible turns sharply down. The head is small and well proportioned, the neck long, but shorter than the grebe's and less rigidly straight. On the contrary, the bird turns with great flexibility until it sees a human close by. As soon as it notices danger it immediately applies its unique capability: it sinks in the water so that only a narrow strip of its back can be seen, with its neck held very straight and its extraordinarily keen, red eyes firmly fixed on the source of danger. In this alert posture the merganser is astonishing! However steadily you may gaze at it you will not observe when or how it disappears! Nor will you observe when or whence it reappears . . . so quickly does it dive. The very word "dive" fails to express the movement of the merganser: it is simply a vanishing act. To fully appreciate the bird's amazing agility it is sufficient to say that in the days of flintlock fowling pieces you could not kill one unless you took it unawares. The instant the flint struck the steel, producing sparks and igniting the powder in the pan, which, of course, was a matter of one second, the bird's neck and head disappeared and the shot struck the empty circle on the surface left by the bird's rapid submergence. This magical speed was the sole reason for the attention paid it by young fowlers in my day, and perhaps even today, for the flesh of the merganser is worse than that of all other fish-eating ducks, and nobody hunts it for its fine down. The apparent opportunity to kill a duck swimming on the surface, within range, and not scared into flight by gunshots, together with the need for speed and a true aim, confidence in one's favorite gun, a desire to shine before one's companions, and, above all, the remote possibility of success, have all tickled the fowler's pride and sometimes caused a whole company to surround a small pond or lake on which mergansers were swimming. In my youth I remember many such times. How we shouted, laughed, and ran about excitedly, firing our guns uselessly! More often than not we returned home having expended all our shot without killing a single bird, to laugh heartily at one another. But occasionally persistence paid off, through only when a single merganser, or at most two, could be isolated on the water, for then the birds had to keep diving. Then the poor bird, finally driven to exhaustion, could no longer keep its body deeply submerged and would begin to surface more often and dive more slowly, so that a true shot could bring triumph to one of the hunters.

From what I have said one might conclude that mergansers

are unable to fly, but I am assured by certain wildfowlers who can be relied upon that they have seen mergansers flying high and fast. And then, where do they appear from in spring? Of course they fly in from somewhere, even if nobody has seen them arrive: they appear in early May on ponds and lakes, always in very small numbers. As for the fact that a merganser surrounded by wildfowlers does not take flight at the sound of shots, no doubt the bird instinctively senses the danger of rising from the water, and it is right: if it took flight it would be killed immediately by several shots. If you can manage to approach the water under some kind of cover it is perfectly easy to shoot a merganser: it rides high in the water, its neck bent as it searches the water for small fish. Then it can be killed like any other duck.

I have tried to shoot mergansers in the same way fish can be shot when swimming close to the surface. You need to take account of the angle of the shot and take aim not at the fish itself, but a little above or below it. The angle of deflection of the pellets, always equal to the angle at which they fall, will depend on the height of the bank the fowler is standing on, and the distance from the target. If the bank is completely flat and the range long—that is, if the angle of fall is acute—the shot will ricochet into the air. Clearly, in this situation you need to aim lower, on the nearer side of the fish. If the bank is high and the angle of fall less acute, the shot will enter the water and go down at the same angle, so you need to aim a little higher. Having observed that a merganser at first dives straight down—not forward like other ducks, or to the side—and then turns in the desired direction, I aimed at the bird just after it had dived, as at a fish in the water, but without success. It was saved by its agility. The merganser's keenness of sight and hearing are astounding: even when swimming with its back to you, without turning its head it sees all your movements and hears the flint striking the steel. Many times I have wondered whether the merganser's eye is designed in some special way, but there is no external sign of this. I suppose it should be easier to shoot mergansers using a percussion weapon, as it produces no spark from the steel, and no flash of powder, and the discharge comes much faster. I have had no opportunity to test this supposition, but I have heard that my view has been confirmed in practice.

I have never found nests of mergansers, but there is no doubt that they build their nests in reeds, above the water, like grebes, coots, and, very likely, other kinds of diving ducks, because the merganser has the least ability to walk. I have often met with broods of mergansers and once saw a female carrying its tiny ducklings, covered in gray down, on its back and swimming very fast. I had heard of this from other wild-fowlers but I confess I did not really believe. One cannot help wondering why other duck species do not do this. Why should the merganser need this facility when its young are more agile than any other ducklings?

I should add that mergansers always occur in small numbers, and by no means everywhere, only on fairly deep water where fish are plentiful. I have not observed any difference in the plumage of the duck and drake. Mergansers depart early in the autumn. Their flesh has an intolerably fishy odor and is bitter and repellent to the taste. I have never seen a fat merganser.

In conclusion I repeat that the bird I have described is the true merganser with all its remarkable distinguishing features, and the diving ducks that are sometimes called the "greater" and "lesser" merganser are merely grebes.[21]

4. COOT

Lysukha, lysena; Fulica atra

The merganser concludes the section on duck. The coot, by the shape of its body, especially its head and neck, its sharp, whitish, utterly chickenlike beak, even its jerky swimming motion and awkward diving, differs from all species of duck, although its permanent home is on shallow water. It may with justice be termed a "water hen." The name *lysukha* [baldpate] was undoubtedly given to it on account of the smooth white shield that seems to be welded to its forehead, like a large almond with the shell removed, making the head, at a distance, look bald. This white shield, which looks like bone, is in fact a protrusion of flesh covered with firm, shell-like hide. All coots without exception, male and female (between which I have never observed any difference), have this protrusion, which gleams in the sunshine. The feathered body looks as big as a medium-sized duck, but the body alone is slightly larger than that of a teal. Seen at a distance, the color is all black but at close range it is blackish-gray or smoky. Although the feet jut out behind like those of the goldeneye, they are not in the same position as those of a grebe or merganser. It is better able to stand on them than the real diving ducks, and can even walk. On its legs, just above the upper joint and just below the soft gray feathers, it has yellowish-green bands the breadth of half a finger. A greenish hue is visible on the lower joint, right down to the foot itself. This color shows through the slate gray that is common to the feet of all coots. In the sun the feet reflect a dirty mother-of-pearl gloss. The webbing between the toes is thick, but cut in lobes, which means that they cannot swim so ably as other ducks. Their feet are covered with straight, whitish lines, forming little squares and latticework patterns; the underside of the feet is dark slate gray; the tail is very short, and dark-colored. It should be noted that it is only the formation of the feet that links the coot to the family of fish-eating ducks; in all other respects, except the fact that it always lives on water, it is unlike them. Coot are weak fliers and take wing only in emergencies: seeing danger, they give a special cry, rather like a groan or a sob, and hurry to hide in the reeds or sometimes run scuttering along the surface, without leaving it, and pattering along with their wings like young ducklings. They also do this when they want to rise from the water, until they gain momentum and assume the usual attitude of a bird in flight. In spring they appear quite late, and depart in early autumn: I have never seen them arriving in flocks or even in pairs. They usually frequent standing water—ponds and lakes with reed-beds. They favor shallow water, even that on the very edges of lakes, as their diet consists mainly of insects, aquatic grasses, and even silt, so they need to be able to reach the bottom. However, they also eat fish when the opportunity arises, and always smell of it, although not so strongly as the fish-eating duck. By autumn, coots are sometimes very fat and would be very appetizing were it not for the fishy smell, which, however, is substantially reduced if the bird is skinned and roasted.

I have said that I once found the floating nest of a grebe: I have also come across a coot's nest of the same type. It stood well above the water with only the bottom in the water. A coot was swimming round it. The nest was made of dry sedge and a special kind of dry, soft, thick reed. The side on which the bird climbed in and out was trodden down and a little lower than the others. Inside, the bottom of the nest and the rounded side walls were smeared and caked almost to the rim with coot dung, applied very smoothly and artfully, and hardened like plaster.[22] The bottom was lined with black feathers and dark down plucked by the mother from her own breast, and there were nine eggs (slightly smaller than hen's eggs) of a lovely, dark gray hue, glossy with a greenish tinge and white speckles. It was clear that the nest had been very firmly attached to the reeds (also by dung), because the tops of two broken reeds and one that had torn free or rotted through were securely glued to the side of the nest and floating with it on the water, indicating that the nest was well above the water before it broke away. At that time I collected the eggs of all birds and was beside myself with joy at this rare find. I carefully took the nest, placed it in my boat, and made speedily for home, pursued right across the pond, almost as far as the millgates, by the parent coot, calling, or piping as it went.

Young coot chicks are covered in almost black down. The mother does not display the same ardor in the defense of her young as the surface-feeding ducks: having concealed her young, she does not show herself to the wildfowler to lure him in the wrong direction and sacrifice her own life, but hides with them, which is far more sensible.

Wildfowlers rarely kill coot unless they have some special reason to do so, and for this reason the birds are very tame. Their flesh is not appetizing, and even their black down is less long and thick than that of the fish-eating ducks. However, they have less need of down as coots spend much time sitting or even walking on the level banks of their pond or lake, and are not constantly on water. The Chuvash, Mordvin, and Tartar people will gladly eat coot-flesh when the opportunity offers, and I have had occasion to provide them with this delicacy. In those places where I have lived in the province of Orenburg, coots are numerous and form an essential attribute of ponds and lakes. It would be strange to approach a reedy pond and not see those black shapes with their white shields (as coot appear in the distance) swimming jerkily off in different directions, and not hear their low, sorrowful piping: the picture would be incomplete.

CATEGORY III

Steppe and Grassland Game

THE STEPPE

Before speaking of the birds of the steppes I feel I should set forth all that I know about their home.

The word "steppe" holds special meaning for us and usually evokes a vast expanse of bare, flat, waterless plain. The steppes are often like this, but in the province of Orenburg, in the Ufa, Sterlitamak, Belebei, Bugul'ma, Buguruslan, and Buzuluk districts, they are of a quite different nature: the ground is mostly not flat but gently rolling, in places quite wooded, even hilly, intersected by gullies with spring-fed streams and rivers, and dotted with lakes. In these parts any expanse of feather-grass–covered virgin soil, never brought under the plow, sometimes stretching for hundreds of versts, but sometimes quite small, is called "steppe." Steppeland such as this is delightful in spring with its lush, fresh vegetation. The black earth is carpeted with rich, tall, succulent grasses and flowers, especially in the valleys and on the open plains between the woodlands. In a good year, cuts of hay in the steppe are better than those from flood meadows. Only on the slopes of the mighty mountain ridges that intersect the rolling plains and low hills at intervals, along the rivers and waterless valleys, can one find the alpine varieties of short grasses: a special kind of feather-grass with a short, friable stem; blue mountain sage, short white wormwood, savory, and mother-of-thyme. These fill the air with a special aroma, and anyone who has not spent a night in the steppe or on a mountainside can have no idea of that gentle, invigorating, and bracing air, which is even healthier than that of any forest. The healing properties of steppe grasses and steppe air are shown by the astonishing revival of physical powers in the nomadic Bashkirs, who go out into the steppe every spring wasted, drawn, and tired after a hard winter; and also by the recovery of many sick people whom the doctors had written off for dead. These recoveries are not attributable to the effects of fermented mare's milk alone, which has little effect without the steppe air, without living in the steppe, and unless the mares have grazed on it.

In early spring, as soon as the snow has melted and last year's grass has begun to dry out, the grass-fire season begins. The practice of burning off last year's dry grass so that the new grass will grow better sometimes has unfortunate consequences. The earlier the fires begin the less dangerous they are, as the fringes of the forests are still damp, puddles still lie on low-lying ground, and there are still snowdrifts in the forests. If everything is dry, grass-fires can lead to disastrous ravages: driven by the wind the blaze travels with incredible speed, destroying everything that will burn in its path: hayricks that have stood through the winter in the steppe, stands of trees, threshing floors with stooks of corn, and sometimes even whole villages. To avert such disasters, forty or fifty years ago there was one method in widespread use: controlled burning round ricks, copses, threshing floors, and habitations. I have seen with my own eyes whole crowds of peasants, men and women, armed with brooms, burning the grass in this fashion. They would walk along each side of a deliberately lit, running fire, beating out any unwanted spurts of flame on the sides and guiding it in the desired direction. In a high wind, which is common in spring, and strengthened by the fires themselves, especially if the grass is dry, this controlled burning is quite difficult. It sometimes happened that the fire got out of control and escaped into the fields, so the precautionary measures produced the very results they were intended to prevent. In the same way, tall weeds are burned off the fallows, as is last year's stubble from cereal fields. This is done not so much to fertilize the soil as to make the spring plowing easier, for on fertile land last year's stubble can be over knee-height. Without entering into debate on the unsound reasons for burning off dry grass and stubble, I shall only say that on a dark night the fires present a splendid picture: in various places, sheets, rivers, and torrents of flame race up steep hills, descend into dales, and spread out on the flat plainland in a sea of fire. All this is accompanied by a roar and a crackling and the anxious cries of the birds of the steppe. It is just as well that the steppes are never completely burned or the grassland birds would have nowhere to live and breed. Damp hollows, belts of woodland, forest fringes with unmelted snow, rutted roads, which hold moisture for a long time, and finally rivers will halt the fires if there is no dry place for them to turn on or let them leap across. In the darkness of night those fiery leaps are also very spectacular. The blaze advances on a broad front, spreading bright light all around and having this reflected in a glow in the dark sky, and suddenly begins to disperse in little rivulets of flame: this means the fire has reached a partially damp surface and is crossing by means of the dry tips of the grass. The fire is weakening by the minute, almost going out. Here and there little starlets jump ahead while darkness veils the scene . . . but a single spark reaches dry fallow ground and in an instant a broad flame flares and spreads, lighting up the surroundings again, and again a crimson glow is reflected in the dark sky.

At first the blackened steppes and fields present a mournful picture of limitless burned desolation, but soon bright green needles break through the black shroud like so many bristles and at an even greater rate they develop into a variety of little leaves and petals. Within a week everything is covered in fresh green. In another week the burned places cannot be recognized at first sight. The steppe shrubs—ground cherry, wild peach and pea-shrub—which are less often and less severely affected by fire because the ground around them retains more moisture, begin to bloom and spread their pleasantly heady scent. The wild peach flowers with particular luxuriance and fragrance.[1] Spreading in dense growth over huge areas of gentle hillsides, it covers them with unbroken pink in which occasional yellow strips or rings of flowering pea-shrub can be seen. On gentler slopes great expanses are covered with a milky white shroud, more matt than gleaming: this is the ground cherry in blossom. All the birds of the steppe, frightened by the fires, reoccupy their homes in this sea of green, of spring flowers and flowering shrubs. The chirruping cry of the little bustard, inexpressible in words, the rippling, bubbling trill of the curlew, the unceasing, urgent call of the quail, and the chatter of sociable plover can be heard all around. At sunrise, when the nighttime mist settles in abundant dew on the ground, when all the scents of flowers and other vegetation are at their strongest and most fragrant, the enchantment of a spring morning in the steppe is ineffable. . . . Everything is fresh, bright, young, and filled with joyful life! . . . Such are the steppe areas of the province of Orenburg throughout the month of May.

If the summer is wet the lush vegetation retains its freshness until the beginning of July and grows to an impressive height, but if June is dry, by the end of the month the grass begins to wilt and the feather-grass gradually starts shedding its downy threads. By Saint Peter's Day, 29 June, the early wild strawberries are ripening and their season is at its height by the second week of July. In some places this wonderful berry, finely scented, and with a delicious taste and valuable healing properties, grows in astonishing abundance. In the open feather-grass steppe it is uncommon, but near woodland, in valleys, and on land left fallow for three or four years and beginning to return to its wild state, wild strawberries come up in profusion, and when they ripen whole fields look like a carpet of red. In July the ground cherry ripens; the wild "orchards" sometimes occupy a vast area and at first look an even deeper red in the distance than the wild strawberries, until the ripe cherries turn darker and acquire their own typical cherry hue. The Russian people of the region only dry the strawberries for sale and to eat during Lent, but the Asiatic peoples make a fruit fudge out of it that can be very tasty if made of the best ripe berries: it is known by the name of "Tartar fudge." The cherries are also dried and the large orchards are let to merchants who come specially for the purpose, hire large numbers of workers, fill dozens of carts with cherries, press the juice out of them, and cart it off in large churns: a splendid vodka can be distilled from the juice. But before this human invasion the birds attack the cherries: great and little bustards and black grouse with their young. The black grouse feed exclusively on berries when they are in season, and at this time of year this gives the young grouse a marvelous flavor.

In autumn the feather-grass steppe changes completely and returns to its special pristine state, which is a wonderful sight to see and unlike anything else. In a light breeze the pearly-grayish fibers, now at full length and at their fluffiest, shimmer and stream in a fine, slightly silvery ripple. But a strong wind, such as has no master in the steppe, bends the weak, supple stems right down to the yellowed roots, lashing them, tugging at them, shaking them this way and that, and buffeting them against the faded ground. It carries them with it, presenting to the eye an endless expanse that seethes and ripples as if it were all flowing in one direction. To the unaccustomed eye the sight is striking at first and quite novel; it is unlike any flowing water. But the eye soon tires of its monotony and it may even induce giddiness and a feeling of dejection. However, the steppes without feather-grass look even more monotonous, lifeless, and sad in late autumn, except for the mown meadows, on which young green aftergrowth springs up besides the ricks of hay, dampened by rain. Droves of great and little bustards like to wander over them and graze on the young grass; even great skeins of geese, on their way from one expanse of water to another, descend on such meadows to feast on the fresh grass.

From spring to early autumn Bashkir encampments, or *kochi*, with their sizable herds of small livestock and horses, form a permanent feature of the Orenburg steppes. As soon as there is grass for grazing, all the Bashkir people and their families, the sick and the healthy alike, with all their possessions, move out into the steppe. They choose a suitable site within reach of water and timber, with plenty of grazing for their stock, erect their felt tents, of the type known as Kalmyk tents, build wicker shelters, and move into them. Human life returns to the steppe, which resumes its age-old appearance, although this is fading with every passing year. Here the scattered flocks of sheep and goats lose themselves in the grass with their young lambs and kids, always born on the steppe grass. Their varied bleating carries over a long distance. Herds of cattle low as they roam and grazing horses neigh; and from time to time on the furthest horizon, now on one side, now on the other, little black specks can be seen moving about—the Bashkirs' sharp-pointed caps. Sometimes these specks appear and disappear again in the far distance; sometimes they draw closer across the steppe, growing in size to assume the shape of horsemen firmly set with crooked legs upon their lean but tough and tireless mounts, their amblers. These are the Bashkirs, in carefree and leisurely fashion roaming, always at a walking pace, over the steppes that are their home.[2] They travel over them in all directions, either for want of anything else to do or to pay visits to neighboring camps, *shabry-kochi*, which may be a hundred versts away, to feast on fat mutton and get drunk on fermented mare's milk. The Bashkirs stay at their first camps until their herds have grazed off all the grass, then they move to new sites, and later will move yet again. In their choice of their first site the Bashkirs are guided by one consideration: they first occupy places where the grass will soon be dried by the sun, that is the higher ground, which is open and dry. Then they move into valleys and wooded areas (where these can be found), to gullies with springs, and generally to lower, damper ground. In earliest spring they collect all their mares except those feeding foals, into one herd and release them in the steppe with a single stallion in charge of them. This stallion takes full command and is truly the master of his own harem. He keeps his wives in strict obedience: if any one of them should stray he brings her back to the herd; he leads them from one pasture to the next, where the grazing is richer; he drives them to water and to their night's resting-place. In brief he minds his herd watchfully, letting no one approach day or night. He gallops round the herd with mane and tail flying, whinnying for all the steppe to hear and dashing to head off any animal or human, and if the imagined foe will not withdraw, he will go for him, tearing with his teeth, thrusting with his fore quarters and kicking with his hind hooves. His temper is sometimes so furious that one such stallion once attacked the team of three horses pulling my hunting *drozhki!* He savaged the neck of my leading stallion and only my gunshots drove him off. . . . When autumn sets in and life in the steppe becomes cold and hungry with the grazing gone, the stallion himself drives his herd of pregnant mares home to his master's yard.

But not all horses are fed in yards in winter: many Bashkir herds spend the winter in the steppe. Only the best horses, those few that are most valued, those needed for riding and for domestic work, the foals born the previous spring and the pregnant mares (which, however, are taken in only in late winter), are kept in the villages. The rest are left to roam the steppe, scraping the snow with their hooves to get at the remaining feather-grass and other vegetation. Although the snow is not deep in the open steppe or on the hillsides, because the wind roves free in the open and strips it from the smooth surface, driving it into deep gullies, hollows, and woodland edges, the scant feed turns the unfortunate horses into skeletons hardly able to walk by spring, and many of them die. If there should be ice on the ground before a snowfall, and the ground is coated with a crust of ice that does not melt under the snow (as sometimes happens), and that the horses cannot break with their hooves, whole herds can perish from hunger. The Bashkirs, being naturally indolent, lay in little hay for the winter. Indeed it was impossible to lay in enough for all the livestock they used to keep. Now they mow twice as much as they used to and keep less than half the number of beasts.

With the onset of winter, snow covers the ground, and the freshly fallen snow is etched with the tracks of hares, foxes, and wolves, as well as those of smaller animals. This is the season of hare-coursing. If there is a sudden fall of heavy snow a foot or more deep—dry, powdery snow in which an animal's paws sink down to the ground—the Bashkirs and other Asiatic peoples, as well as the Russian settlers, hunt hares in large numbers with dogs, not only with borzoi crosses but any mongrel breed. They also pursue foxes and wolves on horseback and kill them with one lash of a thick leather whip, which, incidentally, would even knock down a man. This kind of hunting relies for its success on the fact that snow of this depth does not hamper a horse or a long-legged dog, while a small animal will sink almost up to its ears and soon tire. When it reaches the point of exhaustion it is easily caught. As soon as there is a slight thaw and a hard crust forms on the snow, as usually happens in winter, all such hunting comes to an end in the steppe because the snow hardens and will support the weight of a small animal but not that of a man or a horse. Some winter blizzards, rampaging unhindered on the open plains, lash them from all sides and turn sky, earth and air into a seething cloud of snow and white gloom. . . . God forbid that anyone should have to experience the full fury of a winter snowstorm in the Orenburg steppes!

In addition to the well-known game birds—great and little bustards, curlew, and others—a number of animals are found in the steppe: the whitish steppe fox, smaller than the red fox of the forests and with inferior fur; brown and alpine hares; weasels, stoats, martens, and hamsters. On the spurs of the hills wolves can be found, and sometimes badgers, and on the hillsides there used to be large numbers of marmots. I still remember how, even close to the villages, everywhere you looked there were marmots on their mounds, sitting up on their hind paws like bear cubs and calling to each other in their loud whistle. As the human population of the region has increased the marmots have retreated before the new arrivals into more remote areas, and in some districts all but disappeared. Innumerable warrens that now lie deserted attest to the number of former inhabitants.[3] Foxes often take over the abandoned burrows and rear their young in them, and brown hares use them to take refuge from harsh weather. The thick pelt and wonderfully soft lard of the marmot, which by autumn can be extraordinarily fat, are very well suited to household use. They are difficult to shoot as they sit right above their burrows, so that even if fatally wounded they fall straight into them and manage to hide away so deep down that you cannot reach them, and digging them out is hard work. The local people trap them with snares set over the main entrance of the warrens and clams placed along the runs between burrows. Marmots are fond of visiting their neighbors in whole families and of receiving guests at home: they will gather in a cluster, sit up on their hind paws, whistle for a while, and then disperse. Sometimes when you approach a friendly little gathering of marmots the hosts will suddenly dive into their burrows and the guests will dart awkwardly and comically toward their own. In early autumn they withdraw underground, close off their burrows from inside with dry grass and go to sleep until the spring, until all of nature awakens from the sleep of winter.

In time not a strip of untilled land will remain in the province of Orenburg. Whatever the surveyors' land registers may say, all this land is fertile, all will be populated, and everything I have said about the steppes of this wonderful region will be no more than a story from the forgotten past.

1. GREAT BUSTARD

Drofa; Otis tarda

I do not know the origin of the word *drofa*. In the province of Orenburg the bird is known by its Tartar names *tudak* and *dudak*. I have also heard these terms in neighboring provinces, but in the Kursk area, instead of *drofa*, they say *drokhva*. I remain of the belief that this word is of non-Russian origin.[4]

By virtue of its size and especially its weight (a fat, mature bird may weigh up to thirty-five pounds), by its taste, when it is young and well nourished, by its wariness and the difficulty of bagging one, the great bustard is fully entitled to pride of place among all grassland birds. In size and shape, especially of the head, bill, and legs, it is very like a large domestic turkey. A young bustard in its first year has gray to clay-colored plumage but the color grows lighter year by year as it grows older. The head and neck are ash- or cinder-gray; the bill is stout and strong, turned down slightly at the tip, nearly two inches long, dark gray and not smooth but rather rough; the pupils of the eye are yellow; the ears are unusually large and open, whereas all other birds have them so well hidden under small feathers that you do not notice them. Under the throat is an internal sac of skin, which can hold a large quantity of water. The legs are thick and covered with large gray scales. Unlike other birds, bustards have only three toes on each foot. The male is distinguished not only by his large size, but by the crest or curling tufts of plumes growing on each side of the head; and at chin level along the neck lie plumes about three and a half inches long, forming a mane or necklace that opens out like a fan. The hen bird has none of this, and in the male the gray of the head and neck, the ruddy feathers, and dark plumes on the back are brighter. The great bustard's down is sparse and grayish-pink; even the feathers of the belly and back are pink right at their roots. The bird differs from all other birds in the structure of its internal anatomy, and only the little bustard, as we shall shortly see, shares this characteristic: the great bustard has a stomach and its food is digested in it, not in the crop. Great bustards live and breed in the true steppe, untouched by the plow, but they fly out to feed anywhere: on fallow farmland and cereal fields.[5] I have never found the nest of a great bustard, but, judging by the little bustard, which is very similar in all respects except size, we may believe the reports of other fowlers, that it lays up to nine eggs (some say no more than three), shaped like turkey eggs but slightly bigger, rounder, darker in color, with yellowish spots. The great bustard feeds mainly on grass, rarely eating cereal grain, but also takes all kinds of insects, even lizards, unfeathered nestling birds, mice, frogs, and small snakes, of which the crane is also particularly fond.

In spring the birds appear in small parties but in autumn they gather in large droves: at this time they are even harder to shoot than in spring. In flocks they are very wary and will not let anyone come within even buckshot range, not even if you should use a peasant cart disguised with green boughs or hide in a cartload of hay. When alone, however, or even in pairs, great bustards are somewhat tamer: you can sometimes get close enough to use duck- or goose-shot. The larger grade is more reliable as you will not be firing from close range, and the bird is very resistant to shot. An approach on foot is impossible, unless the lie of the land permits you to crawl along a gully, steal up behind a mound or haycock, or through the cover of unmown crops. A lone bustard, or even a pair, may be "driven down," as fowlers say; that is, on sighting them from afar you can begin riding round them, at first in large circles and then closing in, tightening the ring. The bustard will not let anyone ride toward it, so will start moving away, but whichever way it goes, it will meet the same steadily approaching hunter. It will turn this way and that and then lie down in some slight depression, even if it cannot find one deep enough to conceal its head. In this awkward position, with its neck stretched along the ground and its bulky body sticking up, it will allow quite a close approach. Of course, this unsubtle maneuver cannot be exploited on all types of terrain.

Everything I say about great bustards I have learned from reliable sources. Rather to my own surprise and chagrin, I have little knowledge of the habits of this first-class game-bird of the steppes, or of how to shoot it, although I lived for a long time in districts where it is still found in good numbers. To understand why this is so one must take account of the huge extent of the province of Orenburg. It is a vast area, a whole kingdom of its own. I always lived in districts where they were considered rarities even on passage. At one time they were found everywhere but today they remain only in those places where the human population has not increased greatly, and where there are still large areas of untilled feather-grass steppe little visited by the Bashkir horses. I did occasionally come across bustards, singly, in pairs, and even in small parties, but not only did I fail to kill one, I only ever managed to fire one shot at one bird, in flight, with duck-shot and out of range. My encounters with these birds were marked by total failure and absence of sporting luck. Not wishing to bore my readers, I shall not describe them. Many times, however, I have seen bustards, young and old, thin and fat, killed by other fowlers, and have been able to examine them closely, both externally and internally.

The bustard's flight looks labored, with slow wing-beats and the appearance of a rolling motion from side to side, but it flies swiftly and powerfully.

In spring it appears rather late, after the onset of warmer weather, when the new grass has already grown. It is said that in autumn they congregate in huge droves before departing, and stay for a long time, gradually moving southward. Bashkirs have told me that bustards are fond of roving in large parties over abandoned Bashkir campsites. They are given to scratching the earth and digging on the sites of wickerwork shelters or "Kalmyk tents," and where there is manure and human waste in large quantities.

Unfortunately I am unable to go into more detail about the habits of this splendid bird or how to shoot it, because I do not like to rely on the evidence of others.

2. COMMON CRANE

Zhuravl'; Grus grus

The body of the crane is smaller in mass though perhaps a little longer than that of the great bustard and hardly the size of a large, mature goose, but the long plumes on the back and flanks, and the size of the wings give it the appearance of a very large bird. It stands very tall and its neck is also very long, and if its beak were proportionate to its limbs—as is often the case with the sandpipers—the beak would have to be more than a foot long. But its beak is no more than five inches long, robust, sharp-pointed, of a dark-greenish or flesh color. The head is small. The crane is uniformly pale gray-blue; the front of the head is covered with small black feathers, and the back of the head is bare, covered in small, dark-red warts so that it looks like a raspberry-colored patch. Whitish stripes run from the eyes into the dark gray plumage of the nape. The eyes are small and light-colored, gray to chestnut. The tail is short, and from it, but beginning halfway down the back, soft bushy feathers stick out upward, quite long and gracefully curving. The feet and the three forward-pointing toes are covered in rough black skin that appears to be cracked.

Among migratory birds the crane is the best known and most like a mascot, being the most visible as it does not hide from view. It is part of our language, of sayings, and popular speech. A long-necked or long-legged person may be called a crane. In advising somebody to accept the little that is certain rather than the less certain promise of more, the Russian proverb says, "A tom-tit in the hand is worth a crane in the sky."[6] The phrase "in the sky" shows the height at which they fly. Who has not heard their piercing trumpeting call, like the distant notes of a French horn or bugle, tumbling from the sky, from a height often beyond the range of the human eye? . . . These calls are produced only by the male, whose throat is specially fashioned for the purpose. The peasant delights in hearing these calls in spring, even if the weather is still cold, as he believes they herald the approach of warm weather. But on hot days such as we sometimes experience in late August and even early September, the call of high-flying cranes brings sadness to the peasant's heart. "Winter will be early," he says, "The cranes are already flying." And these forecasts are almost always correct. There is something appealing about the flight and the cry of the crane. Sometimes a group will keep wheeling for a long time at one point, rising higher and higher in the sky with each circle, until they disappear from view, and the call, at first rich, sharp, and ringing, loses its clarity and reaches you in indistinct, softened, muted, yet agreeable notes.

Cranes usually arrive later in spring than other birds, and they form pairs at once. In autumn they gather in large flocks before departing at widely varying times: sometimes in early August, sometimes in late September, always flying during daylight hours. They never fly in untidy flocks, but always in V-formation, in which one arm of the V is usually much longer than the other. In southern Russia these irregular chevrons are aptly termed "keys" of cranes, as their shape is very like the plain homemade wooden keys that the peasants use to lock the wooden bolts of sheds and barns, unlike German metal keys. Only occasionally do cranes form themselves into a blunt chevron with arms of almost equal length.

Strictly speaking the crane is less a bird of the steppes than of the fields. In the true steppe cranes are uncommon; they like cereal fields and tilled land and will happily eat any cereal grains, although they like peas best of all. The crane is a voracious eater, and when food grown by humans is insufficient it will greedily devour anything that comes to hand: the seeds of various grasses, all kinds of berries, small insects, earthworms, and even lizards, frogs, mice, young marmots and hamsters, unfeathered nestlings, and all kinds of snakes. To the latter it is especially partial. If it finds a particularly long snake such as a grass-snake it will tear it into several pieces with its bill and swallow them. Smaller snakes are swallowed whole, having first been tossed several times high in the air. Lizards and frogs are treated in the same manner. It is probable that the bird instinctively wants to kill them before eating them. I do not share the view of those fowlers who contend that it is playing with its food by tossing it in the air. But it is clear that it can digest such food with no untoward effects.

Cranes always make their nests on untilled ground, although the site may be surrounded on all sides by arable land. They choose a raised, dry spot, often an abandoned marmot mound, invariably overgrown with pea-shrub, wild peach, or ground cherry. The nest is crudely fashioned: it is little more than a circular depression in the ground, lightly lined with dry grass. Two huge elongated eggs, the shape of sandpiper eggs, greenish-gray and blotched with dark brown, lie totally unprotected and uncovered. The sexes take turns at incubating the eggs. The bird that is not sitting walks round the nest at a distance, feeding and keeping an eye on it. When its loud cry announces the approach of danger the sitting bird leaves the nest at once and runs a short distance away, crouching as it runs. It calls to its mate, who immediately runs to join it, and together they walk further away from the nest, or fly off. It will be clear that cranes do not display great determination in the defense of their nests or eggs; they show little more in the defense of their young. When the young hatch, the parents lead them into standing crops or meadows with tall grass and bushes. If the meadows are mown the birds take refuge with their young in thinly wooded marshland, thickets and reeds and sometimes at the edges of forests. Depending on the terrain, they will sometimes rear their young in meadows and even marshy woodland. Crane chicks are always clumsy, awkward, and feeble and keep up a ceaseless, pitiful piping. On hatching they are covered in blue-gray down, which they retain for a long time, growing their feathers very slowly. If caught and reared with domestic fowl, they soon adapt to any kind of food and become very tame; but as soon as their wings grow they always fly away, if not in their first year, then in their second. If their wings are clipped they remain tame but do not breed.

On the whole the crane is quite a wary bird, and it is very difficult to approach a flock, even by stealth, but, if close to their nesting site, singly or in pairs, the birds are much tamer, and it is sometimes possible to come within range using a cart or a hunting *drozhki*. It goes without saying that the largest shot should be used, and for a flock of cranes in autumn it is essential to have a supply of cartridges loaded with small buckshot.

Cranes are very difficult to shoot, and ordinary shooting tactics will kill few. One has to resort to particular guile and steal up on them using the cover of bushes, stooks of corn, haycocks, and the like. If you first establish where they fly to feed, roost at night, or spend the day, and by what routes they fly to their roosts, it is possible to prepare a hide and lie in wait to shoot them as they fly over, or catch them at their feeding or roosting grounds. For their roosts cranes select open places, sometimes even close to roads. They usually all sleep standing up, with their heads tucked under one wing, lined up in one or two rows, and with one or two lookouts posted along the sides. The latter only doze, without hiding their heads under their wings, and at the slightest hint of danger they alert the flock with their ringing alarm call, and all fly away.

The crane is, of course, a strong bird, and to its strength must be added the defensive weapons nature has equipped it with. These are the stout bones of its wings, which can deliver a powerful blow, its long legs, strong toes with hard claws, and lastly, a fairly long, stout, sharp bill. Armed with these a slightly wounded crane becomes a very dangerous bird to any fowler or dog who might thoughtlessly seek to catch it. First the injured crane will run away so fast that it will be difficult to catch without a dog. It boosts its speed by flapping its wings, or one wing, if the other is injured. Seeing that it cannot get away, it flings itself at full tilt onto its back and defends itself with its feet and beak, striking deftly and powerfully at its foe. I have seen the sad consequences of this brave defense: a one-eyed fowler and a one-eyed dog, both having lost an eye in awkward attempts to catch an injured crane.

When a crane is in serious mood and is pacing the fields with dignity looking for food, there is nothing at all funny about it; but as soon as it starts running, prancing, crouching, and leaping into the air with wings spread, or when it begins making a fuss over its mate, it is impossible to watch its antics without laughing, so incongruous are its swift and sprightly movements. A group of cranes dancing together or a pair coupling would have even the staidest observer in stitches. Of course, such scenes can only be witnessed from afar, unless you can steal up on them so stealthily that the birds do not notice you.

I have already said that for various reasons cranes are hard to shoot and that you will never kill many of them at once. One shot is most unlikely to kill two or three cranes. For this to happen extraordinary good luck is required, as has twice befallen me. Some peasants returning from their fields once told me they had passed very close to a party of roosting cranes. It was a moonlit night and I took my gun and jumped into a peasant cart, giving orders to take the same track the peasants had followed. The cranes let me approach very close. Although their lookouts were awake they did not raise the alarm. I chose a line of approach that would allow me to fire along a line of sleeping cranes, of which there were about twenty. I took aim at the third bird from the end and killed four with one shot. This was in August, at a time of great heat. On another occasion, during an unusually warm autumn, on 24 September, I saw a huge flock of cranes—migrating birds at this season, of course—descending on a harvested cornfield. The ground was quite open and any approach impossible. I crawled along a field-boundary strip overgrown with wild peach and ground cherry and lay down, having told my *drozhki* driver to go to the other side and move toward me. The cranes began slowly walking straight toward me, while my *drozhki* kept moving to and fro until the whole flock were very close to me. At last I fired: three cranes fell dead and a fourth, severely wounded, flew off and then fell, a verst and a half distant, in a dense, marshy thicket at the confluence of the Bokla and Nasiagai Rivers. I searched for it until evening and finally found it, already dead, with the help of my dog.

A crane cannot take wing instantly. It needs seven or eight yards to build up speed. As evidence of this I can cite a strange incident I witnessed with my own eyes: I happened to meet a hunter making for home with his two borzoi dogs, and as we made our way together we saw two cranes by a large hayrick in a mown meadow. My companion pointed them out to his dogs, which set off to approach them from behind the rick. The hunter, on horseback, for the fun of it, cantered off after the dogs. What do you think happened? One of the dogs, the faster runner, leaped out suddenly from behind the rick and seized one of the cranes by the leg as it struggled to become airborne. The other dog soon ran up and together they held on to the bird, despite being savagely pecked, until the hunter rode up and captured it alive. On the basis of this it is easy to believe reports that in the provinces of Saratov and Astrakhan', where vast flocks of cranes congregate before the autumn migration, the peasants club them to death after driving them into a tight mass and then into an ambush, where hunters on horseback attack them suddenly with long sticks.

The flesh of older cranes is always dry and rather tough but it has a very agreeable flavor and the scent of wild game about it. The flesh of young cranes, on the other hand, is excellent, being both tender and succulent. Cranes are never fat, not even before departure, even when their diet is nourishing grain. The fattest of autumn cranes has a thin covering of fat only on the belly, in two bands, and a small quantity of lard under the wings, but there is more internal fat. To my taste a young crane roasted is very appetizing, but its best use is in pâtés and *okroshka.*[7]

Wildfowlers of old, like peasant fowlers of today, prized the crane for its size, feeling that since it was big it would provide a good meal, although the meat was rather tough. I must confess that in my youth I also pursued them eagerly, wishing to kill them because of their size.

3. LITTLE BUSTARD

Strepet; Otis tetrax

The Russian name *strepet* and its popular variant *strepel* describe this bird's typical manner of taking wing and its level flight.[8] The little bustard seems to give a startled flutter as it rises and takes to the air. It flies with great power and agility, its wing-beats so fast that you can hardly see them. The bird quivers in the air as if standing still, while actually moving swiftly forward. In flight, always direct, its wings produce a swishing whistle, audible from afar and never heard with indifference by wildfowlers. I for one held little bustards in the highest esteem among grassland game, second only to great bustards, which I did not manage to shoot.

The little bustard is a little smaller than an old female blackcock (gray-hen). Of course it is eight times smaller than a well-grown great bustard, but resembles it in all particulars, external and internal, except the coloring of its plumage. It feeds mainly on grass but occasionally eats insects as well. It digests its food in its stomach, not its crop. It has sparse pink down on its body and the fluffy roots of all its feathers are the same color. The head, neck, bill, and all the proportions of the little bustard are exactly like those of a chicken. The speckled greenish-gray plumage is very difficult to describe. Each feather has straight and curving striations running in different directions, though in regular patterns, on a flesh-colored background. All the feathers of the back form a mottled pattern of the same color with blackish spots. The mottled effect results from the interknitting of one vane with the next, with its dark stripes and wavy lines giving the appearance of blotches. The neck is also mottled, with whitish lines running along it; the head is blackish, and the throat and breast have striations running across them on a white background; the lower breast and belly are entirely white, as is the underside of the wing. The first three flight feathers are dark above, the others are white with dark edging at the tips. The tail is short and finely speckled with gray; each tail feather has a narrow dark band across it, a finger's breadth from the tip. The legs are a pale greenish color. The male differs from the female in having dark feathers that appear solid black, on the throat, with a white diagonal stripe. The little bustard's wings are rounded and seem bowed in flight.

The little bustard breeds only in the open steppe, but it flies to farmland to feed and may even remain there for long periods: in spring on stubble fields, fallows, or growing crops, and toward autumn on mown meadows, when the first aftergrowth is rising, and on fields sown with winter crops. It will happily eat all bread grains and likes to peck at horse manure, and for both these reasons stays close to tracks across the fields and steppes, running with great agility along the ruts; but its staple diet is young grass. Anyone who has ridden along such tracks is sure to have put up little bustards and seen them running before the horses. If the traveler is moving steadily the bird will turn aside, tired, no doubt, by much running and not wishing to stray too far from its feeding grounds. To turn off the road it will have to climb over deep ruts, which it does with difficulty, and run a few yards before crouching down in the grass to wait until the cart or carriage has passed. It will lie with its neck outstretched, raising its blackish head from time to time, until, seeing that the traveler is well past, it goes back to the track and runs along it in the opposite direction. If a vehicle is traveling fast and the bird sees that it will be overtaken, it rises, flies some distance off, but sometimes only a few yards, alights, and sits on the ground for a while before returning to the road. Here I am speaking of birds that are tame and not yet gun-shy. At about midday they go out into the steppe but in the morning and evening they stay close to the tracks.

The little bustard has a special cry that is difficult to convey in words. It is rather like "irr." This call is very deceptive: though weak and muted it carries for some distance. At first it seems as if the bird is only a dozen yards away, and an inexperienced fowler will seize his gun and rush toward the call expecting the bird to rise at any moment. But the call grows fainter, and the fowler, his efforts vain, will be obliged to cut short his pursuit. Of course this illusion is assisted by the fact that the little bustard is a very fast runner, but there is no doubt that the call was first heard from afar because it will not call close to humans.

Little bustards arrive in late spring in large flocks just as they depart in autumn, no doubt, but I never saw any on passage. When warm weather arrives and fresh grass springs up everywhere, little bustards suddenly appear scattered over the fields and steppes. Being primarily a bird of the steppes, it makes its nest in the open steppe, almost always under a clump of feather grass. The flat, round nest is woven from dry grass mixed with some of the bird's own feathers. There can be up to nine eggs; at least, I have never found more. The eggs are larger than might be expected, and exceptionally pretty: they are no smaller than large hen's eggs, covered with a bright, green gloss with small yellowish speckles. I am unable to say whether the female incubates the eggs by herself or whether the male shares this work. Wildfowlers very seldom come across nests or young of the little bustard. I myself never found any chicks, probably because the mother takes them out into the remote steppe, where I rarely ventured. The nests I found were fairly close to cereal crops. It is fair to suppose that little bustards form pairs, first, because nobody has ever come across display grounds, and second, because if you flush one bird in spring another will be close by. Between the male and female there are no differences in plumage other than those I have already mentioned, but the female is slightly smaller. It sits extraordinarily tight on its nest, as has been convincingly demonstrated to me. I was once driving toward a little bustard that flew up before I could come within range. I fired a shot without stopping and I thought that I had hit it and that it had gone down some two hundred yards away. Without taking my eyes off the spot, I started running toward it, but before I reached the place I tripped over something and almost fell. I turned involuntarily to see what had tripped me and saw a little bustard lying there with blood on its back. I took it for the bird I had shot and thought I must have misjudged the distance. Seeing that the bird was alive, I quickly grabbed it and picked it up. Imagine my surprise when I saw that there was a nest underneath it with nine eggs in it. It had blood on its back because my hobnailed boot had caught it and torn off a strip of skin the width of a finger. I had never seen a little bustard's nest and, as I collected eggs at the time, I was delighted at this find. Moreover the eggs were new-laid, so it was very easy to blow them. It was clear that the hen bird had not long since laid the last egg and was just beginning to incubate them. On her superficial wound I put some thick pitch from the wheels of my *drozhki* and released her. A few minutes later up sprang the bustard I thought I had winged, before I could come within range and before my dog could catch its scent. It was probably the mate of the female I had released. I take this as tending to confirm my view that little bustards form pairs and share the rearing of the young.

Toward autumn little bustards congregate in flocks that are sometimes very big, numbering up to about fifty pairs. The larger the flock, the harder it is to approach, because birds in flocks are always very wary. They may linger until October, at which time their favorite haunts are winter crops and mown grassland: they like pecking at the late shoots of winter cereals, and at young grass. In raw, damp weather, except for early morning and evening, they remain on fallow land overgrown with tall wormwood, goose-foot, and salsify, where they can keep warm and dry. The measured swish of a flock of little bustards in flight carries far at dawn and dusk. I used to be passionately keen on hunting these birds and often traveled long distances to find them, as there were few in my home area. In spring and throughout the summer, in the furthest steppe, far from human habitation, little bustards are quite tame if they have not been hunted before, especially if encountered singly or in pairs. But they quickly become exceptionally shy and wary, especially in flocks, so that I often rode many versts before being obliged to abandon the chase without firing a single shot, although I could see them flying up and alighting two or four hundred yards further off. Once the birds are on their guard, not even the most effective of methods, the narrowing circle, will work. It sometimes happens that one unexpectedly finds oneself close to a single bird or even a sizable flock; however, once they have flown off and settled again, they are very much harder to approach. I should mention that, after taking wing, they soon alight, and it is rare for them to fly off out of sight. In general the little bustard is wary when standing or running, but tame when lying on the ground, even if the ground should be completely bare. It will stretch out its neck on the ground, putting its head in a slight depression, under some tuft of grass, and consider itself hidden. In this position it will let a wildfowler come very close, sometimes within half a dozen yards or less. (You should never approach in a straight line, but always at a tangent.) There is no need to approach as close as this, but I tried it out of curiosity. Thus success depends on getting the bird or birds to lie down. As I have said, the most reliable way to achieve this end consists in riding in circles round them until they lie down. If a bird is alone and not too gun-shy it will lie down at once. If there are several birds together they will run this way and that for some time before dispersing and lying down in separate places. A large flock that has just alighted will never lie down. It can happen that one or even two shots fired at a lying bustard or one that has taken wing will not put up another hiding close by, so it is not advisable to pick up the kill or make any movement whatsoever before reloading both barrels. It is very easy to hit little bustards in flight, even easier than sitting birds, or so it has always seemed to me. Usually, having ridden within range, I jumped out of my *drozhki* and walked straight toward the bird until it rose into the air, and then fired, without hurrying, at any distance I chose. Only rarely did I have to resort to the second barrel. It is most unusual to kill a number of little bustards with one shot: you need to come within range of a large, tight-packed flock, or to have a flock fly straight toward you. It often happened that I killed a brace, that is, one with each barrel, but only once did I kill three sitting bustards with one barrel and two in flight with the other. It happened by chance. I came upon a substantial flock hiding in dense-growing winter rye, so that none of them could be seen. At a dozen yards two of them raised their black heads and my driver spotted them and pointed them out to me. I fired my first barrel at the sitting birds, and the second at the rising flock: three were left lying on the ground and two fell out of the air from a flock of about thirty.

Only the very best trained dog, staying obediently to heel almost under your *drozhki*, can be used for shooting little bustards by driving toward them. The same may be said of all sitting birds except black grouse and wood pigeons. These sit up in the trees and look down inquisitively at a foraging dog, and thus pay less attention to the hunter and allow him to draw nearer. But any bird on the ground is far more afraid of a dog than an approaching human. Despite this, a good dog with a good nose is very useful for seeking out little bustards, which sometimes sit so tight in grass or growing crops, especially when the birds have dispersed, that a fowler will drive past without noticing them. A dog with a good nose will scent them from afar and lead him straight to them. But beware the overeager dog that runs after the birds! With a dog like that you will not shoot a single bustard.

Number Five shot should usually be employed, as the little bustard is not a large bird, but for warier birds Number Four is needed. For large flocks at the limit of your range the largest shot may sometimes be used.

I have never seen little bustards with much fat on them, but on their arrival in spring and before departing in autumn they are quite well covered. Their flesh has a splendid and distinctive flavor, rather similar to the domestic fowl, with an admixture of the wild about it. Little bustards are considered the most nourishing fare, and at the same time the meat is light and wholesome.

In Little Russia the little bustard is known as "the laughing bird" [*khokhotva*], which is also an extraordinarily expressive name. Whereas in Great Russia it gets its name from its flight, from the visible quivering of its wings, in Little Russia it is the sound of its wings that give it its name. And indeed its swishing wingbeats resemble eerie, distant laughter.

4. CURLEW

Kronshnep; Numenius arquata

The Russian name by which this bird is sometimes known, "steppe sandpiper" [*stepnoi kulik*], needs no explanation, but why the Germans call it the "crown snipe" or "royal snipe" I do not know.[9] On its head it has nothing resembling a crown. Perhaps it is so named on account of its size, in which it really does surpass all other wading birds. The French call it *courlis;* Russian wildfowlers call it *kronshnep,* and ordinary folk know it as the "steppe bird" [*stepniak* or *stepniaga*], since that is its usual home: it breeds in the steppe and that is where the young grow to maturity. Its melodious, bell-like trill enlivens the monotony and silence of the steppe more than any other bird. By size curlews are divided into three kinds: greater, middle (or whimbrel), and lesser (or slender-billed curlew).[10] In body mass the curlew will be roughly the same as a grayhen or domestic fowl; the whimbrel is slightly smaller and the slender-billed curlew much smaller, no larger than a feral pigeon. The latter kind is far more numerous than the previous two. I shall describe the whimbrel in detail, from experience, naturally, and then say how the three kinds differ, as they are exactly the same in their coloration and all their proportions. The whimbrel is entirely speckled gray and covered with light brown spots and striations. On the back and wings, especially toward the tips, the spots are much larger and dark brown, while on the neck, head, and breast they are smaller, lighter, and more yellowish. The belly is almost white except for a few very beautiful arrowhead-shaped spots. The wing lining in the area of the wrist is made up of small pure white feathers and the underside of the remaining large feathers is pale gray, very beautiful, clearly reflecting the pattern of the upper wing. The tailfeathers are speckled above and almost white below. On the rump, under the long feathers, from the middle of the back are brilliant white feathers with fine arrowhead spots. On the neck and throat the feathers are light, almost whitish. The eyes are small and dark and the neck is about five inches long. The bill is a dark flesh color, fairly stout and downcurved, about four and a half inches long. The wings are very long, each sixteen inches, measured from the shoulder to the tip of the longest primary; the tail is short; the legs about seven inches in length. The toes are proportionately long and the leg color is dark. The toes are darker still and the claws completely black, small, and strong.

The distinguishing feature of the curlew family, the downcurved bill, prevents them from drinking normally. When they scoop up water they deftly turn their heads and bills upside down so as to hold the water as in a concave bowl. Then with an even nimbler movement they sweep the head and bill, still in this inverted position, under one foot (which is held up), quickly stretch the neck up, and swallow the water. This is quite a complex operation but the bird performs it with great ease and grace.

In addition to its larger size the curlew has darker brown plumage than the smaller species and its call is short and hoarse. It sometimes rears its young in dry marshland and damp woodland fringes with large tussocks, moss, bushes, and trees, lying close to fields and steppes. Occasionally it will be joined by the whimbrel, but never by the slender-billed curlew, which always stays in the steppe, and which is much lighter colored, with finer speckling. Its call is much purer and more penetrating than that of the whimbrel, whose cry is rather thicker and less drawn out. All three species are very fast runners, especially the slender-billed curlew: when approached it bends its long legs slightly, stretches out its neck, bends its head a little, and starts running so fast that it is hard to keep track of it. Flitting through the steppe grass like a rippling ribbon, it soon eludes even the keenest-eyed fowler.

All three curlews arrive in late spring, in mid- or even late April. At first they fly in large flocks, so high that you cannot see them, but you can hear their sonorous calls, which, however, are less drawn out than when they take up residence for the summer in the green steppes. Soon after the spring passage, curlew begin to appear on plowed fields, on last year's thawed stubble, beside spring freshets, ponds, lakes, and even on the level banks of rivers that have spilled onto surrounding lowland. I have rarely come across them in parties but almost always in ones and twos. At this season any fowler is glad to find and shoot a curlew as they are wary, well fed, and fairly uncommon. Moreover their spring visits to these places are very brief: as soon as the steppe thaws and dries the curlew is there. I even surmise that the curlew we find in spring beside rivers, lakes, and ponds are all on passage and have not yet reached their final destination, while those that live in the steppe make straight for the steppe, having also wandered far and wide on passage to their own breeding grounds. I am persuaded of this by the fact that on my spring visits to flooded river valleys and marshes I found curlew still giving their migratory call, which is shorter and on a single note, whereas when I climbed higher into the steppe, less than a verst away, I came upon curlew that had clearly begun to settle in. They were active at the same sites and gave their summer call, a melodious cry as they rose in the air, and a different, rippling phrase with richer, softer notes, as they descended and alighted. Other fowlers have also observed this. The first phrase of the curlew's call may be said to consist of high notes and the second phrase of lower notes. The bird has another call, more of a soughing note, as if the bird were drawing in air. This call is given only when the bird is sitting on the ground but about to take flight. Often these notes give it away as it lies hidden in the grass.

On their spring arrival, curlew are quite wary, like most other birds, but once they have settled they become less shy and can be approached in a hunting *drozhki* or peasant cart. As soon as they set about building their nests they become quite tame, though less so than black-tailed godwits and the smaller sandpipers. An early mild and dry spring can spell disaster for the curlew. They will build and lay quickly, and then be caught by grass-fires. I have already spoken of this deleterious practice: it causes dreadful damage to the birdlife of the steppe. If spring is late and wet, the fire cannot take hold everywhere and cannot reach far into the steppe, so the birds will be safe, but in an early and dry spring the flames will embrace a large expanse of steppe, destroying not only nests and eggs but often the birds themselves as well. . . . When the hurricane of flame has swept past and the ground has cooled and ceased to smoke, the surviving curlew, sometimes driven far away by the spreading fire, immediately return to their nests, and if they find them destroyed they at once build new ones, as close as possible to the site of the old nests, but always at points that have escaped the blaze. It is beyond question that no bird will build its nest on burned ground. This may seem improbable because the birds obviously live and breed in the burned steppes, but my close observations have persuaded me that they always breed on an unburned site, even if it be only a yard or two in diameter or less, and burned right round the edges. When the grass grows up again a casual glance will not distinguish burned ground from unburned, but if you part the fresh green grass right beside a nest you will always find last year's dry grass, which cannot be present at a burned site, as can easily be seen.

If burning takes place later (as sometimes happens), and the curlew lose their partly incubated eggs, or if the birds themselves suffer in the fire, particularly at night, they do not build new nests and they remain without offspring for the year, though they continue to frequent the area of their lost nest. I have sometimes found and shot such curlew; they always have more flesh on them than those with young. On some I have even found slightly singed feathers.

In late April, then, the curlew reclaim their grassland homes, sometimes surrounded on all sides by plowland, and immediately set about building their simple nests. The nest is very plain: a slight hollow in a dry spot under a clump of last year's feather-grass, with low sides, which, like the bottom, are lined with dry grass—nothing more. The hen lays four eggs, the shape of most other waders' eggs. Their size varies with the species: curlew eggs are larger than hen's eggs; slender-billed curlew eggs are no bigger than those of a small guinea-fowl, but more elongated. The color is greenish-gray and they are covered with speckles or blotches that are larger and darker at the thick end. The cock shares in the incubation and care of the young. The young hatch after three weeks, covered with greenish-gray down. There are almost always four of them, as addled eggs are very uncommon. They very soon leave the nest and begin running nimbly about, but in their first few days the parent birds feed them. The diet of old and young alike consists of various insects, but mostly of worms, which they pull skillfully out of the ground, which may not be soft, with their long, curved bills. Occasionally, however, I have discovered grain and the seeds of various grasses in their crops. When the young are bigger and it is harder for them to hide in the steppe grass, which may not be long, the parents take them to the valleys or to other places where the grass is taller and thicker, or where there is a thin covering of steppe shrubs. There they remain until the young are fully grown and able to fly. At this time they are difficult to find as the parents will not fly from well-grown young to confront a man or a dog, and will not hang in the air over them. They do not make any sound that might betray their hiding place to a wildfowler.

Curlews in the steppe are like black-tailed godwits in the marshes: they also fly out to face a man, dog, or even another animal approaching their nest or young, and also at first fly up close and hang above a human in the air, circling close and landing, trying to lure him away, but all this is done with less ardor and more caution. After a few shots the curlew will retreat and become timid. In steppe areas that have not been shot over, the curlew's first assault, particularly on a hunter riding in a carriage with a dog, can be very determined. In my youth I often traveled the steppe roads of Orenburg and Simbirsk, and whole flocks of curlew, flying in from every hand, would sometimes pursue me for many versts, new birds replacing old as I moved from the territories of some into that of others. The air was filled with their musical bubbling trills: some hovered over my horses while others landed by the roadside and ran at incredible speed. Yet others perched on the milestones.[11] Here I could shoot as many as I wished, as new birds, not yet gun-shy, kept flying in. Many times I found myself in an awkward situation for a keen hunter: traveling on various errands, sometimes urgent ones, I would shoot so many curlew that I had nowhere to put them, and, not knowing what to do with them, I kept vowing to myself not to stop, not to get out, and not to shoot. . . . But then a new flock would descend on me, bigger and bolder than the last—and again they fell to my shots. The slender-billed curlew shows by far the most pluck and determination in the defense of its young; whimbrel are more cautious, and curlew will never fly as close unless this happens by chance. They will immediately move off to a safe distance and start circling, giving short, hoarse, almost grating trills. Here a young and ardent fowler may scatter a lot of shot over the green steppe without killing a single curlew, especially if using smaller-sized shot. It is true that the larger the shot, the more it scatters, the thinner the pattern and the harder it is to hit the target, but the fact is that at long range (that is, at sixty or seventy paces) you cannot kill a curlew even with Number Three shot because the bird has far more resistance to shot than the black-tailed godwit and other related birds. It is astonishing how deceptive visual perceptions can be! As you look at the circular movements a bird makes around you, it begins to appear smaller, and as it twists and turns, sometimes sharply, and as you turn to follow it, it may appear that the bird is flying straight at you. . . . I have many times been deceived by this illusion and fired many wasted shots as a result. Sometimes, after bringing down a curlew and measuring the distance, which looked no more than usual, I found that it was far more than seventy yards, at which range I would never have fired. In such extreme conditions, seeing that duck-shot did not "take," as fowlers say, I used goose-shot, and sometimes, though not often, bagged a number of sizable curlews.

As soon as the young are able to fly the parents begin roaming with their broods over plowed fields, recently fallow, and other places where the ground is soft. They then gather in parties of up to two or three families, before finally assembling in large flocks, in which all three species intermingle, and beginning to visit marshes, large spreading ponds, and the level shores of large rivers. There they spend several hours in the middle of the day, resting, even dozing, sitting on the ground. They like wandering over wet, muddy places trampled by herds. After two weeks or so spent in this manner, even if the weather is warm, or even hot, in mid-August the curlew disappear; that is, they form vast flocks and move south. At least, this is the case in the province of Orenburg.

Curlew shooting is very varied in the size and quality of the bag: spring curlew on passage, before they have formed pairs, or before they begin building, are fairly plump, succulent, and—most important of all—uncommon. Of course, among the spring birds of passage one hears and sees migrating flocks of curlew, but shooting is impossible on account of the extreme range. Later you begin to encounter them occasionally, sometimes with other birds, on the muddy banks of ponds, spring freshets and rivers in flood, but it can be very difficult to come within range, first, because they are very wary, and second, because other, smaller birds constantly fly up as you approach, startling and alerting the curlew. It is impossible to creep up on them under cover, even by crawling along the ground, because the terrain is almost always flat and open. In brief, a curlew on its spring passage is a great prize for the wildfowler. In the steppe, at their permanent sites, they are quite timid at first. Of course they soon become tamer, but only when they have formed pairs, begun nesting, and lost weight at an extraordinary rate. After a while, when they are sitting or have already hatched their young, it is possible to shoot many more of them, and in places that have not been shot over, as I have said, they can be killed in great numbers, but by this time they are even thinner, tougher, and drier, and so a less valuable prize, especially the smallest variety, the slender-billed curlew. Shooting may begin in early spring, from a *drozhki,* at sitting, or more often running curlew, and later at birds in flight, once the birds have started leaving their nests at the first sight of a hunter to fly at him and circle round him.

When the young curlew are fledged and begin to visit the fields in family groups, and then the banks of ponds and lakes in larger flocks, this sport regains its status as the birds are hard to find and even harder to approach, being very wary and sure to fly off to more distant sites at the very first shot. By the time they depart the old birds gain so much weight that the breast is entirely clad in fat, and even the young are quite fleshy. This is the time when curlew-shooting is most satisfying, but unfortunately kills are insignificant in number, and a matter of chance. Strictly speaking, there is no such thing as curlew-shooting at this time of year. If you should happen upon a large flock of curlew while hunting on the banks of a lake or river you will be doing well if you manage to fire one shot at them. Wide open spaces are necessary, in which the flock can fly to the other bank or some other place after your shot, without flying into the far distance. It is possible to bring down several birds from a flock with one or two shots only if the terrain allows you to steal up under cover on a foraging flock, or if the flock flies toward you when you have been able to hide in bushes, a ditch, in reeds, or simply on the ground, but to do this you need to know in advance when they will fly in and where they will settle, in order to wait for them, or at least spot a flock in flight at a distance.

In my neighborhood, some twenty versts away, lay a pond that was visited every day at noon by curlew before their autumn departure. This happened regularly every year in late July or early August and lasted for about two weeks. Fortunately along the flat and open bank on which the whole flock usually landed ran a rickety old wattle fence that had once surrounded a field of hemp, abandoned more than ten years earlier. The fence was always overgrown with tall grass, so it made a good place for me to hide. At about midday I took station in my hiding-place and waited for the curlew to fly in. A huge flock of all three kinds would come sailing toward me unsuspecting, so close that I could hear the turbulence of their heavy flight. A dark cloud would sweep over me, made up of long wings, legs, necks, and curving bills. . . . The first time I lost my head and let them pass, firing only from behind at one lagging bird and wounding it in the wing. After that I was calmer and took aim either at the biggest bird or at the densest point in the flock, before they had come too close or passed overhead. If you fire when they are too close you will kill only one curlew, and quite often blow it apart. Sometimes I let them land and fired at them on the ground and succeeded in killing three or four birds with one shot. The startled flock would fly off in noisy agitation but after circling and not detecting any human presence they would return and alight again as I had not emerged from my hiding-place to pick up the dead or injured birds. This latter factor is very important as a flock will almost always fly down to an injured bird. My second shot increased the kill and the curlew then flew off, not to return until the next day. I never came two days running but only every other day or every third, and always found the curlew there right up to the time they departed, which was never later than 17 August.

The taste of curlew flesh is as variable as the hunt for them: on their arrival they are quite tasty and succulent, but while rearing their young they are tough and dry. On their departure both young birds and old are well covered and of excellent flavor.

5. SOCIABLE PLOVER

Krechetka, stepnaia pigalitsa; Vanellus gregarius

No doubt this bird owes its Russian name *krechetka* to its call, "kretch, kretch, kretch," which it repeats constantly when disturbed by humans and when flying overhead. The sociable plover is a true steppe-dweller, and I have never seen one anywhere else. In size and proportions it resembles the lapwing or green plover but it is slightly stouter and shorter-legged; its head is larger and has no crest. It runs just as nimbly as the lapwing and has the same rounded wings and characteristic flight. Seen from afar, giving occasional flaps of its wings and rolling over in the air, it may easily be mistaken for a lapwing, but its plumage is quite different: the sociable plover is a smoky gray, shot with darker tints and spots.

This is an uncommon bird and neither its arrival nor departure have been witnessed by sportsmen, although it is not a passage migrant, on the contrary, it breeds regularly in our area, and all fowlers have come across it every year in the steppe, where it is found with curlews, just as lapwings are found in company with black-tailed godwits. "Steppe plover" is a name used only by sportsmen, not among country folk, but it will be clear from the foregoing that the name is apt.

It is probable that sociable plovers arrive later than curlew, since, in places where I have found only curlew in early spring, about a fortnight later I have often come upon sociable plover with them, endlessly twisting and turning overhead and apparently leading the intruder away from their nests, which they clearly build very hurriedly. I have never encountered the young, and only rarely found nests with eggs. The nests were very simply fashioned and always contained four small eggs, similar in shape to those of the lapwing, and mottled gray in color. The birds are found in pairs, and the male and female take turns at incubating the eggs for two and a half weeks at the most. Both sexes circle over intruders, trying to lead them away. They approach much closer and are more persistent than curlew, which feed on the same food, at least during the summer. We may assume that the male and female continue to look after the young together until they are full grown, although the birds depart so early that there is no opportunity to observe the young once they are fledged. At the beginning of July, rather earlier than the curlew, they leave the steppes, and none can be found at all.

The sociable plover is not greatly prized by sportsmen since it is met with only at a season when it is very lean, like all birds when rearing young. But I have never passed them by, since they are so uncommon that in some years you may not even see a dozen, let alone shoot that many. Their flesh is dry and tough, and tastes very like that of other waders and lapwings when they are lean.

As I have encountered sociable plovers only at a particular point in their life cycle, in the two-month period between early May and early July, I can unfortunately say no more about the ways of this fairly robust, handsome, and well-proportioned bird.

6. GRAY OR FIELD PARTRIDGE

Seraia kuropatka; Perdix perdix

In its build and all its proportions this bird exactly resembles the domestic fowl, hence its Russian name *kuropatka.*[12] It is known as the "field" and "gray" partridge to distinguish it from its forest congener, which is white in winter, of which I will speak in due course, and also because its plumage is gray and it frequents open fields. In my view, the gray partridge is among the best of all steppe and woodland game, if not the very best apart from the woodcock. Its dark, ruddy yellow, brown and light gray plumage is so very beautiful, and it is so gracefully rounded and robust! How quick and lively it is, how nimble and charming in all its movements, and how rich and succulent its meat can be in autumn and winter! Even in summer the female, thin from incubating her eggs or tending her brood, does not totally lose that flavor and agreeable succulence.

In size this plucky bird looks a little bigger than a domestic pigeon, but much fleshier. It could compare with a pullet or half-grown hen. It has reddish or light brown feathers at its throat and round its bill, undertail coverts of the same color, and a horseshoe-shaped patch on the lower breast formed from slightly larger feathers, brighter in color and darker. On the gray feathers of the flanks it has some reddish stripes. The upper breast and part of the head are slate gray; the upper halves of the speckled reddish wings appear to have narrow white lines along them, as fine as threads. These are simply the white shafts of the feathers. The lower half is speckled with whitish spots, running across a dark blue-gray background. The legs are flesh-colored, feathered only above the upper joint, as befits a bird built for much running over wet ground and snow. The partridge is a true native of the region, not leaving its home even in winter. This is the first nonmigratory bird that I shall write about. It is distinguished by its agility as a runner and the speed of its direct, arrowlike flight. It rises noisily and abruptly, and may cause you to jump if you are not expecting it. Despite the power and speed of their flight, partridges always fly low over the ground and do not fly far.

They have three types of call: the first is given when a whole covey finds food and begins to feed, scraping away the snow or soil with their claws. Here they will cluck like chickens, only in much softer tones, more pleasing to the ear. The second is heard when they espy some sort of danger and prepare to fly off, calling to one another. This cry is also rather like that of hens when they notice a hawk or kite. Last, they have a third note, all their own, given when a startled covey is in full, swift flight.

The partridge's diet consists of grains and seeds. Occasionally I have found small worms and insects in their crops. When not asleep or at rest they scurry ceaselessly about, scratching at the ground and pecking at things. They have a pronounced liking for company and are never met with singly or even in pairs, except when rearing young. In this partridges and black grouse are alike.

Of the life and habits of the partridge between spring and autumn I know nothing, so I avail myself of the observations of another wildfowler. I always lived in places far from the breeding grounds of partridges, and never had occasion to find a nest. In all my life I have only once come upon a brood of young partridges, but I have seen and shot many in autumn, when they congregate in coveys, as I have at the time of the first light winter snow, when you can track them as they run over the stubble, and when the snow is already deep and blizzards drive them close to human habitation—to threshing floors, and even into barns for the night. The family party I found consisted of a female and eight chicks; I shot them all, as they were in the open steppe and they had nowhere to hide, although the young birds flew off some distance. I had a good dog that brought them in one by one. From this experience I concluded that in places where broods are plentiful the shooting must be fine sport indeed: partridge chicks are unlike young grouse; they are quite tough and robust; they are found where there are no trees, and in any case they do not perch in trees; they sometimes fly considerable distances and their flight is very swift; you have to shoot fast as they are soon out of range.

Here is a description by an experienced and utterly reliable Simbirsk wildfowler thoroughly familiar with partridge-shooting, of a brood of partridges, of the shooting of young birds, and of a special method of rearing them at selected sites.

> Partridges form pairs as soon as the fields and heaths begin to thaw in spring, that is, in late March or early April, depending on the weather. The cock and hen stay together and remain faithful to each other; they mate at the onset of warm weather, in late April or early May. The hen builds no proper nest but clears a spot, making a sort of depression in rank grass or winter crops or under a bush, and lining the hollow with small feathers and down plucked from its own breast. A young female lays twelve to fifteen eggs and an old female fifteen to twenty. The eggs are oval-shaped and pale olive in color. Incubation lasts up to three weeks. The young appear in about mid-June, having hatched in a particular manner: they do not peck through the thin shell to get out. Partridge eggshells are always found split along their length into two absolutely equal parts, as if cut by a sharp knife. The chicks at once begin to flutter and run after their parents. The cock and hen together muster, shepherd, and guard their brood. In a few days the chicks begin to fly, as they are hatched with flight feathers. Their down is a reddish-gray color, making the bird at this stage resemble an adult quail. By autumn, when they reach full size, they have molted and their color is paler. As soon as the

young begin to fly freely, every morning at dawn the whole covey flies from its roost to a place a short distance off; there they scurry about for a while, gather together after a few minutes, calling to each other, then make another flight to a place where they will remain all day. In the evening, right after sunset, the parents again call in their young, make a two-stage flight, and settle down at their roosting place.

The shooting of young partridges begins in late July, but the best time is when all the grain crops have been reaped, that is, in August and September. A well-trained and obedient pointer, which is not too eager, is essential for successful partridge shooting. In July broods of partridges stay in the open, in steppeland meadows with a thin covering of bushes, in unmown grass and tall weeds. At first they are very tame and when a dog picks up the scent an old male will start running, twisting and turning, and even fluttering under its very nose to lure it away from the brood. An experienced fowler will realize this from the dog's movements, call it off, head in the opposite direction, and find the covey. In August and September families of partridges cling mainly to hilly and gullied country, or to spring crops, close to stacks and fields of millet, buckwheat, and peas. In October they can sometimes be found in winter crops, and as the weather turns colder they move into meadows, floodplains and willow scrub. Here they are much quicker to fly, exploding suddenly into the air as a covey, almost always out of range. When you have flushed a covey you should follow its line of flight, which is nearly always straight, and walk—or better, ride—in that direction; the covey will not fly far. Once out of sight in a dell or gully, or below a rise, they will usually settle among the nearest bushes, less often in the open steppe—only if there are no bushes nearby. Having alighted they run fast, but a dog, once it catches the scent, will easily locate them. The second time they are disturbed they will permit a much closer approach and often fly up in twos and threes, not all at once. Then, if you succeed in dispersing the covey, they will sit quietly and fly up from under the paws of your dog. In this way many partridges may be shot, even the whole covey, if you have great patience. If you are unable to track down the scattered birds quickly, half an hour after they have alighted you may lure them by means of a special whistle that they will answer, or you may wait until they themselves begin calling to one another, and move straight toward the calls. They will soon congregate again in a covey and then stop calling. A winged partridge runs fast along the ground and may even elude a searching dog. It can happen that after a long search you find a reassembled covey, and your winged bird with the others.

Some fowlers have the peasants bring them live partridges that they have trapped, and place them for the winter in large, specially prepared cages in which they live very comfortably, in order to release them for breeding in spring. This is done in the following manner: in spring, as soon as the ground begins to thaw, the cock and hen partridges are taken from the cage in which they have spent the winter and placed in separate crates, taking care that the birds have enough room and plenty of air. They are then taken to a selected breeding site, preferably with a thin covering of shrubs so that shooting will be easy in season, usually in an area where winter cereals are growing. Here there will be no grazing herds, and the peasants, who let their plowhorses graze among shrubs during their midday rest, will not come here to plow. Fields of winter rye are hardly visited until the harvest season, so nobody will disturb the breeding of the released partridges. At such a site a brace of partridges, cock and hen, are placed under a wicker basket to which a long cord is attached; chaff is scattered at several points around it. Then the basket is cautiously raised by pulling the cord from a distance. The partridges speedily run out and start calling. As soon as they are out of sight the upturned basket is hauled in and the keepers retire, so as not to frighten the birds. They will not usually fly far, and, since they can find food close by, remain and breed at the site of their release. Thus two or three pairs may be released into a small area, and toward autumn they will be found nearby with their broods.[13]

I now turn to the way of life of partridges in autumn, and to ways of shooting them. In early October partridges begin to gather in coveys consisting of two or three families. They gladly run along roads, especially those by which sheaves of grain are carted to the threshing floors. Here they can pick up fallen grain, but I have very often come across them on steppe roads on which grain is never carted. Reaped cereal fields are favored, but especially those sites where buckwheat and other grain crops and peas are threshed (in dry weather the threshing is sometimes done at once in the fields). They often burrow into piles of straw, especially of buckwheat, left in the fields, or into the stalks of peas, and even hide in them if they should espy a hawk, golden eagle, or other predator. I have sometimes come upon coveys that in my presence took cover in this way as they had seen a mortal enemy sailing through the clouds above. The shooting was splendid and most rewarding: partridges flew out of the straw singly, occasionally in pairs, and at very close range, right under my feet. I had to send my dog into the straw or kick it aside myself. I could use hazel-grouse shot, even Number Seven or Eight, which is quite impossible at the usual range, as partridges, especially older birds, are tougher than many larger birds. Only the black grouse is tougher. At forty-five paces, unless you break its wing, you cannot kill a partridge with hazel-grouse shot. It may be severely wounded, but will still fly off out of sight. It may die later, but the bird will be lost, so this is worse than a miss. The colder the weather, the tougher the partridges become. I always used one of the smaller duck-shot sizes, or Number Five, to shoot them successfully.

It is quite difficult to seek out partridges in autumn in open country: from afar you cannot see them in grass or stubble. As soon as they see a human they scatter and hide, so you need to have a dog, but only a well-trained one, as any other will only get in the way. They should always be sought on ground where they have been in the habit of feeding on grain.

With the first light snow, it becomes very easy to find partridges, first, because they stand out much better against the snow, and second, because you can track them. A covey of partridges run widely in all directions, leaving innumerable tracks that meet, disperse, and criss-cross, so that from a distance you see an intricate pattern of lace. The shooting is not always rewarding: if you come across a close-packed covey they will rarely permit you to come within range. They will first scatter and then suddenly fly up, so that most often you will bring down only one—two if you are lucky—from a large party. If you manage to disperse a covey, or find partridges that have individually dug into the snow to hide, you can kill large numbers; in the latter case they sit so tight that you have to winkle them out with your boot. When winter is established and snowdrifts cover the cereal fields, the birds will not be able to run in the deep snow; in any case it would be pointless, as there is nothing for them to eat in the fields. At this time the coveys draw near to villages and appear on threshing floors, where they can find grain scattered round stooks and ricks, run along the tracks along which grain is carted for drying, and round the sites where it is threshed and winnowed. The coveys roost close to human habitation, in woodland gullies, in willow scrub along streams and in any marshy woodland. At the first glimmer of light, when the darkness is still almost total, they rise from their roosts, where they may have been almost buried by snow, and fly straight to their favorite threshing floors. If they should find threshing already in progress—as it often begins long before dawn, by the light of burning brands of straw—the birds fly on to the next threshing floor. If they should be disturbed at this one they will fly to a third. In short, they are not greatly bothered by peasants at work, and can live in harmony with them: they fly on if a threshing floor is occupied, and leave a site when peasants appear there. At about ten o'clock they fly to their roosting site, where they stay for several hours and even sleep, lying half-buried in the snow. An hour before sunset they reappear at the threshing floors and remain there until late at night. During winter blizzards partridges often roost at the threshing floors, burrowing into huge piles of straw amid tall stacks where there is shelter from the wind, or on covered threshing floors and in barns. Sometimes partridges grow so accustomed to life here, especially in steppe villages where there is no suitable roosting-site nearby, that they do not fly away. On seeing a human they will hide in the outermost heaps of straw and the large stacks that always stand apart from the threshing floors, and in secure places. They even hide in the big snowdrifts swept up by the wind against fences. Here they dig small burrows in the snow and roost happily in them at night or rest in them during the day when not searching for food. If a wildfowler should learn of this it will not be hard for him to seek them out, and he will shoot more than half the covey before they abandon the haunts they have grown accustomed to. The birds can be shot in flight or sitting or running on the ground, always at quite close range, so hazel-grouse shot is very suitable. In this manner I have sometimes shot partridges right through the winter, that is, until April, by which time there were puddles of water on the threshing floors.

Partridges are such creatures of habit, and are so easily tamed that I am almost convinced they could be domesticated. They come most readily to any grain bait. So that they can more easily see where food has been spread for them, pathways of chaff are laid out, radiating from a central point, like the rays of the sun. As soon as a partridge finds one of these, it will run along it clucking, and a whole covey will fly straight in and move along the line of chaff, pecking at the grain, toward the bait at the center. There it is usual to trap them, like black grouse, with an awning but partridges are much tamer and given to their habits, in other words, more easily lured. A covey of black grouse will sometimes sit looking intently at the bait without moving to take it. Sometimes some black grouse will peck at the stooks of oats by the bait every day, and others will only fly in to watch. But partridges all rush in immediately to feed on the scattered grain, like hens. Black grouse need a long period of familiarization, whereas partridges can be trapped on the second day. It is never possible to kill a whole covey of black grouse, while with partridges you can bag every last one. I once shot them for a whole month, every day, at the same threshing floor; besides those I killed outright, some of the injured birds were also taken; the covey diminished in number day by day, until only two birds were left, which continued to fly to the threshing floor at the appointed time. . . . I spared them out of respect for their constancy.

7. GOLDEN OR WHISTLING PLOVER

Sivka, rzhanka, ozimaia kuritsa, zolotistaia rzhanka; Pluvialis apricaria

The names *sivka, rzhanka,* and *ozimaia kuritsa* are used in books and among wildfowlers. Ordinary people know this short-term passage migrant as the "field hen" or "field ruff" [*polevoi kurakhtanchik*]. I do not know the origin of the word *sivka,* but *rzhanka* [from *rozh',* "rye"] and *ozimaia kurochka* [*ozim',* "winter cereal crop"] clearly arose because these birds are always met with in fields of rye or winter cereals.[14]

The golden plover is much larger than a starling, broader in the breast and fleshier, although, like the partridge, it is built like the domestic fowl, but less rounded and of more elongated appearance in relation to its size, with a large head. The bill is like a chicken's, usually of dark flesh color. The legs are pale greenish. The bird has dark olive plumage, with white, yellowish, and bright green speckles; the belly is lighter, but the throat, cheeks, and breast are black. It is a solid, robustly built bird, and quite handsome. It flies swiftly and runs with extraordinary agility. The birds always appear in enormous flocks. I have already spoken of the golden plover, particularly of its call or whistle, in my account of the spring migration. It appears later than all other game birds, but no two years are alike. My notes show that golden plover were sometimes very few in number, and sometimes very numerous. There were years when I heard them whistling and saw flocks circling high in the sky, like a dark cloud, but did not see them settle. In 1811 no golden plovers passed through at all.

The movements of this bird of passage are puzzling indeed, at least in the province of Orenburg: it usually appears in May and stays for two to four weeks, before disappearing to parts unknown. If this were its spring passage, as for some other wading birds that I have described, there would also be a return passage in autumn, with the young, but I have never seen golden plover in autumn. Moreover, as they depart in late May they would seem to have already missed the season for rearing their young, though this clearly happens somewhere. We must suppose that they return to their winter quarters by some different route, or fly so high in autumn and so silently that nobody can see or hear them. It would be interesting to conduct a study of the movements of golden plover in other regions of Russia.

I was very fond of shooting these birds and looked forward impatiently every year to hearing their mellow, silvern calls tumbling from the heavens, from an invisible flock twisting and turning high overhead with tireless and astonishing speed. After hearing their long-awaited calls I would start seeking the birds the next day on cereals, sometimes covering great distances to no avail. Occasionally I would see them descending on last year's mown meadows or on fields of rising grain crops. A flock of golden plovers never alights suddenly on the ground: instead they circle endlessly, now gathering in a dense mass, now spreading out in a broad band, circling lower and lower, skimming low, then suddenly settling noisily on a large area. They do not sit still for a moment, but disperse nimbly in all directions. In a moment the ground on which they have settled appears to be moving as if it were alive. To gaze for long on this rippling surface is to dazzle the eye.

As soon as the golden plover arrive, a season of fevered, hurried shooting begins—a time I greatly loved. One's greed and ardor were the greater for the knowledge that the birds might not stay long, and that they could all be gone tomorrow or the next day. It is impossible to approach them on foot: before you can come within range they begin to rise one by one and fly to another spot. They also run so fast that you cannot keep up with them. If you use a *drozhki* they are less nervous and will allow a closer approach, though some of the same difficulties, their constant running and flying up, remain. I rarely managed to kill more than three with one shot: you should not wait for the flock to pack tightly together, in the hope of killing more. It should be a rule to fire at the nearest birds as soon as you are within range. If you take aim at one bird you will usually kill two and occasionally even three. If you hope to kill more with one shot you will tire out both yourself and your horses, and shoot immeasurably fewer, because you will chase them far off and frighten them far more by your constant pursuit than you would by a few shots. Usually the whole flock will rise after each shot, circle once or twice and land again. Thus it is sometimes possible to fire several shots in the same field, because the birds are in no hurry to rise again after they have gamboled through the high sky and settled again. They prefer to make short flights from one spot to another. I once made the discovery that golden plovers circle low over their injured companions, as, in fact, some other birds do. It happened like this: after firing at a flock of golden plovers and killing two I followed the flight of the rest of the flock, which began to rise quite high. Suddenly one bird broke away into downward flight (probably weakened by a wound) and fell or landed some way off. In a moment the entire flock swooped down and began circling very low over the spot. I made my way there as fast as I could and found the winged plover, which did not have the strength to fly, but could only drag itself along the ground, as one leg was broken. The flock rose higher. I at once sent my *drozhki* and horses back and lay down on the ground not far from the injured bird. The flock began to descend and flew quite close to me. I fired and killed five birds, after which the others flew to another field. I subsequently exploited this stratagem many times to good effect.

The best time to shoot golden plover is on overcast rainy days, when they are much tamer: they fly little, run less on damp ground, and sometimes even sit quite still in a tight-packed flock. Before the days of the percussion cartridge, rain not only prevented the wildfowler from shooting but often drove him from the field, because it was so difficult to keep the powder-pan dry: it would soon become damp, and in heavy rain it was impossible to keep it dry. But with modern shotguns rain is no obstacle and many golden plovers may be shot in rain in a single field—or so I surmise: since the new type came in I have not so much as seen golden plover.

As I have said, golden plover are quite hardy, with good resistance to shot, so shot no smaller than Number Six or Seven is needed, although the range is crucial. I have shot them with snipe-shot in wet weather, and large duck-shot in fine weather when they were circling overhead. They are never fat, but neither are they too thin, but always with a covering of meat. Their flesh is very tasty and succulent.

In 1822, in the Belebei district of the province of Orenburg, I once went to inspect some spring crops—with my gun, of course, as I never went anywhere without it. Suddenly my peasant driver pointed out a small flock of golden plover that had just landed. I told him to turn toward them and fired as soon as we were within range. The flock, thirty or forty strong, quickly rose and flew off out of sight. I had killed three. When they were brought to me I was astonished: instead of the usual dark green, speckled birds, I saw birds very similar to golden plover, though a little smaller, and with utterly unfamiliar plumage. How annoying it is that I did not take down a detailed description right away! The peasant assured me that many such birds could be found in the fields. He was wrong: I found no such plovers not only that spring, but in any other year. I call them plovers as they were just like them in lines and build, except that their heads looked to me a little smaller and in better proportion to the overall size of the body. They were very handsome: their plumage was light brown, and they had whitish stripes running from the eye down the neck. . . . That is all I can remember.[15]

There exists another variety of "marsh golden plovers," similar in plumage to the curlew. They do not fly in flocks but occur singly on shoals in rivers and on the banks of ponds, but I am scarcely acquainted with them.[16]

8. BLACK-WINGED PRATINCOLE

Morskaia lastochka, krasnoustik, stepnaia tirkushka;
Glareola nordmanni

I have appropriated the first of these names, *morskaia lastochka* [sea-swallow], from *The Compleat Sportsman.* Whether it owes its name to its resemblance to a swallow and the word "sea" has been added for no clear reason, or whether it really lives near the sea and is there known as the "sea-swallow" I cannot say. Some Orenburg fowlers, myself included, call it the *krasnoustik* [red-lips], while among the peasantry it is known, like the golden plover, as *polevoi kurakhtanchik* [field ruff/field hen], which is not at all appropriate, as there is nothing at all henlike about it. In shape it has much in common with a swallow. We use the name "red-lips" because the gape of the mouth has a bright red border, and this is the name I shall apply.

The pratincole is twice to three times the size of an ordinary swallow; the plumage is dark coffee-color, even appearing black at a distance. The belly is a little lighter and the bill yellowish, the neck short, the head rather large and rounded, the legs thin and short and of an indeterminate dark gray. They are clearly not built for much running. The tail is white and the tips of the tailfeathers blackish. It has long wings with sharp, pointed tips, which are folded over each other when the bird is seated, as in all birds that have long wings, such as the hobby and even the common swallow.[17]

The arrival of the pratincole and the duration of its stay in the province of Orenburg is even more mysterious than in the case of the golden plover. I have rarely encountered them in two successive years, more like every third year, but once I observed them occurring twice in a single year: in June, when the fallows are being plowed (the time when they usually arrive), and in early August, the time of rye sowing. This latter factor has me utterly baffled. What should we call the first appearance of the pratincole? If it is their spring passage, the return passage follows too soon, giving them no time to breed and depart with their young. In that year I shot several of the birds and one of them was carrying an egg; assuming that it was not a wind-egg, or unfertilized egg, we may suppose that pratincoles breed in autumn, in some warm climate of course, and that they fly there in August.[18] The egg was very beautiful, with brown speckles on a pale flesh-colored background.

Pratincoles are swift fliers and skim endlessly over freshly plowed land, hawking for the midges and other flying insects that swarm over it, as well as feeding on insects crawling on the ground. For this they have to alight, but they walk little and slowly. On the one occasion when I came upon pratincoles in August it was not on arable land, not in a field of any kind, but skimming to and fro over a pond late one evening. I killed four; early the following morning the remaining pratincoles were gone.

For a wildfowler like myself, who from earliest youth had an ungovernable passion for observing and studying the life and habits of birds whenever possible, the arrival of pratincoles was a matter of particular interest. It always surprised me that they arrived as soon as the plowing of fallows began. This season and that of the sowing of rye do not coincide everywhere or always, and it cannot be assumed that the birds knew it by instinct and flew long distances for the occasion. We must therefore conclude that they were already present somewhere close by, although this also seems somewhat improbable. Pratincoles always appear in small parties and can be quickly spotted from afar as they constantly circle or flit back and forth over the same spot, alighting only for brief periods. They are not particularly shy, especially at first, and must almost always be shot in flight. I usually took station in the middle of the area around which the birds were circling, taking a dog with me—a well-trained one, of course—and they flew toward me and sometimes came well within range. After a few shots the birds would move off some way, and I would follow them until they left the fields altogether and flew right away. They are quite difficult to shoot as they do not fly close and will not circle over your head, but fly somewhere nearby, skimming low over the ground just like swallows. This means that the target cannot always be clearly seen, especially on a dull day, and for a fowler who is even slightly short-sighted, as I have always been, shooting becomes more difficult. Moreover they fly very fast. I never managed to shoot many of them, although I sought them avidly. They fly separately, not in compact groups, so it is impossible to kill more than one with a single shot. As they are not particularly tough, a fine hazel-grouse shot, Number Seven or even Eight, is more than enough. Like golden plovers, pratincoles are never fat during their brief sojourn on passage, but well enough covered, and their flesh is tender, succulent, and very tasty.

9. CORNCRAKE

Korostel', dergach, dergun; Crex crex

It may seem strange to assign the corncrake to the category of "birds of field and steppe," because its usual home is in meadows thinly covered with bushes, not only adjacent to marshes, but often themselves quite wet. All this is true. This is where they live in spring and where they raise their young, but after this they remove their young into standing crops, then to grass-covered dividing strips and fallows, and finally to woodland fringes. So in which category does the corncrake belong? Perhaps we should create a special category of marshland-meadowland game. But this too would be incorrect. In the marshes that it sometimes inhabits there lives another crake that lives there permanently—the spotted crake, of which I have already spoken.

Korostel' is a wildfowling and literary term, whereas the folk names are *dergun* and *dergach*. City folk, especially those of the capital, are largely unfamiliar with this bird, but all country-dwellers, young and old, know its restless cry. But what a pleasure it is to hear those hoarse, unmelodious notes in spring and summer, especially when it first begins to call! This is never early in the spring; tall grass and bushes in young leaf are a precondition for the song of the corncrake, which does indeed resemble a monotonous croak or "crake."

The corncrake is slightly larger in the body than a quail and only a little longer in shape, but at first glance it looks much larger because of its long neck, legs, and plumes. In spite of this, its proportions are also those of a domestic fowl. Its plumage is russet, with fine dark barring and striations. The wings are much redder; right along the back lie long feathers, darkish along the shaft and with light brown edging. The belly is much lighter; the throat has a kind of sheen, tending to blue-gray; the bill is of the usual flesh color and the legs pale; the underwing lining is red and the axillaries speckled. This speckling extends toward the tail and even the upper leg, which is covered in small feathers; the tail is short and also speckled. The flight of this bird is quite different from all other birds: the hindquarters always droop as if the bird had been shot, so that it does not fly in a horizontal position but travels through the air almost in a standing position. Furthermore it has the peculiarity that, on taking wing, it does not try to fly into the wind like all other birds, but readily flies with it. This makes its feathers turn back and gives it a shaggy appearance. But perhaps this choice is imposed upon it, and it flies with the wind because of its short wings, lack of strength, and feeble flight, which always caused me to wonder how a bird that flies so heavily and awkwardly could cover vast distances and even cross the sea to winter in a warm climate. Moreover, nobody has observed corncrakes on arrival or departure in flocks, or even in twos and threes; in spring they appear singly and in autumn this is the way they are last seen. How easy it would be to believe that they seek refuge in autumn in some remote woodland fastness and spend the winter there in a torpid state, like kites, for example, which can be found frozen stiff in hollow trees, but which thaw out and revive in the warm, as I myself have seen! Yet there is no doubt that corncrakes do depart.

To return to my description: corncrakes fly feebly, but are surprisingly nimble and tireless runners. If a dog should scent one in tall grass, the bird will rely more on its legs than its wings. It will be in no hurry to rise, but will wear out the fowler, especially in hot weather. The better a dog is trained and the more patience it has as a pointer, the harder it will be for it to put up a corncrake: when it scents the bird nearby, exuding that particularly pungent odor that makes any dog unusually keen to find it, it begins to point at once, while the corncrake, almost deliberately, pauses for a moment and then takes to its heels. By the time you tell the dog to "Take!" and before the dog can race to the spot where the bird was hiding, it will be twenty to forty yards away. Again the dog will follow the warm scent and point again, and the whole exercise is repeated. The dog will get carried away and will start pursuing the deceptive bird by leaps and bounds until it finally flushes it out, but this is extraordinarily damaging to a dog's training. This is why fowlers do not let a good young dog seek corncrakes, and this is why they do not shoot them in large numbers. However, the training of an older, well-schooled dog will not suffer from chasing corncrakes, especially if it has a very good nose. Without tiring itself out by trying to follow all the twists and turns of the bird's trail, it will lead you to it quickly and directly, and the bird will be obliged to take wing. On ground covered with short, thin grass the corncrake will rise much sooner, as it fears to allow the dog to come too close. But here is a paradox: like me, other fowlers have often flushed corncrakes unexpectedly without any dog, in long grass when we were not looking for them. One might have thought that they could very easily have hidden or run away.

The most remarkable thing about the corncrake is its voice or call, which has won it nationwide renown. The call sounds like "creck, creck," repeated up to fifteen times in succession. A fervid ardor can be heard in these hoarse notes. If you listen carefully, you realize at once that this is not the calm singing voice of a bird, but a cry of passion. It is a distinctive feature of this call that it seems to come from different directions and distances at one and the same time. At first I thought several corncrakes were calling at once, but later was able to establish that it was the same bird, and I saw with my own eyes the cause of this illusion: the corncrake produces this cry with all the fury of a thing possessed, straining, craning its neck, thrusting itself forward with each cry as if about to hurl itself at something, and constantly turning in different directions without moving from the spot. This accounts for the varying power and apparent proximity of the call. When the bird turns its head away, the cry seems much further off, and vice versa. Furthermore, after calling a dozen times from one position, the bird immediately starts running hither and thither and then starts calling again from another spot a few yards away, so its position changes constantly. In the voice of the corncrake I have not found the same variation in volume and power that one hears in the quail, but there is some variation in the number of calls. From the foregoing I conclude that the cry of the corncrake is simply to attract a female and give voice to a powerful concupiscence. I went to great lengths to try and discover more detail but despite all efforts I was never able to observe their copulation, because amid rank grass and bushes you can see nothing, even with a powerful telescope such as the one I armed myself with for my observations. A peasant told me that he was once asleep in some bushes and awoke to see a pair of corncrakes copulating close by in the accustomed manner, after which the female shook her feathers down and ran off, while the male, after waiting a while, began to call. This supports my contention that the male attracts the female by his call, and she runs to him or gives an answering call, like a quail. However, no wildfowlers have heard this answering call.

Notwithstanding the sketchy nature of the information, the following conclusions may be drawn: (1) corncrakes do not form pairs; (2) they do not have communal display grounds; (3) random copulation takes place with several females; (4) the male does not assist the female in rearing the young.

My close acquaintance with corncrakes has caused me to get somewhat carried away, but, to return to my usual order: I have already said that nobody has witnessed the spring arrival of corncrakes. To judge by the time they begin calling one might suppose that they arrive very late, but this would be an erroneous impression: they arrive only a little later than great snipe but do not emerge in open places because these are as yet bare of grass. They hide in thickets, skulking at the very roots of the bushes, sometimes on very wet ground where a hunter will not venture at this season. I realized this a long time ago, while watching my dog searching eagerly for something. I even glimpsed some birds flitting through the bushes and took them for woodcock on account of their russet plumage, but later I realized that they were corncrakes. I have shot them in late April, but they begin calling only in late May. At this season I have twice found nests, lovingly woven from dry grass and well concealed in impenetrable coverts along woodland edges. I did not find more than ten eggs, but I am told there may be as many as fifteen. I do not quite believe this, as it would mean that corncrakes would be more numerous than they are. The eggs are small and slightly elongated, whitish to blue-gray in color, and covered with pretty brown spots. Only the female sits. The baby birds are tiny on hatching and covered in down as black as soot. They soon leave the nest and run with great agility. Nests and broods of young are very rarely found. As soon as the young have grown a little, the mother leads them into fields of standing cereals, and from this season until late autumn I have never found them in broods, but only singly.

The male birds, as well as the unpaired birds, remain close to meadows, even at hay-making time, sometimes moving to neighboring fields, fallow land, woodland fringes, and marshland, if not too wet. Corncrakes cease to call before quail, in mid-July. I do not know when they sleep. They call day and night, mostly in the twilight of dusk and dawn, which at this season are hardly separated. It is probable that they sleep at midday.

Corncrake-shooting as such is not practiced. The birds may turn up among other game birds: among great snipe and black-tailed godwits in hay meadows; with quail in open fields; or with young black grouse in thin belts of trees. They will never be shot in large numbers: ten in one field at the outside—first, because they are scarce, and second, because they are difficult to flush, with a dog or without.

I have described the flight of the corncrake, and from this it can easily be seen that they are quite easily shot. They have little resistance, so a fine snipe shot is more than sufficient. They usually rise so close and always fly so slowly that you have to give them time to pull away. Eager young fowlers who forget this rule often blow the birds to pieces, or else miss, which is a cause of great annoyance, and which (I must admit) has happened to me. Near or among bushes it is harder to shoot them, as the bird will immediately take refuge behind one, and when a bush is in full leaf you cannot see through it or shoot through it.

In spring and summer, until the end of July, corncrakes are quite lean, but when they move out into the fields they build up fat so quickly that by the end of August they have a thick covering, and at this time they taste wonderful, as the fat is less cloying than that of quail. At all seasons, however, they are tasty. In marshy meadows they eat anything at all, including all kinds of insects, while in cereal fields they eat pure bread grains and the ripe seeds of certain grasses, which are very nourishing. Throughout August they cling close to cereal crops, hiding at midday, when not feeding, in broad, grassy dividing strips thinly covered with shrubs. These places are their favorite haunts, but in their absence they will stay in nearby fallows, wooded dells, and woodland fringes, which they take to before their departure, or rather, before they disappear. I have encountered corncrakes up to the tenth of September, at which time, I confess, I considered them a rare prize.

Corncrakes and quail can be hunted with hawks, but it cannot be said that any hawk will successfully take a corncrake, for the following reason: as soon as a hawk closes on a corncrake and extends its talons to seize it, the corncrake lets out a loud cry, similar to the chatter of a magpie or the yapping of a ferret. If the hawk is startled and overshoots the first time, it will never take corncrakes in the future. Of course this applies only to "fledglings"—hawks taken as young birds from the nest and reared in cages—whereas older birds that have already hunted in the wild will not be scared off. Sometimes a hungry "fledgling" will take a corncrake if it has plenty of experience at hunting other birds before encountering a corncrake.

10. QUAIL

Perepelka; obyknovennyi perepel; Coturnix coturnix

This appealing bird is much better known even to city-dwellers than the corncrake, being more common. It is heard and seen frequently by peasants at their farm work, whether weeding, plowing, hay-making in the steppe, or harvesting. The diminutive form *perepelochka* is sometimes used as a term of endearment, although not nearly so often as the names of some other birds, and the word has even found a place in a folk song: a young man tells how speedily and lightly he will run to his beloved's side, using the quail as a colorful metaphor for speed and grace.

The quail is slightly larger than a starling, but fleshier. Of course everybody is familiar with the bird, at least from the table. Who has not tried its succulent, tender, tasty meat, sometimes cloyingly fat? In the proportions of all its parts the quail is a chicken or partridge in miniature, but it looks even prettier and more pleasing to the eye than a partridge, perhaps because it is so much smaller. Like partridges, quail have all the attributes and habits of domestic fowl: just like them, they ceaselessly scratch and scrape at the ground, raking away dust, sand, and loose soil with their claws. They do this both to seek food and to sit down and rest more comfortably on the ground.

It is difficult to describe the gray, speckled plumage of the quail, and in any case it is too well known. It is not strikingly beautiful, but to me that quiet, unvarying speckling is so agreeable that I prefer it to the louder beauty of more colorful birds. The female differs from the male in having a lighter, whitish throat, while the male has a ruddy-colored throat with a black mark on it. The male's bill is also longer, with the appearance of whiskers at the base. The quail is not only a fast runner, but also a swift flier when it is lean and light. It is a real bird of the steppes, and, although it is very partial to food grains and fields sown with them, especially millet, it is found in abundance and always favors the real, remote steppe, often far from any arable land. There it feeds mainly on insects and grass seeds.

Neither the quail's spring arrival nor its autumn departure have been observed. They do not flock together. They appear singly, unobtrusively, and disappear in the same way. In late April, or more often in early May, when the young grass is rising, they begin to turn up, never in large numbers, in meadows and fallows, but never on last year's stubble. At this time they are not very tame, do not tolerate the set of a dog for long, and fly at great speed to alight a long distance off. Their flight is very direct, but even so they are quite difficult to shoot in spring. In autumn it is quite different, and the shooting becomes very easy.

No sooner has the grass grown tall, so that the quail can easily hide in it, than they begin to call. The call consists of two phrases: the first resembles the syllables "va-vva, va-vva," repeated up to three times, but never more, at least in my experience. This is followed by the typical cry resembling the words "weed the plot," or so this is interpreted by the Russian peasant.[19] This call is repeated four to ten times without pause, but ten times is exceptional. The bird calls as heatedly as the corncrake, and with the same movements. Some quail have very clear, loud voices, and can be heard over long distances. The Russian people are fond of the cry of the quail, although there is nothing particularly pleasing to the ear about it, and the bird is often kept as a cage-bird. Even today in Moscow, in some side streets and back streets, above the rattle of wheels and the hubbub of human voices, you can often hear the call of a quail. Of course this pitiful little call, drowned by the noise of the city, is far from the resonant cry of freedom in the open fields, in the fresh air and silence. Be this as it may, in Russia and perhaps elsewhere quail have had their passionate admirers, mostly among merchants: the louder and purer the call and the higher the number of calls, the more valuable it is considered. I have heard that in the olden days they paid up to a hundred rubles for a good quail. Some quail go on calling until mid-August.

As soon as the quail start calling, their amorous adventures begin; in other words, this cry is the expression of the irrepressible urge to mate. In the case of the corncrake, I said this without confirmation, but the mating of the quail I know at first hand. As a boy I often went out with an old fowler to trap quail with a net and "quail pipes"; that is, I went to watch him trap them. This procedure, which fully reveals the mating process, is carried out in the following way: the trapper takes to the field armed with his "quail pipes" (whose design I shall not describe but which produce notes similar to the low musical call of the female) and a fine net some twenty-five yards or more square with a mesh large enough to allow a quail to put its head through. Having selected a meadow where quail can be heard calling, where the grass is tall, or better, where there are low bushes of wild peach or pea-shrub, the trapper carefully spreads his net over them and lies down by the edge of it. As soon as he has sounded a few notes on his pipe, quail will reply from all sides: some fly in from afar, and those closer come running. When he can see several quail under his net and very close to him, he leaps to his feet. The quail fly up and are caught in the net.

This is not the place to describe the details or the nicer points of this method. The point is that this gave me the opportunity to study at length the courtship activities and copulation of the quail, because hen birds also sometimes responded to the call. The male birds are furiously determined in their mating: they fling themselves upon a female time after time and one after another, but they do not fight among themselves, at least, I never witnessed any fighting.[20] Such episodes usually ended with the more than satisfied female taking to her heels or flying away, pursued by several males. Clearly, with mating of this kind no pairs are formed, there is no bonding, and the male takes no part in the rearing of the young. When the females disperse to nest and incubate their eggs, the males vainly seek and call their temporary partners, who now have other matters to attend to: now the ardor of the males reaches a level of wild intoxication. At this period they come most readily to the net, answering the pipes, and, I am told, will fight among themselves. My companion, an old hunter, tried to use a live female instead of the pipes, placing her under the net in a small cage, and I saw with my own eyes how two or three males at once leaped at the cage and struggled against it, trying to get at the female. As if this were not enough, the mischievous old man crumpled his glove into a ball and tossed it toward the males when they ran up close. In blind fury they leaped upon it and trod it as if it were a female.

In mid-May some females are already sitting: these are the early broods, the "early-hatchers," but others (the "late hatchers") hatch their young in late July. This means that very young quail can be found over a period of two months. This unusual feature leads many to think that the same female rears two clutches in one season. Although the great increase in quail numbers toward autumn lends some credibility to this theory, I, for my part, cannot support it.

The nest is made of dry grass, on the ground, preferably in thick feather-grass. The nest, always lined with the down of the mother, is too wide and deep for such a small bird, but this is inevitable as she lays up to sixteen eggs—some say up to twenty. To my mind this large number is proof that they rear only one brood per year.

Quail eggs are very similar to sparrow eggs in having light brown speckling, although they are twice as large and rather greener. After a three-week incubation period the young hatch, covered in gray down, with stubby winglets, from which feathers grow within a few days. The chicks are thus able to start fluttering a little while still down-covered, and are called "flutterers" [*porshki*]. I have often found "flutterers" of different age and size in one and the same brood. Fowlers explain this by saying that the hen bird does not hatch all her eggs at once, and that she removes the first-hatched chicks from the nest and continues to incubate the others. I have not witnessed this myself, so cannot confirm that this is the case. It seems to me that it would be a little difficult for the bird to sit on her nest and find food for herself and her young at the same time, when the young in their first days are very weak and would have to be left unattended outside the nest, unprotected at night or in the rain by the warmth of their mother's body. I have also found young fledglings still in the nest and seen the mother feeding them out of her own mouth, and all were the same age. Might it not be more satisfactory to account for the curious occurrence of broods of varying age by the supposition that if the mother should perish the young disperse and join other families, possibly older or younger? This would explain the great difference in age between chicks apparently of the same brood.

As soon as the crops begin to rise, especially millet, quail flock in from all sides and remain in them constantly. Amid such abundant and nourishing fare, not only the parents, but also the young wax plump at an amazing rate, particularly the males and the unmated females. By this season they are most reluctant to fly; their flight is very slow and labored, and they soon alight again a short distance away. They will allow a dog to point for a long time, and sit tight right under its nose, so that the dog may often take them there and then, as may a falconer.[21]

Quail have a particular fondness for millet, and when reaping is nearing completion in a field of this crop several quail will leap out at each stroke of the sickle. In hot weather, not wishing to take my dog out, I sometimes took advantage of this, taking my stand among the harvesters and shooting quail as they flew out. Often I shot two dozen or so, and well over a hundred quail could be flushed from one three-acre field; but a bevy of this size gathers only in the evenings, just before sunset. It will stay together in one place all night, and the birds will scatter in all directions in the morning, to hide in nearby fallows, dividing strips and meadows. Once the cereals are harvested, the quail remain on the stubble to feed, and often hide in stooks, or under bunches of unbound millet. Many times I have turned these over with my foot to flush the quail underneath. They continue to visit even those fields from which the crops have been cleared, especially those in which there is a good growth of meadow saxifrage and bur-marigold showing green among the yellow straw, and they feed on the overripe seed that has fallen from the ears. Thus they spend the whole of August and even the first days of September; but then they begin to decrease imperceptibly in numbers, and by mid-September they are sometimes all gone; their departure is hastened by frosts and cold weather, of course, and delayed by mild weather. I should add that quail do not all disappear at once, but rather little by little. Having been from an early age a "quail-hawker" (that is, a falconer who pursues quail), I was able to observe their gradual departure many times. Had I been only a shooting man, I would never have been able to discover the details of this, as I would not have spent so much valuable shooting time every day in pursuit of quail alone.

The first drop in quail numbers, after a medium frost or a sudden north wind, is quite noticeable. This happens sometimes at the end of August, but more often at the beginning of September. Every day after that you find quail numbers gradually diminishing by a dozen or so, from seventy or even eighty birds until finally there are three, two, or one. Sometimes I was left with this one last bird for several days, and finally shot it, having tramped until footsore over all the places quail favor in autumn: the broad, bushy dividing strips with thick, drooping grass, and the gentle feather-grass–covered hollows in the steppe, where a particular kind of fluffy, silky grass grows with the feather grass. At this season a well-fattened quail is a delight! Long after I had forsaken falconry for the shotgun, I still enjoyed shooting the scarce quail still to be found.

There is no doubt that quail depart in autumn for warm, southern lands. We have much evidence from eyewitnesses of vast quail flocks setting out to cross the Black Sea and often perishing from exhaustion in it, after battling the headwinds. The question then arises: When and where do they assemble in these flocks? Clearly there must be such assembly points somewhere, although, to my knowledge, in none of the provinces of Central Russia has anyone observed the arrival, departure, or passage of quail. Nor has anyone even flushed them or seen them in these great flocks. We cannot suppose that each individual bird flies separately to the seacoast many thousand versts away. This is why many fowlers believe that they congregate in flocks and make their aerial journey at night and spend the days dispersed on the ground, seeking food wherever they happen to be. I should mention that I knew one wildfowler who assured me that quail did not fly away, but departed on foot, and that he had seen them leaving one spot and appearing in large numbers in another, though not in a flock, at a place where there had previously been very few. He added that they were heading due south, and that this movement took place not at night but during the day. This fowler followed their progress and noted that they appeared at new sites not in early morning, but more often at noon or toward evening. I do not presume to judge which view is closer to the truth: for this we would need the precise observations of not one but many fowlers. I have also heard from reliable observers that quail have sometimes been known to turn up in winter, in the shelter of long, dense grass on dividing strips and even in marmot burrows, always tightly sealed off deep inside by the marmots themselves. The birds were alive but in a semitorpid state. When taken into warm habitation and placed in a cage, they quickly revived and set about feeding. Hence the false notion that I have met with among old-time fowlers and among the peasants, that quail winter in our province. It is my view that these birds found in winter were late-hatching young or sickly specimens: these were too weak to depart in time, on the wing or on foot, and were thus obliged to over-winter. Whether they would have survived the whole winter or perished of cold remains an open question.

From all I have said of the life and habits of the quail it may be seen that they must always be shot in flight and must be put up by a dog. All smaller shot sizes may be used, as the quail, especially in autumn, may be shot at any range. Given open fields and their habit of sitting tight and rising at close quarters—factors for which one may prepare in advance, if you have a good pointer—you have full control of the range: you may allow the bird to fly off to the desired distance, depending on the type of shot you have loaded. Clearly it is essential to let the bird pull away, just as it is with corncrakes. On the whole, considering their numbers and their value as game, quail are little shot, and ordinary hunters who simply seek large bags never bother with them, thinking it not worth wasting a shot on such a small bird; and many are unable to shoot a bird in flight. True wildfowlers, on the other hand, quite understandably prefer marshland game, which is at the peak of its season in August, at the same time as the quail; but in places where there is little or no marshland, quail-shooting is a most enjoyable and rewarding sport. Besides, one may sometimes take an hour or two from marshland shooting and devote that time to plump autumn quail.

I have said that quail are shot relatively little. They are trapped or hunted, however, in great numbers: using quail-pipes, of which I have spoken; with drag-nets, which are hauled over them; with a dog to locate them and point; and above all with falcons. Those caught by the first two methods are placed in coops, or large cages, where they live very comfortably and grow very fat. In such cages they may be transported live over long distances. To preserve the fatty meat of those taken by the latter two methods they are lightly salted, placed in tubs, and butter is poured over them. Many maintain that freshly salted quail are superior to birds just shot.

CATEGORY IV

Woodland Game

FORESTS

All woodland birds spend most of their lives in forests and some never leave them, so I shall first consider and define to the best of my ability the various types of forest and of woodland species.

Speaking of water, I said that it was nature's crowning glory; I might almost have said the same of forests. The beauty of any particular locality lies in the combination of woodland and water in it. That is the way of nature: rivers, streams, brooks, and lakes almost always have trees and bushes growing round them. Exceptions are few. Another of nature's great purposes may be seen in the combination of woodland and water: the forest is the guardian of the water. The trees shield the ground against the searing rays of the summer sun and from the drying power of the wind. Cool and dampness thrive in their shadow, in which flowing or standing water cannot dry out. The falling water levels of rivers, which has been seen throughout Russia, is generally thought to result from the destruction of forests.[1]

All types of resinous trees, such as pine, fir, spruce, and the like, are known as "evergreen" trees, and are distinguished by the fact that instead of leaves they have needles, which they do not lose in winter, although they shed and change them imperceptibly and gradually in spring and early summer. In autumn they become fuller, fresher, and greener, so that they are at the peak of their beauty and strength as winter draws on. There are woods consisting exclusively of pines. All other varieties of trees, those that lose their leaves in autumn and grow new ones in spring, such as oak, elm, black poplar, lime, birch, aspen, alder, and others, are termed "deciduous." These include the berry-bearing trees: bird-cherry and rowan, which sometimes reach considerable height and girth. The deciduous trees include all those bushes that lose their leaves in autumn: guelder rose, hazel, mezereon, honeysuckle, wild rose, bay willow, dwarf willow, and others.

Coniferous forest favors clay or silt soils, while pines prefer sandy soil. On pure black earth, pines are scarce, except in mountainous country where loam and bare rock is exposed. I am not fond of coniferous forests, with their endless monotony, gloomy green, and sandy or clay soil, perhaps because from earliest youth I grew to admire the varied and jolly deciduous forest about me, growing on rich black soil. Pine trees were rare in those districts of the province of Orenburg where I spent more than half my life. For this reason I shall speak only of deciduous woodland.

Deciduous woods usually consist of a mixture of various kinds of tree, and this mixture is particularly pleasing to the eye, but sometimes one comes across pockets in which a particular species is dominant, be it oak, lime, birch, or aspen, growing in far greater density than other species and reaching large enough size to provide building timber. When trees of different types grow together, forming a single green mass, all of them together are equally beautiful, but some stand out more than others.

The spreading, white-boled, jolly, bright green birch is handsome, but handsomer still is the slender, curly, round-leaved linden tree, sweet-scented at blossom time, soft green rather than bright green—the tree that provides the roofing bark and bast shoes for the Godfearing folk of Russia. The maple, with its pawlike leaves (as Gogol called them), is handsome too—tall, slender, and beautiful, but it does not commonly grow in those districts of Orenburg province that I know, and it does not attain its full height there. An ancient oak, sturdy and robust, tall and mighty, may be several yards in girth at its base, but such majestic specimens are rarely found, and a grove of small oaks has no particular attraction: the foliage is a dark or dull green, and the carved leaves, though thick and healthy, show only the first signs of the might and endurance of these trees. Aspen wood is held in least regard as construction timber, owing to its appearance and intrinsic properties.[2] Quite unnoticed, the trembling-leaved aspen becomes beautiful, even striking, only in autumn: its early fading leaves are covered with gold and crimson, making it stand out from the green of the other trees, and it lends great charm and variety to a forest at the season of the fall.

Scrub or brush (that is, young woodland) is pleasing to the

eye, especially from afar. The green foliage is fresh and bright but casts little shade. The trees are thin, but may grow so close together as to be impenetrable. With time most of the trees will die, being too close together, and only the strongest will claim the nutritive powers of the soil and begin to grow not only upward but in girth.

Black in the distance stands the tall, shady, old woodland—the "dark forest"—but the word "old" should not be understood as meaning leafless or dying: the sight of such trees in great numbers would be dreary indeed. In nature everything proceeds gradually. A large forest always consists of trees of varying ages: those that are dying or completely dead may not be noticeable in the mass of others that are in leaf or blossom. Huge trunks lie scattered about the forest, of oaks, limes, birches, and aspens that first died, then rotted at the root, and were finally felled by a high wind.[3] As they fell they bent and snapped the young trees growing nearby, and these, though deformed, continue to grow and put out leaves, picturesquely twisted to one side, bent double, or laid flat on the forest floor. The corpses of these forest giants preserve the same outward appearance for a long time, while rotting inside; moss and even grass grows over the bark; I have often jumped in haste onto just such a fallen tree and fallen right through to the ground below, enveloped for several seconds in a cloud of wood-rot, similar to puff-ball spores. . . . But this in no way disturbs the beauty of the mighty, green, sylvan kingdom, growing freely in the cool, silent gloom. The sight of a dense forest at a time of noonday heat is pleasing, its cool air refreshing, the stillness soothing, and the rustle of the leaves is pleasing to the ear as the wind occasionally stirs the treetops. There is something mysterious, something uncertain, about the gloom; the cries of animals, birds, and humans are altered and sound different, and strange. This is a world that is somehow special, and the popular imagination peoples it with supernatural beings: with forest goblins and nymphs, like the water sprites that are said to haunt deep places in rivers and lakes. During a gale a large forest is eerie, although all is quiet under the trees: the trees creak and groan, and boughs crack and break. A man may be gripped by involuntary fear and feel compelled to flee to open ground.

In the forest, on the branches, and amid the dense green foliage lives an infinite variety of colorful and beautiful birds, all calling in their distinctive voices. Black grouse and capercaillie give their courtship notes; hazel grouse whistle; woodcock in their roding flight grunt; all the varieties of pigeon coo, each in its own voice; thrushes whistle and cluck; golden orioles call to one another in melodic but mournful tones;[4] speckled cuckoos lament; assorted woodpeckers tap and drum on tree trunks; black woodpeckers give their resonant cry; jays scold; waxwings, woodlarks, hawfinches, and a vast array of small avian songsters fill the air with their varied voices, bringing life to the silent forest.[5] In hollow trunks and in the branches the birds make their nests, lay their eggs, and rear their young. For the same purpose, martens and squirrels, the enemies of birdlife, and noisy swarms of wild bees, also take up residence in holes in trees.[6] Flowers and grasses are scarce in a large forest: the deep and permanent shade does not favor vegetation that needs the light and warmth of the sun. Bracken, the thick green leaves of the lily-of-the-valley and the tall stalks of the faded forest gillyflower are the plants most often met with, and clumps of ripe, red stone bramble add color. The musty scent of mushrooms hangs in the air, but the most striking is the pungent and, to my mind, agreeable scent of milk-agaric, because these mushrooms grow in family groups, nestling in thin bracken, under last year's decaying leaves.

Deciduous woodland also provides a more or less permanent home to bears, wolves, hares, martens, and squirrels.[7] Among the squirrels are some that are almost all white, known as "flying squirrels." These have a fine membrane of skin between the fore- and hindpaws on each side. When stretched, this membrane helps them to leap over long distances from one tree to another. I once shot one in midair during one of its flightlike leaps, thus killing "an animal on the wing."

Birds of prey—goshawks and sparrowhawks, harriers, white-tailed eagles, hobbies, and others—also breed in the forest, building their nests on the main boughs, tight against the trunk.[8] In the deep shade of the woodland depths various owls hide and breed, including eagle owls, whose wild, mournful, eerie cry would frighten even the boldest spirit who might be caught in the forest at night. It is no surprise that the peasants consider these cries the hooting and laughter of a wood-demon or goblin.

If you should chance to travel through lightly timbered country, where copses alternate with fragrant open glades, as soon as you emerge into the latter a hobby may appear in the sky overhead. If it has a nest nearby, it will usually follow a traveler, even a walker, sailing above him in wide, daring circles in the sky, watching with its astonishingly keen eyes for any small bird that may fly from under the feet of the traveler or his horse. With lightning speed it plummets from on high upon the fluttering bird, and, if the latter is too slow to take cover in the grass or in a tree or bush, the hobby spears it with its sharp talons and carries it off to the young in its nest. If it fails to capture its prey it will soar up again in a steep arc to make a second stoop if the same bird reappears or if another is flushed. The hobby strikes from above, like the peregrine, which it so closely resembles. It sometimes happens that both parents, tercel and hen, will leave well-grown young and go hunting together, and when they do so they will entertain any observer, be he a wildfowler or not. It is impossible to watch the speed, grace, and agility of this handsome little raptor without admiration and without becoming engrossed. Strange to say, even the most compassionate person will feel little for the poor little birds caught by the falcon. The process is so elegant and exciting that you cannot help wishing it success. If one of the hobbies succeeds in catching a bird it will immediately carry the prey off to its young, while its mate remains, wheeling over the traveler in the hope of being rewarded by more prey.

It can happen that both hobbies kill birds at almost the same time and fly off with them, but a minute later they will return to the traveler on the road. The hobby is a puzzling bird: in freedom it is a wonderful hunter but a tamed bird will catch nothing. I have tried many times to train hobbies (as one would a dog), both those taken from the nest and those captured as adults. They are very easy to train: in three or four days they will be fully accustomed to the routine, and will fly to your hand even without the bait of a piece of meat; you have only to whistle and wave your hand and if the bird sees this and hears your whistle it will alight on your hand, and if you do not hold out your hand it will land on your head or shoulder, but it will never take a live bird. This characteristic is familiar to all falconers, but I did not believe it until my own numerous experiments convinced me that it was entirely true.[9] Having given up hope that my hobbies would start killing game I usually released them, and could see them flying round my house for a long time and hear their piteous cries of hunger. Whether the birds recovered their ability to hunt or starved to death I do not know.

Patches of damp woodland with bushy undergrowth along watercourses that often flood are known as "carrs." These are of various types: along large and medium-sized rivers, which always have sandy banks, they consist mostly of elm, black poplar, willow, and occasionally oak, which grows to vast size and girth; bird-cherry, rowan, hazel, and wild rose almost always accompany them and fill the air with their rich scent at the time of spring blossom. The elm is not so tall, but very stout: its gnarled bole may be up to twenty feet around. It spreads picturesquely, and its dense dull green mantle of oval leaves, which look as if printed, is a beautiful sight. The black poplar, on the other hand, grows to colossal height; it is majestic, slender, and leafy; its pale green leaves are like aspen leaves and, like them, flutter on their long stalks with the slightest breath of wind. Its thick but light bark, which is soft and red inside, has several uses, mostly as floats for fishing nets and lines. Carrs of this type are not dense. They have many deep pools, which are rich in fish and waterfowl. Along the banks of rivers and lakes, on sandy rises and slopes, the prevalent forest berry, the blackberry (known also as bramble), grows in abundance, its supple, slightly barbed, creeping stalks clinging to everything. In spring it is decked with little white flowers, and in autumn with wonderfully flavored blue-black berries, outwardly similar in shape and size to large raspberries. The huge trees need plenty of room, so they do not grow close together: beneath them and around them, for as far as they cast their shade, there are no young saplings growing, and their majestic beauty is in full view.

Along rivers that are of less than medium size, though swift-flowing and carrying a substantial volume of water, a different type of carr is formed. Along rivers flowing not through infertile sandy soil, but between green flowering banks over rich black earth, you will find few elms, oaks, or black poplars. Instead there are young birches, aspens, and alders.[10] Besides bird-cherry and rowan, there is a variety of bushes: guelder rose, honeysuckle, hawthorn, osier, blackcurrant, and others. I am especially fond of this type of woodland. Many of the trees, especially the osiers, are picturesquely entwined and entangled to their very tops with the clinging shoots of wild hops, and enveloped first by its green leaves—rather like vine leaves—and then with pale yellow or gold cones that look like bunches of grapes. Inside are the small, round, bitter-tasting hopseeds. The dense green thickets are frequented by large numbers of nightingales, bluethroats, and other songbirds. The song of the nightingales drowns out all others. Their whistles and peals continue uninterrupted day and night. When the sun goes down the tired nightingales, which have sung all day, are replaced by others that sing through the night. Only here, to the accompaniment of a gently murmuring river, amid trees and bushes that are blooming and turning green, on a warm and fragrant night, does the nightingale's song have its full richness and charm. . . . But it produces a painful effect when heard in a city street, amid the dust and rumble of carriages, or in an airless room in the hubbub of human conversation.

Along small rivers and streams, especially on low-lying marshy ground, alder and osier beds with a growth of fine reeds are common. Here and there lopsided birches, which are just as much at home on wet ground as on dry, stand out. Woodland of this type is sometimes very dense and marshy, and sometimes dotted with pools that are well suited to the breeding of marshland birds and waterfowl. Many animals also find safe refuge in them.

These woodlands, which I have described so superficially and inadequately, this jewel of nature, this cool haven in hot weather, this home of animals and birds, these woodlands that provide timber for our houses and fuel in our long harsh winters, are treated by us with the utmost extravagance. We are rich in forests, but the very abundance makes us so wasteful that poverty is but a step away. We think nothing of felling a tree for no reason. It may be true that in the truly forest provinces, the sparse human population could not destroy the forest even if it wished to, but in many other places where forests once stood we now have open steppes and straw has replaced timber. This may yet be the fate of the province of Orenburg. Here I am thinking not of the peasants' generally merciless treatment of the forest, of the fact that they usually fell young trees for firewood instead of taking branches brought down by the wind and rotting uselessly, as these are thick and heavy to handle; or of the old trees from which they cut only the branches and the tops, leaving the bare boles to die and rot; or of the way they mow the grass or graze their herds quite needlessly in places where tree growth has just begun. None of this is as harmful as the extraction of potash or the distillation of tar. For potash it is mostly elm and lime trees that are burned to ash, although other kinds of tree are not spared; while for tar the outer bark is stripped off birches. It might appear that the removal of the bark is not fatal to the tree, as it does not die at once, and if removed carefully, about ten years later new bark will grow, which can then be removed in its turn. But do the hired laborers take care when they remove it? Besides, no tree stripped of its bark, even with the greatest care, will grow to its full height: it will wither gradually and die before its time.

Of all the vegetable kingdom it is trees that demonstrate most of all the visible manifestations of organic life and are most evocative of human feelings. Their huge size, slow growth, long life, the strength and solidity of the trunk, the sustaining power of the roots, always ready to renew dead boughs and put up young shoots from a dry stump, and finally their enduring usefulness and beauty should, one might think, inspire respect and compassion . . . but the timber-merchant's axe and saw know no such feelings, and the landowners themselves are tempted by the prospect of short-term gain. . . . I could never look with indifference not only upon a felled grove, but even upon the felling of a single large tree; there is something ineffably sad about this fall: at first the ringing ax-blows produce only a slight tremor in the trunk, but the tremor grows in intensity with each blow, until every branch and every leaf shudders. As the ax bites into the heartwood the blows become more muffled and painful. . . . One more stroke, the last stroke of the ax, and the tree sways, sags, cracks, and the treetop begins to rustle; for a few moments it seems to wonder which way to fall, and at last it starts to tilt in one direction, at first gradually, gently, and then, with increasing speed and a rising roar like the rush of a strong wind, it crashes to the ground. . . . It took many decades to reach its full maturity and beauty, and in minutes it perishes, often at the merest whim of man.

1. CAPERCAILLIE OR WOOD GROUSE

Glukhoi teterev; glukhar', mokhovik; Tetrao urogallus

By virtue of its size, scarcity, wariness, and the difficulty of making a kill, the capercaillie may be called, without fear of contradiction, the pride of woodland game. It does not depart for the winter, but remains in good numbers in the very coldest regions of Siberia. It is known as *glukhar'* not because it is deaf, but because it inhabits the most remote and inaccessible forest places; and it owes the name *mokhovik* to the damp, mossy forests in which it lives.[11] In my youth I encountered elderly fowlers who believed that the capercaillie was deaf because the birds showed no fear of noise, especially during their display. This view is utterly erroneous. In the first place, no bird shows any fear of noise if it cannot see the source of it; in the second, during display no grouse, and least of all a wood grouse, hears anything at all, and nor does it even see anything. There was a popular belief that persists to this day among the peasantry that the capercaillie is deaf. This is demonstrated by the well-known reproachful saying likening a person who is hard of hearing to a wood grouse. This bird, on the contrary, has exceptionally keen hearing, as any fowler of experience knows.

In the province of Orenburg the capercaillie does not grow to great size. I have weighed many male birds: the biggest weighed twelve and a half pounds, while one from the Saint Petersburg region, for example (here I am repeating what I have heard), may weigh up to seventeen pounds. The male capercaillie differs from the blackcock, although they are of one family, but the hens are completely alike in their plumage, differing only in the fact that there is more red in the plumage of the female capercaillie, and its speckling is darker. The male capercaillie has long, curving black quills in its tail (less curving than the blackcock's).[12] It is roughly the size of a year-old turkey-cock, which it resembles in shape. At full stretch, from bill-tip to the tip of the tail, the male would measure about three and a half feet. Of this the body takes up about fourteen inches, and the tail and neck, with head, are also about fourteen inches each. The beak is stout and strong, slightly down-curved at the tip, of pale green-tinted flesh color, just under one and three-quarter inches long. The eyes are dark, the eyebrows broad and red. The head is small and the neck quite thick. At a distance the male may appear black, but this is incorrect: the head and neck are covered with very dark, but actually patterned gray plumage; the throat has a green gloss, the belly is speckled with white spots on a black background, and the back and especially the upper wing has long brown patches against a background of gray. The lower tailfeathers are dark with white speckling on the upper surface, while the upper tail coverts, projecting from the rump, are shorter and gray. The underwing shows brilliant white, flecked with black at the scapulars, but is otherwise slate-gray; the legs are heavily feathered right to the toes with long, soft, ash-gray feathers. The toes have a membrane-like covering and a coating of light-colored protective scales, and are edged with tough skin; the legs are large, dark, and strong.

The hen is very much smaller than the cock: I have never killed one more than six pounds in weight. I shall not speak of the courtship of capercaillie, or of the rearing of the young, because in these respects the capercaillie is just like the black grouse; as I know the latter better I shall give a detailed account of them.[13] Capercaillie prefer to frequent coniferous forests: they need pines, firs, spruces, and junipers, as their diet consists chiefly of the young shoots of these trees. This almost always gives the flesh of the capercaillie the scent of pine resin. In deciduous woodland, however, where pines are few, capercaillie may sometimes keep company with black grouse, and with them they are sometimes caught by net-traps, but never in large numbers. For this purpose, the tops of young pines are stuck into the ground round the usual bait of oat-sheaves. Capercaillie eat little grain and rarely visit cereal crops. They are on the whole much more solitary and austere than their smaller cousins the black grouse. They remain permanently in deep forest, where the hens build their nests on the bare ground, in shallow depressions. Their eggs, almost always seven or eight in number, are twice as large as hens' eggs, of reddish color with dark brown speckles.

The capercaillie is a very solidly built, tough, and robust bird. Although some fowlers maintain that it has less resistance to shot than black grouse, I do not share this view. I can only say that, given their size, they are less resistant than might be expected, but I am quite convinced that they are tougher than black grouse. As proof I can adduce the fact that all fowlers use the biggest shot size to shoot them. I am referring, of course, to late autumn or early winter shooting, and mostly of cock birds.

I have already mentioned that the capercaillie is uncommonly timid and wary. It likes to perch in the tops of huge pines, especially those growing along inaccessible gullies and on hills. Here of course it is perfectly safe from the fowler: if you go up to the pine tree, the lower branches will conceal it from you. If you move away so that you can see it, the range will be so great that not even the largest shot will kill such a large, robust bird. From this it follows that shooting capercaillies, especially males, is the most difficult sport. The females are much tamer and less robust, and often perch on smaller trees. The easiest way to kill the males is with a small-bore rifle, as is done not only by Siberian hunters and trappers, but by the Votiak and Cheremis peoples of the provinces of Viatka and Perm'.[14] But how many of our fowlers are skilled in using a rifle? Here speed and dexterity are not enough, nor is a good eye: above all, one needs a very steady hand. I know this from experience: I was a good shot with a shotgun but given a rifle I could not come anywhere near the mark. The same may be said of most of our skilled fowlers. But a passion for hunting will overcome all difficulties. Unlimited patience is required, but I have often used an ordinary shotgun loaded with ordinary goose-shot and killed up to six wood grouse in one morning. I was rarely able to approach them in a *drozhki* or sled, owing to the unsuitable terrain. Instead I stalked them, hiding behind trees. If the bird was completely invisible and it was impossible to shoot, I would run right up to the tree it was perched on and scare it off, sometimes firing one of my two barrels, and using the other to bring down the prized booty in flight, aiming at its wings. But this can only work if the tree is not too tall. I also used another maneuver successfully: taking note, from the direction the first bird took, which way the others would fly—since capercaillie invariably take their lead from the first bird to fly—I would take up position in their path and send a companion or my driver with the horses to flush the remaining birds. Sometimes I had to wait a long time, standing in the cold, as my companions had to take a long route, negotiating hills and gullies, to flush the birds, but I could then succeed in bagging two capercaillie from a small party. This method is particularly convenient because, when a capercaillie flies down from a tall pine tree, it always drops low and flies to the top of a smaller tree: the range is therefore not great if it flies directly over you or passes a short distance away. Of course quite a lot of my shots missed and many more winged the wood grouse, which I sometimes found dead the following day, as I visited the same sites several days running. I must confess that during autumn shooting of wood grouse it is mainly those with broken wings that one succeeds in claiming: this is not solely on account of their strength but also because of the difficulty of shooting among tall pines with dense needles. It is clear that you need to be most careful to check whether the bird is injured and whether it lags behind the others in flight. Does it leave bloodstains in the snow along its path? Has it perched halfway up a tree instead of at the top? Was there a sudden dip in its flight? If any of these signs are observed you must follow the injured bird and finish it off. A winged bird will be tamer and more easily approached.

In early spring it is possible to stalk a displaying male not only by hiding behind tree trunks, but even across open ground, if you take care to make your movements only while the bird is calling and to stop as soon as it falls silent. For as long as it is silent you should stand stock-still; when it resumes calling you should advance boldly until you are within range.

There is little more that I can say definitely about the wood grouse, other than to repeat that in all other respects it is just like the black grouse, and therefore shooting young birds is exactly the same, except that they never land on the ground but always in trees, and that they are always found in the forest, not in the open.

All are agreed that the flesh of young capercaillies is very tasty; older birds are dry and tough and have that special flavor of large game, which not everybody likes, with a hint of pine, fir, or juniper berries. There are those who are very partial to it.

I was always passionately keen on the difficult and unprofitable sport of shooting mature capercaillies in late autumn, before or just after the first snowfalls. I sought them avidly and tirelessly. I must confess that the substantial size of the bird, especially in view of its strength, timidity, and scarcity, is a powerful incentive to all hunters, not just ordinary folk out to kill as much game as they can—or so I always felt.

2. BLACK GROUSE

Teterev; Lyrurus tetrix

Is there anybody who is unfamiliar with the ordinary, common black grouse? The wood grouse, or capercaillie, is a different matter. It does not enjoy such fame or popularity. Many people have probably never even seen one except on the table, but I have already spoken of the capercaillie. I do not consider it necessary to describe in detail the size, shape, or plumage of the black grouse, particularly as in speaking of its life cycle I shall mention the changes in its appearance. I should only say that, of all the birds of its size, the black grouse is the toughest and most robust. It is a very swift and tireless flier; its wingbeats are so rapid that they produce a loud, sharp sound, especially when the bird rises.

Black grouse are found everywhere: in forests large and small, coniferous and deciduous, in small groves, in lightly wooded country, and even in treeless areas as long as all the land has not been plowed, for the gray-hen will never build her nest on ground touched by the plow. In provinces that are not densely populated, in places where cereal crops and especially woodlands are extensive, black grouse are found in great abundance. Like wood grouse, they do not fly away for the winter. Fierce frosts cause them no harm; in fact, they seem to breed even more successfully in colder climes. But let us begin at the beginning.

In May the gray-hen builds her nest on the edge of a wood, among thinly growing trees, and usually in fresh coverts. In the steppe a patch of scrub is selected. The hen lays up to ten, sometimes even twelve eggs, so hunters say, but I myself have never found more than nine. The hen sits very tight on the nest, so tight that not only any predatory animal but even a domestic dog may sometimes catch the bird on the nest. I myself have sometimes driven in a troika right up to sitting hens, and once my shaft-horse even crushed one of the eggs under its hoof. For three weeks the hen hardly leaves the nest, day or night; only at noon does she leave it for very short periods, always covering the eggs with grass and feathers to keep them warm. The eggs usually hatch in about mid-June, though this may be later if the first clutch should be lost for any reason. They are often destroyed by grass-fires when these occur late in the season, as I have already mentioned. At first all the chicks are a speckly grayish-yellow, and the male and female cannot be distinguished. In late August the male begins to acquire some dark feathers, rather like bunches of dark brown flowers. At this period he looks distinctive and very handsome, and fowlers say "the chicks are mixing." The blackcock is already larger at this stage than the gray-hen and has broader, redder eyebrows: this is a feature he will retain throughout his life. An old male is always a pound heavier than a female of the same age. In early winter the male turns a deep coffee color and the black plumes of the tail grow out until the tips curl—half to the right, and half to the left. Their shape is very like that of the curving blade of an old table knife. The plumage of the male grows darker year by year, until in the third year it is completely black except for a gray stripe down the back between the wings and a steely gloss all over the body, especially on the neck. The underwing, however, is lined with fine white feathers, as are the tail plumes, and a white band runs across the primaries. The hen does not alter much in color, except that with the approach of winter her feathers grow coarser and bigger, and the mottling is darker, with more yellow.

Black grouse chicks are distinguished by the fact that

within a few days of hatching they begin to fly a little, or rather flutter, so that in some areas they are called "flutterers," like young partridges. At first they feed on various grass seeds and small insects, and later on berries such as wild strawberries, stone bramble, and cherries, of which they are very fond, and—in wooded areas—on forest berries of all kinds. Young grouse have a highly original way of eating cherries, which grow well out of their reach. Clinging to the branches, they gradually move along them, bending them down until the cherries hang within easy reach of their beaks. At this season the young have a specially fine flavor in those places where berries are abundant enough to comprise their exclusive diet or the greater part of it. Later they eat mainly bread grains, and finally, when the crops have been harvested and the ground is covered with snow, they obtain plentiful nourishment from the buds of trees, acorns, birch catkins, alder cones, juniper berries, and the shoots of pines and firs.[15]

The shooting of black grouse is on a small scale in early spring and it ceases when the hens start to sit and the cocks take cover in forest gullies and other inaccessible places, which happens in late May. In June the cocks and the unpaired hens molt. The females with young molt when their broods are reared, which is much later. The shooting season for the young opens in July and continues until the beginning of September, always with dogs, of course. When the trees lose their leaves and the grass wilts in the rain and frost, the black grouse begin to perch in trees in the morning and evening, at first in family groups, and later in flocks in which older birds mix with the young. These flocks often consist entirely of males or entirely of females. As autumn wears on they sit longer and longer, if not driven away by strong winds. In still weather, especially when drizzle is falling, they will only fly down at midday onto the ground in a clearing or open space, far from the raindrops ceaselessly dripping from the wet branches. When the sun begins to sink toward the west, the grouse rise from the ground and resume their perches in the trees, where they sit with feathers puffed out as if dozing until dusk has gathered. Then they remove themselves to the halfway point down the tree, and then come down to roost: they always roost on the ground. They will also perch halfway up a tree and close to the trunk during windy weather, so as not to be violently rocked by the wind in the branches, as they dislike this. When they descend to roost, they do not so much fly as tumble silently to the ground, so that if from afar you see a large tree, full of grouse, and ride up to it warily, you will suddenly see that there are no grouse present, although they have not flown away! If you go right up to the tree you flush the whole covey, which has settled down to roost. During winter blizzards they are completely buried by snow, and the bird needs all its strength to dig its way out. Here they fall prey to foxes and wolves, which are led by the scent to this delicate prize. Roaming early in the morning, I have often come unexpectedly on the site of a black grouse roost; the first time I was actually startled: several dozen of them leaped vertically into the air without warning, showering me with powdery snow, some of which they themselves threw up, but most of it was shaken down as their wings grazed the snow-laden branches sprinkled with rime. Late autumn and early winter are the best and most profitable times for shooting black grouse, whether by riding up to them or by luring them to decoys. This sport ends only when the snow is deep, so it may last until the end of December.

This is a general picture of the black grouse. When I speak of the sport of shooting it, I shall have more to say about its habits, which change with the seasons, and I shall have to repeat myself to some extent.

In late March the sun begins to give more warmth, the blood in the blackcock's chilled veins warms up, his irresistible urge to mate awakens and he begins to give his mating call; that is, sitting in a tree, he produces his muffled notes, sometimes resembling the hiss of a goose but more often the cooing of a dove, which can be heard over a long distance in the silence of dawn and at sunrise. Many people, no doubt, and not only hunters, have heard "the blackcock's muted, distant courtship song," and experienced a vague, agreeable sensation on hearing it.[16] There is nothing pleasing to the ear about the notes themselves, yet in them one subconsciously senses and understands the harmony of life in nature as a whole. . . . So the blackcock begins his courtship call: at first only briefly, languidly, in a low voice, as if muttering to himself after a hearty breakfast, when he has filled his crop with ripening buds. Later, as the air gradually warms, he calls louder, more ardently, and for longer periods, finally working himself into a frenzy. His neck is puffed up, the feathers on it rising like a mane; his eyebrows, usually hidden in slight hollows and covered by a thin, wrinkled membrane, swell up and distend to an improbable degree, showing a brilliant red. Before sunrise, after taking a little food (clearly, even birds have little interest in food when love is in the air), the males gather at a chosen site suitable for the deeds of heroism to be performed. This may be a clearing in the forest, or a meadow on the edge of a wood or among trees on otherwise open ground, usually on higher ground. This site, unchanging, and regularly frequented, is known as a lek. Determined human efforts are required to compel the grouse to leave it and choose another. Leks remain at the same site for years on end. The blackcock sit on the upper branches, ceaselessly extending their necks downward, as though making low bows, curtsying and then straightening up, stretching their distended necks to the limit, hissing, muttering and calling, and letting their wings droop during their more energetic movements in order to maintain their balance. As the hours pass they work themselves into more and more of a lather: their movements become faster, their calls blend into a constant clucking, and a white foam spatters from their ever-open beaks. . . . Hence the hoary old myth—no longer believed by anyone—according to which the gray-hen run along the ground and catch the saliva flying from the mouths of the displaying males above and are thus impregnated.

But it is not for nothing that the locality resounds to the ardent calls of the males, who for some time display on their own: the females have long been hearkening to their calls and at last begin to fly toward the lek. At first they perch in trees a little way off, then move in closer, without, however, ever perching next to a male, but always opposite one. As they listen with interest to the passionate hissings and mutterings of their black beaux, the speckled ladies begin to feel the commanding urge of nature and make provocative movements: they preen and wiggle, flirtatiously inspecting their plumage with their bills, trembling, spreading their tails, fluttering their wings as if about to fly down from their perches, until suddenly—quite carried away—they do indeed descend rapidly to the ground. . . . All the males immediately fall upon them. . . . And now the usually peaceable and phlegmatic blackcock seethe with jealousy and hatred, for there are always far fewer hens than cocks, sometimes only one female to many males. Furious fighting erupts: the males seize one another by the neck and drag one another about, pecking and scratching mercilessly, while blood spatters and feathers fly . . . and at the edge of the arena the lucky ones, or the nimblest, copulate with the females, who are utterly indifferent to the battles being fought for their favors.[17]

The fertilized female immediately takes steps to safeguard the future of her progeny: on lightly timbered land she selects a dry spot—not too low—scoops out a shallow depression, collects last year's dry grass as nesting material, fashions a round nest, which she lines with down plucked from her own breast, and lays her first egg. The next day, after carefully covering the nest with grass and feathers, she flies to the lek again to be fertilized again by the first eager male. Then she lays her second egg. This pattern is repeated until the nest is full of eggs, or until her temporary appetite is fully satisfied. For some time the males continue to gather at the lek, while the females gradually desert it, and the displays diminish day by day until they cease altogether. The season of love is over, the distended skin on the necks of the males subsides, their eyebrows no longer stand out, and they begin to lose their plumes . . . it is time for them to seek close cover in remote places, in forest gullies. Soon the molt will begin, that is, all their old plumage will be replaced. This is a time of weakness, if not sickness, for any bird.

Spring shooting of black grouse is neither rewarding nor easy. As soon as the sun begins to provide a little warmth and the surface of the snow, warmed by its rays, begins to thaw imperceptibly at midday, a hard, thin crust, sparkling like diamonds, forms on it. Over this crust, in March, and sometimes in early April, it is possible to steal up on the displaying males, perched singly in their trees, and on the females as they listen to them. The greatest care must be exercised in approaching them, keeping behind other trees, in complete silence, always ensuring that the head of the bird you are stalking is hidden by branches or the trunk. While the grouse is calling you may advance more boldly, but as soon as its call ceases you must stop, or advance only if shielded completely from view by the trunk. While calling, the male in his ardor sees and hears nothing, but the moment he stops, whether from weariness or because he is suddenly startled, his hearing and visual acuity return. You do not need a dog but you do need a gun that keeps the shot in a tight pattern, and with good carrying power and range: although at this season the grouse has less resistance to gunshot than in late autumn or early winter, you almost always have to fire at long range and often through twigs and branches. This is not like approaching in a *drozhki*, when the bird is within easy range and unprotected. Here things are very different: once you have crept up to the nearest tree and cannot step out without frightening the bird you have to fire whatever the range and whatever the situation. It is obvious that you will often miss, and that the number of kills will be small.

When the snow melts, or at least thins, so that driving becomes possible, you can then drive a *drozhki* up to the grouse: at first early in the morning at the leks themselves, and later, when the shots have dispersed them, close to the leks, for the birds do not fly far. They remain close to the same spot until it is time for them to leave the leks and scatter, which happens at about nine in the morning. Of course, you can shoot more by driving up to them than by stalking on foot, but the number will remain small.

So much for the spring shooting of black grouse, with its thin pickings. It lasts until the beginning of May, or mid-May at the latest. Few wildfowlers go in for it, and then not often, for at this season the shooting of all kinds of spring migrants is in full swing.[18]

Thus from early or mid-May at the latest the black grouse completely disappears from the wildfowler's view. The males and unpaired gray-hens seek the deepest forest cover where they molt throughout the month of June. In July the chicks appear. While they are very small their mother keeps her brood close in woodland shaves and forest edges, where there are plenty of young shoots, especially of oak, whose broad, thick leaves reach almost down to the ground. Here the grass grows thick and it is easy for the defenseless chicks to hide. As soon as they hear their mother's call they nimbly run to her and hide under her spreading wings, like the young of the domestic fowl, if she should espy a kite overhead and begin clucking anxiously. Here I should say that black grouse are very similar to domestic fowl. In all their habits and behavior the same nature can be seen: partridges and quail are even more like them. Although in all species the female birds are more devoted to their young than the males, those females whose mates have no such devotion and actually destroy their nests (such as the drakes of all duck species) display even greater dedication. I cannot say for certain how blackcock behave but many wildfowlers assure me that they also destroy the gray-hens' nests. Whatever the truth of the matter the gray-hen is no less determined than a duck in the defense of her brood and when in danger will give her life for them. She may be beset by all sorts of worries, for not only the least noble birds of prey but also crows and magpies will take grouse chicks, to say nothing of wolves and especially foxes, which often claim them. When the young are half-grown, the mother takes them into more open places, where they can feed on berries.

At this time the season for young grouse opens in earnest. To many it is the most rewarding, the easiest, and the most enjoyable shooting, but not to me: I prefer autumn shooting from a *drozhki*. In shooting young grouse one relies chiefly not on one's skill or prowess with a gun, but on one's dog. Its scent, its pointing, and its training are critical. Although a brood of grouse produces a strong scent, so that even a dog with a weak sense of smell will follow them eagerly, the heat at this season severely hampers a dog. In early morning and late evening a heavy dew dulls the scent, and in the daytime a dog soon tires in the heat and humidity. Moreover the dust from some wilted flowers and dry leaves confuses the trail, so a dog with good stamina as well as a keen nose is needed. If it lacks these qualities, as it tries to follow a tangled thread of trails, it will soon become fevered and then tire, as young grouse run with extraordinary vitality.

This means that a fowler should take his pointer and make

for those places where the broods of grouse should be hiding. A good dog with a superior sense of smell will not scratch for long at the traces but will circle and scout close to its master, soon picking up the scent of a covey, pointing—sometimes at distances of a hundred paces or more—and lead its master straight to the birds. If the covey is surprised when tightly packed, all the birds often rise at once. If it is dispersed, that is, when the chicks are spread some distance from one another, the mother will usually take wing first, not in order to get away, but so as to distract attention and lure the foe away. To do this, after rising noisily with much clucking, she barely flies at all, but hangs in the air with little forward movement, as if sickly or injured, constantly alighting on the ground and flying up again. An ill-trained dog will immediately give chase and be led a verst or more away, while the young scatter in all directions. Even an inexperienced fowler may be deceived and try to catch the bird in his hands, without wasting a cartridge. But the fowler who knows these ploys will kill the mother straight away; then his dog will seek out all the young one by one, and a good shot—if he keeps a cool head and lets the birds fly off to the desired distance—will bring them all down without fail.

When a covey takes wing all at once the young will scatter, making for the cover of trees if possible, and after flying some distance, depending on their age and strength, will drop to the ground and lie motionless, like stones. When this happens, the last to rise is the mother, when all the covey has flown, always very close to the hunter. She then begins her decoying action. Of course she is shot straight away, but it is much harder for the dog to locate the young, since, as I have said, when they settle they lie motionless, hidden under young saplings, in bushes or tall grass. Furthermore, it is harder to shoot them among trees and bushes. Young grouse usually sit very tight but a dog will seek them all out if it has been trained to do so.

When the young have grown a little more and are better feathered, they will more often rise as a covey, especially in open places, and begin to perch in trees: sometimes in different trees, and sometimes all in the same large tree. They usually perch halfway up, close to the trunk on stout branches, and lie along the bough, stretching out their necks along it. Here the greatest difficulty lies in spotting them: nothing is easier than to shoot every last one, as nothing will induce them to fly from the tree.[19] By the end of August the young are so large and strong that when flushed by a dog they fly far off into the forest so that they cannot be found. This means you can only fire one shot. The shooting of the young is over, but a month later a different kind of shooting begins.

In the interval black grouse are difficult to shoot as they hide in the forest. During this time the young grow to full maturity: the males assume their full first-year plumage, dark with a bluish glint; and the gray-hens' tails grow out and spread. Family coveys gather, first as small parties, and later in large flocks. In the morning and evening they fly to grain stooks in the fields; they are especially fond of buckwheat and continue to visit fields of this crop long after it has been harvested and threshed, when only heaps of straw are left. In late September the trees are beginning to lose most of their leaves and the grouse perch in them morning and evening. Now the autumn shooting season opens.

Grouse-shooting in autumn and early winter, before the snow is deep, has its own particular features. This is the season of shooting from mobile cover, using transport. The autumn rains, wind, and morning frosts have stripped the trees of leaves. The wet ground is soft, so it is possible to drive up to the grouse, even in a wheeled vehicle, without much noise. But once the first fluffy snow has covered the ground the conditions for using transport are ideal.

Even at six in the morning it is still completely dark. The hunter has long been up and dressed by candlelight. His gun, ammunition, and equipment have been ready since the previous evening and lie waiting on their own table. The horses are readied. The shooting ground is some way away; it is time to set out; day will dawn along the route. The hunter climbs into his low sled with high sides, on which he will be able to rest his elbow as he takes aim, and carefully covers his gun with its canvas case or simply with his overcoat to protect it from the snow thrown up by the horses' hooves. The troika starts out briskly.[20] The first covering of snow lies over the road: hills and gullies are no obstacle to a plain, stoutly built hunting sled. At last the cereal fields come into view, not yet completely snow-covered, where the black grouse are accustomed to feeding on rich, satisfying fare. Here is the woodland fringe with young aspens and birches, in which the grouse will certainly have roosted, if not driven to some more distant place by a goshawk or golden eagle. Here the hunter must pause to rest his horses and look around in case the birds should fly. Now it is completely light, the crows are cawing and moving out from their roosts, magpies are chattering in the distance, excited by the unusual spectacle. . . . The hunter looks all about him impatiently, as does his experienced driver: there is nothing to be seen. Suddenly, in the branches of an old birch tree in the distance they see a dark, round shape, then another, and another. . . . It is the black grouse just awaking. The hunter rides toward them at full tilt to catch them while still hungry and before they have gathered in a large covey, as a large covey may sometimes travel a very long way to its feeding grounds in the cereal fields they frequented in autumn. The hunter begins his approach, selecting the nearest bird or one on the edge of the party. The main point to remember is that one should never drive straight toward a grouse and never approach from behind, if the lie of the land permits, of course. One should approach as if intending to drive past. Black grouse, like most other birds, do not like to see anything driving straight toward them, especially from behind. They start looking about them ceaselessly and will soon fly off before you can come within range. It may sometimes happen, if the birds feel a need to fly from their trees, that they will turn to face the approaching fowler, but this is exceptional. If the bird sits on its branch pecking at buds, or sits motionless with its plumage fluffed up, this means the bird feels at ease and has no thought of flying away, so the hunter may come closer. But if it stretches its neck, rises to its feet, constantly turning its head this way and that, or if it sidesteps toward the end of its branch, clucking softly like a hen, you should fire at once if you are within range, as the bird intends to fly off; it will suddenly crouch and then take wing. Unless absolutely necessary, you should not fire at long range, least of all at a grouse in flight. The ideal range is thirty-five to forty-five paces. It is of course possible to kill a black grouse at sixty or even seventy paces, but this is unusual. They have exceptional resistance to gunshot, especially the males, and at long range it is very rare to kill one outright, and a bird that is slightly wounded, or even fatally wounded, flies off a long way and disappears. I have sometimes seen an injured black grouse with blood dripping from its bill (a sure sign of a fatal internal injury), yet still flying. More surprising still, a grouse may still fly with its hindquarters so badly injured that its intestines hang out! Only those who have actually witnessed this or heard of it from reliable sources will believe this.

It follows from all I have said that after every shot, if a grouse does not fall, one should observe it carefully until it is out of sight. This is an important rule that should be adhered to for all types of game. It very often happens that a seriously injured grouse will fly from its perch apparently unharmed but after flying some considerable distance it will suddenly rise vertically upward and drop down dead. It is very uncommon that an injured grouse will fly straight downward without first soaring up. One should take good care to observe the spot where it fell and drive straight toward it, particularly if the snow is fairly deep and the bird falls among trees or bushes. Soft snow will conceal it completely and if you lose sight of the spot it will be impossible to find it again, unless it is revealed by the crows and magpies that immediately converge on a dead bird when they see it drop.

The fowler should pursue and shoot any hungry grouse he might come across, until they disperse and fly in different directions. Then he will hasten to seek other coveys at their usual feeding grounds. If they are not there, he should locate them somewhere nearby. Having eaten their fill, the grouse will perch and rest, either in one large tree, filling every part of it, or in several trees, but always facing into the wind. Here the same process will be repeated: if the grouse are sitting close together they will not permit any approach, but will fly off one by one, all perching in different trees nearby. The fowler should always approach the one at the edge of the party, preferably perched on its own or with one other bird, because the smaller the number in a tree the tamer the bird and the closer it will allow you to approach. Shooting of this type may continue into the evening, if the terrain permits, of course, and if the grouse have nowhere further off to fly to. Coveys that have not been exposed to shooting are often very tame, especially when not tight-packed. You can shoot one while the others sit quietly round about, but once frightened by frequent shots they become very wary and will allow a close approach only in the morning, when they are hungry. It is best to leave a gun-shy covey alone and seek another; you may return to it after a week, when the birds will be tamer. On the whole grayhen are tamer than blackcock, and both sexes are tamer in calm, damp, and misty weather than at times of fine, dry, windy weather.

A black grouse's resistance to gunshot increases with the frosts and is sometimes so marked as to reduce the hunter to despair, as my companions and I have frequently found. I have often wondered whether there was a flaw or a bend in my gun-barrel, or if the powder was weak or the cartridges badly loaded. I have sometimes fired twenty-five shots to kill three or four grouse, without even wounding many. On my return home I would open the breech and lay a cord along the barrel, run a light cleaning rod through it, and find everything in good order. I would fire it at a target and find the gun was firing no worse than before. I would load my cartridges again with great care, and go after grouse again with the same lack of success. It was the same with a second gun, and a third; yet in spring these same guns would work as well as ever.

The real reason for the extraordinary toughness of the grouse, especially the blackcock, lies in the fact that the feathers of the breast and upper belly, to say nothing of the large wingfeathers, become so tough and smooth in cold weather that at a certain range the shot skids over them and glances off. This may seem hard to believe, but I invite anyone who doubts it to conduct an experiment, for the sake of comparison, in autumn or winter, with a domestic cockerel. The bird should be placed on the ground at thirty paces with its head tied under its wing while you fire a charge of duck-shot at its breast. The bird will be unharmed. The blackcock is a wild cockerel of very similar type, so it is not surprising that an old bird, toughened by the hard November frosts, that will not permit a fowler to approach closely, is very seldom harmed by shot.[21] The fact that the same male, when flushed by chance in the forest in late spring, summer, or even early autumn, drops like a stone when hit, even if your gun is loaded with fine hazel-grouse shot and if the range is quite long, directly proves my point. Late in the year I always used a large goose-shot and avoided aiming at the breast, and this sometimes paid off. This is where a hard-hitting shotgun, placing the shot in tight star patterns, really comes into its own, and grouse-shooting becomes truly absorbing for the hunter.

Finally the season of shooting from a troika comes to an end. The snow is deep and the black grouse retreat in huge coveys into deep forest and thickets, where they find more warmth and food. However, I have occasionally shot them as late as December, even in twenty-five degrees of frost. At times of hard frost they are tame, and your shots sound no louder than the crack of a knout. At first I thought the charge was too small and could not believe my eyes when I saw a bird tumbling down, although it had been more than half-hidden by the thick rime that lines all branches at that season. During hard frosts the principal difficulty lies in the awkward movements you have to make when dressed to keep out the cold. The worst of it is the difficulty of reloading, especially with a flintlock, when you have to tip your powder into the pan. But it is most unusual in the province of Orenburg that there should be so little snow in December that you cannot travel where you will by sleigh.

There are many who are fond of using decoys to shoot black grouse, but I am not among them. It is very like luring drakes to a tame duck or a farmyard duck and shooting them from a hide. What pleasure can be found in deceiving a bird and having it settle right under your nose, or swim right up to you, so that you can kill it at a range of a few yards? It is more like commercial trapping, and is in fact a step closer to the trapping of grouse as practiced in spring at their leks by means of snares, in autumn with springes or gin-traps and balance-top traps, and finally, in winter, with large tentlike nets. By this last method dozens are caught at a time and such mass destruction is loathsome to the true sportsman; however, for the benefit of a few lovers of decoy shooting, which I myself have tried, I shall recount all I know of it.

Black grouse have a singular characteristic that I have already mentioned: wherever the first bird flies, the rest of the covey will unfailingly follow; wherever the first one alights, all the rest will also alight. This being the case, the following method is employed: on open ground, or even in lightly timbered country which is often visited by black grouse, a spacious hide is constructed, of round or rectangular plan, not too low and not rising to a pointed roof. A hunter should be able to stand upright, or nearly upright, and load his gun in it. In a semicircle around it, not more than a dozen yards away, young saplings eight or ten feet high are set in the ground and stripped of leaves and superfluous branches to provide perches. Some stakes with artificial branches attached are also driven into the ground. On two, three, or four of these perches (according to choice), dummy grouse are fixed, having been produced by one of three methods. The first and most widely used is simply to cut a shape roughly resembling a grouse out of cloth and stuff it with wool or hay, sew on some eyebrows of red fabric, add two white canvas strips to the flanks, and finally stick in some real grouse tailfeathers if there are any to hand, although they can be dispensed with. The second way is to fashion a dummy out of papier-mâché, paint it, and varnish it. The third is to take real grouse skins, carefully removed with the plumage, and stuff them with wool or cotton wool. The first method is the simplest of all. In every village the material and the talent to make it can be found. The second is the hardest and most costly, as papier-mâché dummies have to be ordered from Moscow. The third is inconvenient as one needs the skill to stuff it; moreover, the dummy always turns out smaller than the live grouse, whereas they need to be bigger and visible from afar. Furthermore, raptors such as golden and other eagles, and goshawks sometimes seize them and carry them off, if they are simply placed on a perch and not attached to it. (In this way I once killed a huge golden eagle.) Hides and perches are set up in early autumn to give the grouse time to get used to them. Before dawn the hunter places his decoys facing into the wind, and enters his hide with his gun and ammunition, using straw to shield the doorway behind him. As soon as the grouse stir from their roost to seek food they see the decoys and land beside them. Startled by a volley of shots they fly off to the cereal fields and on their return they notice the decoys and alight again. As if this were not enough, they can be driven to the perches by as few as two mounted beaters.

Black grouse are easily duped into taking the dummies for their fellows and, when they have flown to nearby trees after hearing a shot, return to the decoys as soon as they are startled again. In this respect black grouse are so stupid that if you put a charred stump, a tussock, or a cap on a perch they will fly to join it, or so I am told. What is more, as long as they cannot see a human, which they fear more than all other animals, even after hearing a shot and seeing one of their number fall, the grouse will rarely desert their artificial perches, but merely flit from one to another.

If there are several grouse on one perch it is usual to shoot the lowest one first; the birds higher up often sit and look at the dead one, clucking to one another in surprise as if discussing what caused it to drop down dead. Tamer grouse, unaccustomed to gunshots, behave like this, while more gun-shy birds scatter after the first few shots and do not return. In places where they are numerous but the terrain is ill-suited to an approach by vehicle, the use of decoys ensures rewarding shooting. It has the further advantage that a fowler who is lazy, elderly, or in no condition to travel dozens of versts in a hunting *drozhki* or sleigh, circling round his quarry and endlessly approaching it in difficult country, often to no avail, may undoubtedly sit in his armchair in his hide, without the slightest exertion, with all creature comforts, smoking his pipe or cigar, drinking tea or coffee prepared for him on a traveling stove by his servant, even reading a book when there are no grouse to hand. And when they do appear (his companion will be watching for them), he can poke his shotgun through one of the openings designed for that purpose and calmly pick off the grouse. . . . But where is the sport in this?

To return to my interrupted narrative, grouse shot from hides should be picked up while no grouse are perched in the vicinity, preferably when the shooting has finished; otherwise the grouse may be scared off—although I must confess that, even with a good gun, large shot, and the short range (conditions good enough, one might think, to kill the birds outright or mortally wound them), it is in fact uncommon to collect all the birds that were fired at and that fell from their perches, apparently dead: there will always be one or two that recover and escape.

Shooting can continue only until midday. Before sunset the grouse appear again and perch beside the decoys but they are wary and do not stay long: they seem to be in a hurry and there is too little time.[22] In places where they are common and where beaters can be employed, one fowler may kill up to twelve brace in a morning. However, I often shot up to thirty-five in a morning by using transport to approach them, and other fowlers may also have reached this number. But can shooting from a hide compare with driving up to the birds? Where is the constant activity, the movement, the anticipation, the apprehension as to the outcome? Will the bird admit you within range, or not? Where is the agitation you feel on seeing your quarry preparing to take flight? And lastly, where is the pleasure evoked by brilliant feats of marksmanship, in extremes of range and conditions overcome by an accurate gun and a sure, skilled hand? These are shots that quite often occur in this kind of shooting, and they remain forever in the memory. Black grouse are very wary and constantly fly off before you are within range. . . . It is possible to approach so that they will fly over you, or close by, if they follow the usual flight-path that you have observed: without dismounting you can fire two memorable shots and sometimes bring down a brace of grouse, one with each barrel! And what pleasure can be found in knocking a blackcock down from the very top of a tall tree with a well-aimed shot and watching it slowly tumble, "counting the branches," as the saying goes, that is, bumping against them one by one until it finally crashes to the ground! It can happen that the bird will be caught in the branches. In that case there is nothing for it but to climb the tree to recover it.

I shall not dwell on the devastating commercial hunting practiced by Moscow and Petersburg merchants. To me, as to all true wildfowlers, it is repugnant. I shall only say that they are highly skilled in decoying and killing all kinds of game, even including hares. Their main prey consists of coveys of black grouse, hazel grouse, and willow grouse; first they lure the mother, using the call of a chick, then they exterminate all the chicks by luring them to the call of the mother.

The flesh of the black grouse chick remains white, like that of the hazel grouse, until their adult plumage begins to appear.

Then it grows gradually darker until it has the usual appearance of grouse meat. As everybody knows, black grouse chicks are considered a delicacy, but fully grown birds, especially in their first or second year, are very tasty, nourishing, and wholesome. Later they become tougher, but a plump bird—and they are often plump—will always have a splendid flavor. Black grouse are eaten in large numbers, most of them having been caught by netting; predatory birds and animals also take many, so it is a wonder that so many are left. One must remember the vastness of Russia and its limitless forests.

To conclude my account of the black grouse I shall tell of a surprising incident that I witnessed as a boy. I was once sitting in a hide with an elderly fowler who trapped grouse in nets. The birds were coming closer and he was watching them, holding the cord in his hand, ready to release the net when enough of them were under it, while I watched through a chink I had opened with my fingers. Suddenly the whole flock flew up as if somebody had frightened them. The old hunter leaped out of the hide and I after him, to see who it was, and what should we see? The grouse flew straight toward the nearest trees and one gray-hen suddenly soared upward as grouse do when hit by a gunshot. It rose quite high then fell to the ground, and a weasel jumped clear and darted away. This little predatory animal, known to us all, is no more than eight inches long and only slightly thicker than a man's thumb. The grouse did not struggle for long: an artery in its neck had been severed. Imagine the daring and determination! The weasel had evidently sunk its teeth into the bird's neck as it sat in the snow, and risen with it when the bird took flight. I later established that this tiny animal kills hares and drinks their blood in exactly the same manner. For a long time I was reluctant to believe it, but once, having followed a fresh trail, in a burrow in the snow I found a hare, already dead and cold: the animal's jugular had also been severed, and there was no track leading to the burrow but that of the weasel.

3. HAZEL GROUSE

Riabchik; Tetrastes bonasia

The Russian name *riabchik,* or in many places *riabets,* is well deserved as the bird is entirely speckled, or mottled.[23] In size a mature bird is slightly larger than a feral pigeon but a little more solid and fleshy. Its shape is exactly that of the black grouse. Its eyebrows are red and its eyes quite large and black. The feathers of the head are dark and may sometimes be raised slightly, giving the appearance of a crest. The legs are well feathered, except for the claws. The speckling on the neck, breast, and belly is of varying color: blackish, white, yellowish, and even reddish, especially on the flanks below the wings. The down on the body and at the feather roots is dark; the speckles are in the form of rounded and slightly arched blotches; the back and tail, which consists of quite long, stiff feathers, are mottled with only gray spots; and short bars of the same color run across the wings; the cock has a dark spot on his throat, his brows are redder, and he is more heavily mottled than the hen, which appears grayer. The wings are small and short; thanks to this the bird takes wing noisily and with much effort. Nature evidently intended it to make only short flights, but it runs very nimbly.

The hazel grouse, which winters in our part of the world, deservedly belongs in the category of forest game. All other varieties of woodland bird leave the forest occasionally, for short periods, whether to seek food or to avoid dripping rain in wet weather. But the hazel grouse never leaves it. It will not even frequent scattered copses: its permanent home in summer and winter is in unbroken forest, preferably deciduous, occupying vast areas, though it will sometimes breed in large coniferous forests. In those districts of the province of Orenburg where I have lived and hunted there are no hazel grouse so I am poorly acquainted with its ways. I have shot them in the province of Viatka, where the dense forest reaching right up to Arkhangel'sk has an abundant hazel-grouse population. I have not found their nests or broods of young, as I have not hunted them during the breeding season, but I have been told by Viatka wildfowlers that hazel grouse begin incubation in early May, on very primitive nests, always on bare ground in the forest. The nest is fashioned of dry grass, leaves, and even small twigs. Courtship takes place in March. The hazel hen lays ten to fifteen eggs and incubates them alone, without the hazel cock, for three weeks. The young very soon begin to run about. Until they are full grown the mother stays with them, mostly in forest, more or less dense, in cloughs and along woodland streams. It is said that at all seasons the birds are fond of running water and like listening to the babble of a stream as they perch in their trees. As soon as a hunter or his dog flushes a covey of young, partly grown birds, they will always scatter and take refuge on low branches, pressing flat against the main boughs and lying so still that it is very difficult to make them out, especially in fir trees.

Hazel grouse are never very fat. Their diet consists of the buds of many kinds of deciduous and coniferous trees and the latter give the meat a special, resinous flavor. They are also very fond of all kinds of forest berries.

In spring, as early as March, hazel grouse begin to "whistle back" or "come to the whistle," as fowlers say. I have already mentioned this simple instrument, which produces notes similar to the whistle of the hazel hen. The whistles are fashioned from limewood sticks the thickness of a goose quill and about two and a half inches long. The pith is extracted over half this length and the end fashioned into the shape of a reed-pipe mouthpiece. Similar whistles are also made from goose quills and even cast from tin. There are some successful fowlers who are able to lure hazel grouse by mimicking their calls.

The season opens in the second half of March, when skis are used—later the hunter can move on foot over the hard snow crust—and lasts until midsummer, but the late season differs from the earlier part. In early spring the males not only reply to the call of the hen but fly eagerly toward it, so they will perch on trees quite close to you and present easy targets; from late May until mid-July they respond readily, but move less eagerly. Later still they cease to come to the hen completely, though replying to her call, so the hunter must seek them out with his dog. In autumn pointers are used to find them, first in coveys, later in pairs; in late October and November they again begin to respond to the whistle by flying toward it.

When flushed from the ground hazel grouse immediately perch in trees, and a sharp eye is essential to locate them as they hide in the dense dark green of the pines and firs. The natives of Perm', Viatka, and other heavily forested provinces have this ability in the highest degree and I have often been astonished at their uncommonly keen sight.

Hazel grouse have no great resistance to gunshot: Number Six or Seven shot is more than enough, but the ordinary folk of Perm', Viatka, and Arkhangel'sk usually use large or small duck-shot in a small-bore gun, loaded with the smallest possible charge. They sometimes even use cast iron. Often they shoot hazel grouse with a very small-bore weapon that fires a bullet only slightly larger than a large shotgun pellet. Their marksmanship is so superb that they often hit the bird in the head. They use small charges for reasons of economy. The report is so feeble that even at close range you would suppose you had not heard a shot but the pop of a small detonator. These hunters still use flintlocks and hunt hazel grouse until midwinter, on skis when the snow is deep.

Hazel grouse are often caught in special snares fashioned from a bent branch with a loop of hair attached to the end. A bunch of rowan or guelder rose berries is hung behind it, since these birds are very fond of them. The trappers—mostly Chuvash, Cheremis, and Vostiak people—stock up berries in autumn and continue trapping throughout the winter. The snare is set so that the bird cannot take the berries without putting its head through the loop and releasing the catch that holds the branch down. The branch springs up immediately, tightening the noose and throttling the bird.

Country folk will not eat birds that have been throttled, but in the cities nobody pays much attention to this, and how is anyone to know whether the birds in the market have been shot or snared? Besides, before selling them the traders break their wings and pierce their skulls with a quill, to give them the appearance of birds shot and finished off in the field.

In Saint Petersburg, Moscow, and all provincial and even district centers hazel grouse are consumed in vast numbers, but, thanks to the forested expanses of northern Russia, they are not threatened with extinction. To my surprise they even live close to Moscow, though in small numbers.

The white flesh of hazel grouse is tender, nutritious, and has that well-known, superb flavor, though a little dry. The innards and legs have a slightly bitter tang that is particularly savored by gourmets.

4. WILLOW GROUSE

Belaia (lesnaia) kuropatka; Lagopus lagopus

This bird is sometimes known as the "white wood grouse"; "white" because it loses its color in winter, like a hare, eventually becoming snow-white; and "wood" because, like the hazel grouse, it lives in the forest the whole year round, mostly in damp deciduous forest.[24] I have not heard of them inhabiting coniferous woodland. In the province of Orenburg, as in the whole central belt of Russia, willow grouse are not found; even in the environs of Moscow there are none, despite the preponderance of broad-leaved woodland; but in the province of Tver' and in the northwest generally they begin to occur. In the Petersburg area they are still plentiful.

The willow grouse is much larger than the partridge and has very different plumage, even in summer. It is entirely rufous-yellow and mottled and at first sight bears some resemblance to a gray-hen, which is of similar shape and has the same reddish brows and similar tasting flesh, though the willow grouse is slightly smaller. It has very bright black eyes, and legs covered with white feathers right down to the toes. It is distinguished from all other birds by the fact that in winter it is pure white, as I have said. As soon as cold, wet weather sets in, white feathers begin to appear and it begins to shed the mottled gray summer plumage, so that by the beginning of an early winter or the end of a late autumn it presents a strange picture that I would not call handsome, with blotches of rufous-yellow scattered unevenly over a white background. I am utterly unfamiliar with the habits of the willow grouse, having seen a live one only once, but I know that they are shot in late autumn, just like winter hares, when they are obvious to the eye. In vain do they seek cover in forest thickets; their brilliant white plumage betrays them. A hunter can easily see them in the distance and shoot them on the ground. The flesh of the willow grouse, which is never fat, and always dry and rather tough, cannot compare with that of the partridge, let alone black game. However, when the latter are molting and are very lean, almost sickly, their meat tastes very much like that of the willow grouse. In Saint Petersburg, willow grouse is often served at the table at any season, but in Moscow it is found on sale only in late autumn and winter.

The willow grouse is the last of those few game birds that do not leave us for the winter.

5. PIGEONS

Wild doves are of three kinds, but they differ so greatly that I shall speak of them separately, after a few general words about their common features.

The pigeon has stood from time immemorial as the symbol of purity, humility, and love, and with good reason: the bird possesses all these characteristics. The sacred words of the Old and New Testaments attest to its purity. The love of the male for the female and their love for their young is recognized by all the Russian people, as their songs and folk sayings demonstrate, and there can be no more convincing, indeed irrefutable, authority. The caressing words of endearment *golubchik* and *golubushka* may be constantly heard in the speech of ordinary folk, and often describe the mutual affection of man and wife or brother and sister.[25] They may also describe somebody's goodness of heart and any peasant woman is likely to use these words to express sympathy for someone in distress.

The very appearance of the dove expresses its qualities. It is always clean and tidy, and its body is so well proportioned in all its parts, so well rounded and with such gentle lines! In its movement you will see nothing jerky or abrupt: everything about it is gentle, serene, and graceful. Ordinary folk are profoundly aware of the pigeon's inner qualities and nurture a special affection for it. Many householders feed grain to feral pigeons, which are beyond doubt descended from the wild variety, and put up nesting boxes for them, considering it a good omen if the birds prosper and multiply in their yards. The peasants never eat pigeons and in many villages will not allow anyone to shoot them.

5A. WOOD PIGEON OR RING DOVE

Viakhir', vitiuten', vitiutin; Columba palumbus

This bird is the largest of the pigeons. The origin of its two Russian names is difficult to establish. Both are used among ordinary folk, reproachfully, of a person who is slow or clumsy in his movements, and one may apply related terms to oneself or another when one makes a silly mistake. But there is nothing in the character of the wood pigeon to justify this misuse of its name. Perhaps its lack of aggression and its timid nature gave rise to this. Being so ill-equipped to defend themselves, pigeons cannot be brave in the face of predators and well-armed enemies.

The wood pigeon is about half again as large as a domestic pigeon. Its plumage is very beautiful: it is all a smoky shade of gray, with a pinkish tinge, especially on the breast and neck; seen in the sunlight, this plumage reflects two colors, a greenish-gold, and a pinkish-gold sheen. On each side of the upper neck is a white patch, which, however, does not meet at the throat, so the German name "ring dove" (*Ringtaube*) is not quite accurate; there is also a somewhat elongated white patch at the bend of the wing, which forms a white bar when the wing is extended; the tips of the primaries and tailfeathers are dark; on the undersurface of the tailfeathers is a transverse white band, formed from white spots on each of the feathers.

On the upper surface these spots do not show at all. The legs are pink, like those of the domestic pigeon; the bill, pale reddish to pink. The eyes are bright, neither dark nor gray, but of an ill-defined pale slate color.

Wood pigeons do not arrive early in spring, almost always in late April. By "arrive" I have in mind the time when they descend on trees and thawed ground. A week or two earlier they can be seen passing over quite high in the sky, in large flocks, but rarely landing on the ground. I have always found them in small parties of up to ten birds in spring, but mostly in twos and threes. Soon after arriving they form pairs, mate, and begin building their nests on the stout limbs of large trees. All varieties of doves make tender and devoted couples. Long before the female begins to lay the male becomes attached to her and will not be parted from her for a moment. There is frequent billing and cooing as he kisses her with feeling and at length, walking round her, constantly bowing and straightening up, fanning his tailfeathers and puffing up the feathers of his neck like a mane. The kissing of doves is a distinctive feature that places them above other birds, a clear expression of heartfelt feeling. I have closely observed many birds: there are some that have something similar to kissing, but in doves it is performed in a more definite way. Sometimes the female does not want to kiss, and the male keeps trying to open her closed beak; but usually both bring their open beaks together and often close their eyes with pleasure . . .

When the female feels the eggs growing larger inside her a nest is hurriedly constructed on a stout branch, right next to the trunk. It is made of small twigs and lined with soft dry grass and down. The female lays only two eggs (some fowlers claim three, but I have seen more than ten nests, always with two eggs). The eggs are pale pink or flesh-colored, of the usual shape of chicken eggs but much larger and rounder than those of domestic pigeons. "Cooing" is not exactly the word to describe the call of the wood pigeon. There is something mournful about its notes; they are drawn out, and more like a kind of murmur or moan, very loud yet pleasing to the ear. This can be heard from afar, especially in twilight and when there is a breeze to carry it, and it often gives away the bird's nest, as it like to perch on a branch of the tree nearest its nest, usually a dead one, to give voice to its contentment by prolonged cooing. When the female wishes to stretch her weary wings after much sitting, or find something to eat, the male immediately takes her place.

On arrival the wood pigeon is not particularly tame, and it is always more retiring than other pigeons. But when nesting it does not fly far from the nest, becoming tamer, and permitting you to come quite close in a vehicle; you cannot approach on foot, however, unless you can stalk it using trees as cover. The wood pigeon is a very strong bird, with much resistance to gunshot. In this it is exceeded only by the black grouse, so duck-shot, Number Four or even Three, should be used.

The male and female take turns at incubation for two and a half weeks. Many hunters aver that all species of pigeon rear three clutches in a season. I cannot give definite confirmation of this, but consider it likely, since in May, June, and July I have found pigeons sitting, and also because they only ever have two eggs. The chicks hatch covered in pale yellow down; they do not leave the nest until well feathered and even then cling for a long time to the branches of the nest-tree, at first hopping from bough to bough, and then making fluttering flights. Throughout this time the parents constantly ply them with food and water from their own beaks, so they have to keep flying away to seek food for them. While the chicks are small, the parents leave them by turns, but when they are bigger both will leave together. Their diet consists of the seeds of various grasses and trees; their preference is for cereal grains, but since these crops are not yet ripe at the time when they are feeding their first brood and few of the grass seeds have ripened either, the chicks depend mostly on a variety of insects that their mother and father bring them. These efforts take the parents' whole day, from early morning till late evening. Pigeons have the remarkable ability, unmatched by any other birds, to fill their crops with food and, on returning to the nest, to regurgitate it all and feed it to their young. The parent bird places its bill in the open mouth of the chick, and, with no visible effort, the foods passes into the throat of the chick so quickly that the young bird scarcely has time to swallow it. This is repeated several times a day. As a result of this ample feeding, the young become uncommonly fat and tasty before they have even left the nest.

The wood pigeon has a distinctive manner of flight: on leaving a tree it first rises steeply upward. Then it slaps one wing against the other, or both wings against its flanks, producing a sound very like hands clapping, repeated several times. Then the bird points its head somewhat downward and launches into normal level flight, but always very swift and powerful. By the time the young are fully fledged and flying like adults, the cereals are ripe, and old and young form small flocks and spend all day, from morning till evening, in the grainfields. They most frequently visit fields on which the crops have been reaped: before the grain is gathered in they flock round the clustered stooks, then the long frame ricks; when the stooks have been carted away, the wood pigeons roam over the stubble, foraging for any remaining ears of corn and spilt grain.[26] Of course they will most readily eat exposed grain with no husk or ears, such as rye, spring wheat, and peas, but when these are lacking they will feed on spring cereals of all kinds. Of course, on this nourishing food they very soon wax fat, and this is when the best season for wood-pigeon–shooting begins. They should be shot from a vehicle, as on foot one can rarely come within range unless the terrain provides stalking cover. Stalking is, however, possible when standing stooks are numerous in the fields (as happens in a good harvest), and often you may kill several birds with one shot. Wood pigeons are much tamer early in the morning, before they have had time to fill their bellies. At this time they are reluctant to abandon their rich breakfast and do not fly right away, but only flutter a short distance. If there are any trees in the vicinity, after the first shot they will often perch in them, to return to feeding when the hunter has passed on. They are used to doing this, as they constantly repeat this maneuver when the peasants are carting the stooks; that is, they perch in the trees when the peasants come to load the grain, and fly down again when the loaded carts leave the fields. In mid-September wood pigeons form huge flocks, become very wary, and soon depart. Before they leave they become very plump and tasty, especially the young, whereas in the breeding season the parent birds have dry, tough flesh.

5B. STOCK DOVE

Klintukh; Columba oenas

The name *klintukh*, which is not of Russian origin, is used by hunters; to ordinary folk the bird is known as the "wild dove."[27]

The stock dove is very similar to the blue-gray domestic pigeon; its plumage is quite unmarked by spots or speckles, even under the tail; when it is perched and even when it flies overhead, it shows no white at all. I repeat that it cannot immediately be told from a young domestic pigeon, though it is slightly smaller than an old one. Its plumage is a dull dark gray; seen in the light it has a small area of greenish sheen on the neck; the bill is light flesh-color, the legs pale flesh, described in hunting manuals as "apricot color."

In its mode of life and all its habits the stock dove is exactly like the wood pigeon so there is no need to give a separate account of these. The only difference that I have observed is the following: stock doves appear exceptionally early, long before all other birds, always in March, and I once even found a brace at a threshing floor in late February, as my wildfowling notes show; but I do not know whether this early sighting can properly be called "arrival." I usually came upon my first stock doves singly, sometimes in pairs, and very occasionally in groups of four. These occurrences sometimes precede by two or even three weeks the main spring arrival, when stock doves begin to fly in and alight in vast flocks. This arrival too is much earlier than that of wood pigeons. In late March I have found flocks of several hundred sitting by the few thawed patches that have appeared by then, and have killed ten with one shot. They are much tamer than wood pigeons.

Stock doves also nest on the main boughs of large trees, but seek remote sites deep in unbroken forest. I have not heard their call and nor have other fowlers whom I have asked about this. There is nothing distinctive about the bird's flight. In summer they are rarely seen, but from mid-August to late September they occur in parties and soon pass through in huge flocks. It is curious that at the height of the autumn passage and even after it stock doves again appear in ones and twos, and remain until October. In other words, they depart in autumn in the same way as they arrived in spring. I have always regarded the autumn stragglers as either late hatching or ailing birds, but how is one to account for the appearance of individuals in March, sometimes during twenty-degree frosts, and even in February, which even the calendar terms a winter month? My theory is that stock doves begin their migration flight earlier than we suppose, even as early as February, but they fly at night and fly high—like many other species—so we know nothing of it. In large flocks there are probably always some tired or weak birds that fall behind on the journey, and, having nowhere else to go, settle at threshing floors to wait for spring proper to arrive. These are the birds the hunter finds so early in the season.

The flesh of the stock dove is of just the same quality as that of the wood pigeon or even tenderer, and therefore superior. They have far less resistance to shot than their larger cousins. Fowlers have little regard for these birds when they appear singly, but when it is possible to bring down several brace from a large flock, particularly on their arrival in spring, they do not spurn them. I have already mentioned how pleasing it is to find them in early spring.

5C. TURTLEDOVE

Gorlitsa, gorlinka; Streptopelia turtur

The third variety of dove is known in the literary language by the name of *gorlitsa* and among ordinary folk as *gorlinka*. I am unable to explain the derivation of these names, unless they are connected with the dark spot on the throat of the bird.[28]

The turtledove enjoys no particular prominence in folk sayings, being subsumed in the broader concept of the dove family, yet it is well known to the public. Our poets and novelists of the late eighteenth century and even the early nineteenth made much of the passionate and devoted love of turtledoves for their partners, claiming that, should one of them die, the other would kill itself in the following manner: after paying

its final tribute to its mate by mournful cooing, the surviving bird would soar up as high as it could over a rocky crag or over water, fold its wings, and plummet like a stone to its death. The tenderhearted reading public believed this tender tale. . . . The turtledove has not only done duty as an ideal of true love, but has been obliged to sympathize with ardent and especially unhappy lovers. As one poet has written, with true feeling, and without blushing,

Two turtledoves will show you
Where my cold ashes rest.
They'll coo and softly tell you:
He died by tears oppressed.[29]

And his readers took up these lines with genuine sympathy. . . . But that time is past, and I am afraid I must tell the bald truth of the matter: that the touching tale of the suicidal pigeon is without foundation. I have kept turtledoves in cages and bred them. When one of a pair died, its mate very soon paired with a new friend and started building a new nest.

The turtledove is much smaller than the stock dove, and less than half the size of a wood pigeon, in fact little more than one-third its size. Its plumage is very beautiful and sharply distinguished from all other pigeons, although it maintains the same proportions. As for appearance and particular qualities, the turtledove stands out most prominently, or most visibly, as it is a confiding bird that has little fear of man, does not hide from him, and offers every opportunity, even to the least curious, for the study of its habits. Not only does it visit gardens and vegetable patches, but it often perches in the broad green gardens of country estates and sits on their plain fences.

The bill has a knob on the top of it, of pale flesh color. The head, neck, and breast are a grayish pink. There is a fairly broad, light red ring of bare skin round the beautiful dark eye; on each side of the neck, a finger's breadth from the eye, is an elongated and very pretty coffee-colored patch, cut through by white bars, or rather by three dark brown spots ringed with white. Along the wings from the shoulder run dark, elongated blotches, edged with brown; the pinions are light coffee-brown, and the tail, which is quite long, is the same color; two of the upper tailfeathers have no edging, while the lower ones end in a white band the breadth of one finger; there are small, indistinct speckles on the back; the belly is pure white, and the legs pink.

It will be clear from this description that the turtledove is very similar in size and plumage to the Barbary dove, with which it readily mates.[30] There is even some similarity in their cooing, but the turtledove's coo is softer, gentler, less deep and heavy. At a distance the call of the turtledove sometimes resembles the intermittent babble of a distant brook, very pleasing to the ear. It has its own special place in the general chorus of avian voices, producing an involuntary feeling of rather doleful, sweet reflection.

Turtledoves arrive later in spring than all other doves, or at least they show themselves later. I have never seen them flying in migratory flocks, although this certainly takes place, and other fowlers have seen it. I have always encountered them when they have already paired and started building, which they do at woodland fringes, in copses, and usually in trees close to streams or small rivers—never in the depths of dense forests. They mate, nest, lay, and rear their young in exactly the same manner as wood pigeons and stock doves; I have not observed the slightest deviation in their habits from those of other doves, so I shall not repeat myself here. The only difference—if one can call it such—is that turtledoves are much more confiding than their cousins, and can always be approached not only in a vehicle but on foot. They are almost as tame as sparrows, jackdaws, or domestic pigeons. They are easily tamed, especially if taken from the nest before they are fully feathered. You only need to put them in a large wooden or mesh cage (it does not matter which), and feed them plenty of grain. When full grown they will breed and live just like domestic pigeons. In autumn they depart quite early, in August, long before cold weather sets in. I have never come across large flocks before departure but I have quite often encountered small groups of three to five pairs. At this season they are often quite plump and very tasty. Indeed at all seasons they taste better than other doves. They have less resistance to gunshot, and hazel-grouse shot is sufficient to kill them.

Turtledoves are rarely shot: ordinary folk leave them alone out of respect for the dove family, and also because they are not very big, while true sportsmen regard them as too tame.

One point needs to be added to the general picture of the dove family: the way they express their feelings is so gentle, meek, and timid, that even their love for their young when the latter are threatened is not manifested by any rash or daring behavior. I have many times approached a nest-tree with young, and even climbed up it, and the parent birds did not mob me, like black-tailed godwits, or try to lure me away by feigning injury, like ducks or gray-hen. Instead the doves flitted timidly from one tree to another, anxiously turning this way and that, sidestepping along the branch they were sitting on, ceaselessly changing their position and approaching me as I drew near the nest. I could hardly hear their sad, soft, murmuring notes, quite different from their usual cooing. In brief, even in this situation the meekness of the dove family was fully in evidence.

6. THE THRUSH FAMILY

There are seven kinds of thrush:

(1) the mistle thrush [*Turdus viscivorus*], the largest of the family, almost the size of a turtledove; it is light gray all over, except for a whitish breast and belly covered in fine darkish speckles; the back and upper wings are grayish, even tending to green; the eyes are dark and the bill a light flesh color. This thrush is fairly uncommon in the province of Orenburg;

(2) the fieldfare [*Turdus pilaris*], which is slightly smaller than the mistle thrush; it is fond of rowanberries, hence its Russian name.[31] It has quite large speckles, rather like elongated dark brown blotches on a yellowish-gray background; the feathers of the back and upper wing are brown with dark gray tints; the eyes and bill are dark, almost black. It is common everywhere, especially in the province of Orenburg;

(3) the redwing [*Turdus iliacus*] has plumage just like that of the fieldfare but is half the size and very much rarer. It feeds mostly on the berries of juniper, where juniper is common, hence one of its Russian names.[32] In Orenburg it is known by the name of "lesser hazel grouse" [*malyi riabchik*];

(4) and (5) are the blackbirds, which are a little smaller than the fieldfare; they differ from each other in that one has dark, almost black plumage, with a yellow ring round the eye and a reddish-yellow bill, while the other has dark brown plumage, a bill that is lightish toward the tip, and no eye-ring. This kind seems to be a little smaller than the first;[33]

(6) the song thrush [*Turdus philomelos*], which at first glance is very like the mistle thrush in plumage, but only half the size and with larger speckles, rounder, almost black, but thinly scattered, so that from afar the bird looks gray. It sings very beautifully and can even mimic the nightingale;

(7) the water ouzel or dipper [*Cinclus cinclus*]; about the size of a song thrush or slightly smaller, and dark slate-gray; the legs are almost black; there is a white patch at the throat. It clings to small rivers and streams and runs along the banks. Often it crosses from one side to the other by running over the

streambed underwater at a depth of two or three feet, and even catches small fish. Its beak is straight and tough, of light flesh color.

I know little of the sixth and seventh varieties. I have seen song thrushes in cages, and dippers only in the distance, so I repeat the reliable descriptions given by other fowlers.

All thrushes are the same shape, which is rather like that of the magpie, and all hop with both feet together. This hopping is unknown among game birds, and therefore, in the popular view, thrushes should not be eaten, any more than crows, magpies, jackdaws, sparrows, and other hopping birds should. Of course, in the country those who seek to fill their bags do not shoot them—less because of popular prejudice than because they are small and not worth a cartridge. Near large towns, however, especially the capitals, the peasants shoot thrushes in large numbers, and trap many more to sell at a profit for the dinner tables of well-to-do city-dwellers.

Thrushes are cheerful, lively songbirds. The fieldfare, with the elongated speckles, and the blackbird, with the yellow eye-ring, are considered the best singers after the song thrush. I can say nothing definite about the blackbird, but I did keep a fieldfare in a cage for a long time; it sang agreeably and softly, which one might not expect, given its harsh call, resembling a loud, clattering cluck. All fowlers know the calls of the thrushes, sounding like the syllables "chok, chok, chok," and I always listened to them with pleasure.[34] A thrush will often thus betray its presence as it sits amid dense foliage or at the top of a tall tree. A large flock perched in trees will raise such a racket that you can hear it a long distance away. The thrushes I know best are the fieldfare and redwing, so in speaking of the thrush family I have these two principally in mind.

These two thrushes arrive in spring earlier than almost all other birds, usually in late March. I always found them in bushes, close to thawed springs or warm manure heaps. Some fowlers maintain that thrushes do not fly away to warmer climes for the winter, because they have often come across them in winter, occasionally in quite large numbers beside unfrozen springs, but this proves only that they can endure our winters. There is no doubt that ducks migrate, but it is always possible to find a few mallard and even gadwall wintering on unfrozen streams. It is my belief that these are birds from late-summer clutches that for some particular reason did not depart. The thrushes that turn up in winter besides springs may stay behind for the same reasons. I am prepared to accept, however, that duck do not fly very far south, because they sometimes depart very late, often after the first snow. Speaking for myself, I have never ever come across any thrushes in winter.

Be this as it may, thrushes appear very early in spring, singly at first, but soon in huge flocks that disperse in scattered woodland and the mown meadows separating it. It cannot be said that they are very timid on their arrival, but all birds are wary when gathered in large numbers, and they can be very difficult to approach when scattered over a wide area, whether of open ground or thin woodland. They immediately start clucking loudly and hopping and fluttering about, so much that they scare one another. This means that you can never shoot very many at this season, although one does particularly prize them on account of this.[35] Here I have in mind the fieldfare; the redwing arrives later and always in small numbers. It is much tamer, and will usually perch or hop about very low down in dense thickets. It would be hard to find if it sat in silence, but its soft notes, "tsu-tsu" help the fowler to locate it.

After a week or so, during which they are everywhere in large numbers, at the time of their spring passage, thrushes suddenly disappear, and throughout the summer it is unusual to find single unpaired birds. They form pairs and build their nests on the branches of trees in woodland and copses, and near Moscow even in neglected parks and gardens. The female lays four eggs, slightly smaller than pigeon's eggs, but elongated in shape and speckled green. The male and female take turns at sitting, and the eggs hatch after three weeks. The parents feed them constantly on green berries—only just beginning to ripen at this season—and various seeds and insects, until they are fully grown. Thrushes with nests and eggs, and especially nests with young, are less retiring, or rather bolder, and if they do not attack an intruder, at least they do not fly away, but flit from branch to branch and tree to tree, clucking ceaselessly and trying to lure you away. The young hatch quite early, in the first week of June, but they remain for a long time in the nest or in the branches of the nest tree until able to fly like their parents. After this for some time they remain well concealed, skulking in dense woodland thickets, before beginning to fly in small parties in search of berries. Toward autumn they form large flocks.

The thrushes' favorite food is berries of all kinds, so they like to frequent orchards, and if these are guarded during the day they will make their devastating raids very early in the morning, even before sunrise. In the forests of Orenburg, especially in the large riverside carrs, their favorite and most nourishing delicacies are bird-cherries, rowan- and guelder-rose berries. The latter two become sweeter after the first frosts and the thrushes greedily feast on them right into winter. The more berries they consume, the tastier their flesh, and they become very plump. They should be shot with hazel-grouse shot, since they have good resistance to shot, in proportion to their size. The main shooting seasons for thrushes—mainly fieldfares—are in spring and autumn. They may also be shot in summer, when rearing their young, but they are very lean at that season. The spring season is very short, but the autumn season may sometimes last a long time. Here no dog is needed. On the whole thrushes are not retiring birds, but they constantly flit from bough to bough, from tree to tree, and always perch among thick branches and foliage, where they are hard to see. It is usual to approach them by stalking on foot, when the birds are perched or moving in the trees. It would be easier to hit them in flight, but among trees the branches always get in the way.

In the province of Orenburg thrushes are trapped, using bunches of ripe rowan- or guelder-rose berries, which show up as bright red from afar, especially against the bright white of the first snow. The birds get caught in snares, hung all about with bunches of berries. They are even trapped in nets, into which they are lured by the same bait of rowan or guelder rose.

Near Moscow blackbirds of both varieties are common. They frequent only places where coniferous woodland is found, and particularly where there are firs. They are even more determined in their raids on berries than fieldfares. I have never found blackbirds' nests, and have not observed them flocking, although they can be present in large numbers when scattered. They cling mostly to thin coniferous woodland, usually perching on the lower branches or hopping on the ground, just like redwings. They are easy to shoot, though difficult to pick out in the firs.

I have shot only three mistle thrushes in our province. They were in a flock of fieldfares and stood out even at a distance by their larger bodies and much lighter plumage. Near Moscow I have never seen mistle thrushes and have no knowledge of them in that area.

A fat thrush is considered a dainty dish. It was renowned for its fine flavor even in ancient Rome, at the banquets of Lucullus, who would pay fabulous sums for mistle thrushes. The thrush is alone in sharing the famous privilege of the snipe family—of being roasted whole and ungutted in a pan. Why it merits this honor I have no idea. Perhaps because of the fame of its ancestors. But in any case this method of cooking is highly commendable, and I have already recommended its use with all game species. In my view a plump thrush is very tasty, though not more so than all other plump birds. There is no doubt, however, that thrushes, as they feed exclusively on berries and fruit—or, in warmer lands, grapes—have a splendid flavor.

7. WOODCOCK

Val'dshnep; Scolopax rusticola

With regard to its quality, the woodcock is the finest game. Since by habitat it is a woodland bird I thought it best to deal with the woodcock after all the other species of woodland birds, although it differs from them in every respect—in its proportions, which are those of a wader, its food, and its habits.

I have already said enough elsewhere about its Russian and foreign names, but I should note that in Poland, as in southern Russia, it is called *slonka* or *slomka,* which may perhaps have the same origin as one of its Russian names, *sluka.*

There is something curious about the fact that the woodcock with its long legs and bill lives in forests, often where growth is thickest. Its build requires space, and when one thinks of waders one thinks of marshland, or at least riverbanks, ponds, and lakes. To be sure, the curlew lives in the steppes, which are dry and open, but at certain times of year the bird regularly visits wet and muddy banks. One would think that the woodcock might find it difficult to fly, or even run, in the forest. Its long bill and legs might catch on branches, but in fact it runs along the ground and darts through the air in dense forest, mature or half-grown, with astonishing ease.

Without any doubt the woodcock is in all respects the most

superb game. It even holds pride of place in the noble family of the snipes, its close affinity with which is shown by the excellent flavor of its flesh, the similarity in its mottled plumage, the beauty of its large, dark eyes, the speed and agility of its flight, its manner of feeding, and by its elusiveness as a target. Its long legs, neck, and bill notwithstanding, the woodcock is a plump and fleshy bird, about the size of a large pigeon. Its build resembles that of the great snipe, and its mottled plumage, apart from that with a reddish or tawny tint, also resembles the great snipe's.

The woodcock is a very beautiful bird. All the spots and speckles consist of a mixture of dark, reddish, and ash-gray hues, difficult to describe adequately, as with the other species of snipe. The crown of the head is barred by four dark stripes, or extended blotches across it. The ruddy tint is more evident on the back and the upper wings. The underwing, breast, and belly are lighter and barred with straight, ash-gray streaks. The tail is short, with the lower tailfeathers slightly longer than the upper ones. They are very dark, almost black, and each one ends with a little white spot below and a reddish-gray one above. The upper tailfeathers are finer, slightly shorter, and light brown. The bill is two and a quarter inches long. For a wading bird of its size, the legs are short. The beak and legs are flesh-colored.

Lone woodcock sometimes first appear very early in the spring, before the first signs of thaw. Where they can live and what they find to eat is difficult to imagine. Perhaps they find springs and spring-fed pools that do not freeze over in winter, and around which the spring thaw gathers pace. I have often flushed and shot woodcock in deep snow that shows no sign of melting, as early as the end of March. It is notable that early woodcock are fairly plump. Later, with the onset of milder weather once spring is well established, the birds begin to arrive in numbers (in Orenburg region, almost always about 12 April). "Falls" of woodcock, as they are known, are sometimes extremely large, particularly at woodland edges, in felled clearings, in younger woodland and heathland, and in the Moscow area in orchards and berry fields. The sportsman must seize this opportunity because woodcock on passage rarely stay longer than three days in one place. No one has ever observed migrating woodcock in flocks: no doubt they fly at night. In a week the spring passage is over, falls are no more to be found, and the established birds have occupied their forest territories. Roding begins at once. I have already explained this term and shall treat this aspect of the bird's behavior in more detail when I speak of woodcock as game birds. In mid-May the birds begin nesting, and in mid-June the eggs hatch. The nest is built of down and dry grass, on the ground in extensive woodland. The female lays four eggs, slightly larger than pigeons' eggs, elongated, like those of sandpipers, and speckled with brown. I cannot say for certain whether woodcock form pairs or whether the cock and hen share in nest-building and incubation. Some sportsmen assure me that both invariably take part in rearing the young, but I have not been able to verify this for myself. Nor do I know anything of the details or of any peculiarities of their mating behavior.

I asserted in the first edition of this book that the roding of woodcocks was not their courtship flight, but a number of sportsmen have offered objections that I recognize to be so well-founded that I cannot cling to my original belief. Here are some observations communicated to me by reliable sportsmen: (1) flying woodcock, always males—as I myself have noted—sometimes drop suddenly to the ground on hearing the call of the female. When skilled fowlers imitate this sound the birds approach very close; (2) if you stand in the roding territory and throw up a hat, cap, or rolled handkerchief when you see a woodcock approaching, the bird will alight at the spot where it falls; (3) no roding occurs in places where the birds do not breed, even if they are present from early spring in good numbers. On the basis of this persuasive evidence we may conclude with certainty that roding is the woodcock's courtship flight: the males fly through the forest calling to the females; the latter reply, the males go to them and mating takes place. Once one accepts that roding is courtship flight, there can be no doubt that it is the females who incubate the eggs. As for the question of whether roding woodcock catch midges and small insects that swarm at treetop height—something that many sportsmen question—there is no doubt that they do. I have often cut open the crops of freshly shot roding birds and always found flies, large mosquitoes, moths, and flying beetles that have only just been swallowed. There is nothing to prevent a woodcock catching insects it encounters while roding.

When the young have grown a little the female leads them from the tall forest into lower but if possible denser growth. There they remain until fully grown, or even until autumn, at the start of which they move, either to the fringes of large woods, adjacent to fields sown with winter cereals—the rootlets of rye shoots are their favorite food—or from younger woods into marshy thickets and boggy scrub, and particularly to springs. Here they may stay for a considerable while because the muddy ground beside a spring will not freeze for a long time. At this season woodcock will boldly approach human habitation, millponds, and weirs, especially hemp fields and vegetable gardens. By day they hide in well-grown gardens, parks, spinneys, and alder and willow carrs, which almost always grow beside pools, weirs, and rivers. At night they fly out to market gardens and cabbage patches, where they can easily find food in the soft, broken soil. They are also fond of visiting places where cattle have roamed during the day. They happily peck at fresh cow dung, consisting of digested grasses and small worms, which quickly infest it. In forests where woodcock are common, you cannot find a single one of yesterday's cow-pats that has not been thoroughly probed by their bills, while older dung that has dried and hardened is untouched. (Some sportsmen maintain that woodcock do not eat the dung itself, but merely probe it for small worms.) The woodcock's diet, like that of other species of snipe, consists from preference of the rootlets of certain forest and marshland grasses, which it adroitly pulls out with its long and fairly stout beak, and also of various insects.

I have mentioned that on their arrival woodcock are fairly plump, but subsequently they quickly lose weight and by autumn their flesh is dry, tough, and of poor quality. But as autumn advances the birds become plumper, until they are very well clad in fat. This does not happen every year, however. As a rule they disappear before they have had time to gain weight. In this connection I particularly recall the year 1822. Autumn lasted a long time. At first it was clear and cold, before turning mild and wet. All the woodcock gathered in scattered brakes on boggy ground and stayed there until 8 November, growing extraordinarily plump. Abandoning all other game, I went after woodcock every day without fail. On 6 November I shot eight of them, and on the seventh, twelve. The next night seven inches of snow fell with fifteen degrees of frost. Supposing that all the woodcock could not have flown on the same night, I took a good gun-dog and rushed to explore the springs that had not frozen or been buried in snow and where there had still been a good number of woodcock the day before. But although I paced the area all day I did not find a single one. Only as I was returning home, among the roots of some impenetrable bushes beside a boggy patch fed by a spring, did my tireless dog put up a woodcock, which I shot. The bird turned out to be sickly and utterly wasted. I expect it would have perished from cold within a day. The twenty plump birds that I had shot on 6 and 7 November and hung in the shed froze solid. A harsh winter then set in and I regularly dined on perfectly fresh woodcock until the very beginning of Lent. This, of course, can be regarded as exceptional.

It has always surprised me that the woodcock can grow so fat at a time when its sources of food are diminishing daily, but perhaps it is because the grass roots become particularly nourishing, as at this time of year that is where all the goodness lies. The last woodcock usually disappear in about mid-October. The spring and autumn passage, with accompanying falls, varies greatly. Sometimes numbers are high, and autumn passage may last about a fortnight. In other years the birds are so scarce that in a whole day you can hardly find two brace. Occasionally they turn up everywhere, and vanish the same day. This is rightly regarded as a sure sign that winter will soon take firm hold, but the birds can withstand a brief and even heavy snowfall without frost, and often stay for a long time after it has melted. I have often found the fresh, moist autumn snow among trees and bushes laced with the intricate patterns of woodcock tracks. This can also happen in spring, during sudden, late snowfalls such as sometimes occur in early May.

The open season begins as soon as the birds arrive. Since they first appear singly such sport is a matter of choice. Suddenly you may flush a woodcock where you least expected to find one, and on the other hand find none in the most suitable places. At this season the woodcock is a gift to be prized, a bonus, but it is too early to speak of the woodcock season as such. When they begin to pass through in large numbers and substantial falls occur, woodcock shooting presents the very best sport, particularly as it is short-lived, and at this early period, after six months of inactivity, the hunter's passion is far from spent. Besides this, the woodcock itself is first-class game and no hunter is indifferent to it. In spring, as soon as you flush two or three birds in one spot, you may be sure that many are present. Naturally the true sportsman will abandon all other migratory birds and pursue woodcock.

Here a good, sensible, level-headed pointer will be essential. Although spring parties of woodcock will not allow a dog to come close, so it has to point from afar, it frequently happens that some woodcock will rise at a distance, while others closer will sit so tight that without a dog you would walk straight past them. You can shoot at a bird rising some way off, and others will take wing just a few yards behind you or to one side. A keen-scented dog, and one that does not chase after rising birds, will do much to overcome these difficulties. It will immediately catch the scent, and show from afar where a woodcock is hiding. The sportsman will not walk past and will be able to find a position where no bushes or trees obstruct his line of fire. Sometimes parties of woodcock are so large that even an experienced, cool-headed sportsman can be at a loss, and a young enthusiast can lose his head completely. If, in addition, you have a dog that runs after the birds, a flock of a hundred will take fright and disperse in minutes in all directions. When you unexpectedly come upon a flock the birds begin to rise with a loud clatter of wings, darting in all directions. If they are not yet gun-shy they will describe a small arc, up to the height of the treetops, and land again. It must be an inviolable rule never to run toward those birds that alight again within view, or those first seen running or standing. It is necessary to advance steadily, at a measured pace, looking about or making one's dog search thoroughly on each side, and trying to hold a position in which trees and bushes present as little obstacle as possible. This rule is vital, since woodcock that have just alighted are so watchful for the first few minutes that they will not admit a sportsman within range, and if he runs after them he will pass by other birds much closer to him, sitting tight.

If you have no choice but to hunt with a dog that runs after the birds it must be put on the leash as soon as it locates a flock, because you will shoot far more without it, especially if several guns or beaters advance in line abreast. You must inspect every little covert and hollow, every nook, always taking care to adopt a comfortable firing position. Only then will the shoot be successful and the bag large during the spring passage. The problems vanish if the shoot takes place in dense low scrub or undergrowth half the height of a man, which does not shield the rising bird from the hunter's eye or his gun muzzle. The extensive berry fields near Moscow, of raspberry, gooseberry, blackcurrant, and barberry bushes, are the best place for shooting woodcock in their spring and autumn flocks, which, I have heard, can be fabulously large. Here it is best if several members of the party walk in line abreast. Even without dogs (if the line closes up), there will be a large bag, but with sensible dogs it will be larger, and better sport. The woodcock is not a strong bird and since it is usually shot at close range (though sometimes through a screen of branches) there is no need to use shot larger than that used for hazel grouse: even Number Eight shot is large enough, and sometimes Number Nine will suffice.

Shooting woodcock is both easy and difficult: in open spaces it flies straight and level but among trees and bushes it twists and weaves with great agility; it is no exaggeration to say that it sometimes darts like a flash of lightning. To shoot it in tall, moderately dense forest therefore demands extraordinary speed and skill. It has to be shot as it rises, before it reaches the understory; if it rises at an angle, you have to seize the moment when it emerges into a relatively open space. This is not at all the same thing as shooting in fields or open marshes, where you can let it fly while you take aim at leisure at a bird in the open. With a woodcock darting through the trees you have to be just as quick as with a merganser diving in a lake. With woodcock, many shots miss, but on the other hand no other sport affords so many inexplicably lucky shots. Often I have been unable to believe my eyes when after a desperate shot into a bush or thick branches in the general direction of a disappearing woodcock my dog has suddenly brought me a dead bird. I still fail to understand how it is that densely interwoven branches, though bare of leaves that might conceal the bird, do not always protect it from the shot.

In spring, as soon as the birds have taken up territory, the shooting of woodcock at their roding begins. This always takes place in the forest, over glades, clearings, and woodland rides. The height at which the birds fly depends on the height of the trees, as they always fly just above the treetops. In spring roding begins at sunset and continues until it is completely dark, or sometimes throughout the night until sunrise, as I have often observed. As spring turns to summer, roding begins later, so that in early July it begins only when it is quite dark and shooting is impossible.

The woodcock's flight is accompanied by a special cry, rather like a grunt or a snort, which can be heard long before the bird comes into view. This is of great assistance in shooting, since without that warning note the sportsman often does not notice the bird flying past, especially if he is standing in a confined space; even if he does, he may have no time to raise his gun and take aim. The call is divided into two phrases: the first consists of brief, hoarse notes repeated two or three times, and the second of a rather longer note, similar to "tsu." At all other times, outside the roding season, the bird is completely silent. In places where woodcock are plentiful, and where the field of fire is unobstructed, shooting roding birds is quite jolly, especially if there is a large shooting party. This is the only instance where the more guns there are the better. Well spaced at their stations, they do not hinder one another, but on the contrary help one another, as a bird startled by a shot from one gun will fly toward another, then toward a third, and so on, until somebody hits it. If the party is large and the birds numerous, the shots ring out constantly, like running rifle fire. Sometimes they resound sonorously in the forest in the thin, cool air of spring, sending echoes rolling through the forest gullies. A passing traveler would halt in astonishment, amazed at such rapid and furious fire, like an exchange in the front line during a battle.

The darkness of night puts an end to it. The sportsmen

congregate, each looking intently at the others' bags and trying to make out in the darkness how full they are. One will tell in a loud and merry voice of his lucky shots, another, with vexation, of his unlucky ones. However, this sort of shooting is never very productive in proportion to the number of guns, and cannot compare with that of spring flocks, to say nothing of autumn flocks. During roding even the luckiest seldom manage to bag more than two brace, and some bag none at all.

Clearly such shooting is less appealing on one's own, although it can be very peaceful: you can sit down, have a smoke, stroll up and down, or even lie down for a while if you wish, although this may become a little wearisome. As the birds' flight path may often be unsuitable, it can also be unproductive. Their calls can be heard from all quarters, yet none will fly within range, and after waiting for up to three hours the sportsmen is obliged to return home without firing his gun even once. Nevertheless I used to love to stand at the roding ground alone on a fine, still May evening. In dull or windy weather the birds are hard to see or hear, as they do not rode very much. A warm spring or early summer evening in broad-leaved woodland in late May has ineffable charm. The trees and bushes have just come into leaf, including the lime and oak, which are later than other species. After sunset the air is filled with the delicate fragrance of fresh leaves, sometimes overlaid by the heavier scent of the bird-cherry in flower. All the birds, from the nightingale to the tiny blue-tit, are hurriedly and spiritedly singing their twilight song, gradually falling silent with the gathering dusk, which falls sooner in the forest. At last all is quiet. In the silence you can hear not only the hares hopping, but even the scurrying movements of small animals. At times you can lose yourself in your own thoughts, and then with a start hear the hoarse grunt of the woodcock, louder and louder as it draws near. Gone are the unfurling leaves, the splendid evening, and all of nature. . . . How tensely one awaits the appearance of the bird above the crowns of the trees, and what joy when the shot is true!

Once high summer comes on, the woodcock season closes until autumn. Young woodcock are hard to find in the forest, and in any case the half-grown birds are so beautiful that one would regret shooting them. For this reason nobody hunts them at this time of year, but at the end of August the young attain full size and begin to appear in young woodland and on the fringes of mature woods. But enough has been said about this already. On about 6 September, or sometimes a little later, the real autumn woodcock season begins.

Here a good pointer becomes the central figure: without one it is impossible to do anything. The woodcock sit tight in deep cover amid the roots of trees and bushes, in dense, low undergrowth or tall, thick grass. They are also very fond of dank woodland fringes close to stubble fields, as well as little gullies with ruts and pools, thickly overgrown with young willow and alder, especially if there is a brook flowing along the gully, with springs feeding it at intervals. This sort of terrain is best worked in pairs, one walking on each side of the gully, while a dog combs through the bushes. The woodcock will fly out to left and right.

Along woodland fringes, on the other hand, it is best to shoot alone, with a dog, of course. If there are many such sites the shooting can be wonderful and extremely rewarding. This relates to those birds that have hatched in neighboring woodland and emerged into scattered bushes and carrs. But besides these, and long before the departure of the locally bred birds, autumn falls of passage migrants appear, chiefly in young woodland and bushes. In some years these are unusually large, in others scarcely noticeable. It is during these autumn falls of woodcock that the shooting is busiest and most productive. One regrets only that these flocks rarely stay long and that sometimes, after one day of good shooting, the next day the same locality will not yield a single bird. Furthermore the migrating flocks select different places every year. This may well be a matter of chance. Some years there seem to be no migrating flocks, because you do not locate the chosen spots in time. I am at a loss to explain why the local woodcock do not depart with the passage migrants but instead linger on sometimes for quite a while.

Sometimes the autumn hunt for woodcock takes on a special character. At this time of year the birds keep to dense vegetation on woodland fringes and in marshy brakes, except for rare and almost exclusively nocturnal sorties for food. They venture into the open at one time only: on wet autumn days when gray clouds lour heavily and a fine drizzle falls day and night; when all distant objects appear as in a mist, and the light seems like endless twilight; when everything is soaking wet, and heavy drops fall steadily and sonorously from the dark, drooping boughs. These drops, which all birds and animals dislike, drive the woodcock not only from the forest depths but also from the fringes and the bushes. Indeed there is something mournful and frightening about the monotonous, incessant drip of raindrops in the forest. I have often had occasion to listen to that strange sound, and involuntarily lose myself in thought, to be roused with a start as a large, cold drop painfully struck me in the face. . . . Thus, quite apart from the alarming sound of it, the dripping moisture disturbs the birds and compels them to keep moving from one place to another.

However, the shooting can be wonderful when the woodcock come out of the forest into open meadows or marshland. By "open" I do not mean places offering no cover at all. The woodcock is not a small bird. It needs tussocks to take cover in, or thick, unmown grass, or field boundaries where wild peach and pea-shrub grow, or the deep furrows plowed for winter crops, and this within a short distance of woodland or scrub. As soon as the rain stops, if only for a while, and the dripping from the trees becomes intermittent, the woodcock return to the forest, whence they rarely emerge further than a few paces and to which they speedily return if startled, in spite of rain and ubiquitous moisture. At such times the birds are lethargic. They sit tight, permit a sportsman to approach closely and are slow to take wing when a dog is pointing. They are easy targets, particularly because in wet weather they themselves are wet and slow on the wing in the open, like crows. Only a very bad shot, or a very hot-headed one, could miss them. One might suppose that such easy sport could bring no pleasure to a true sportsman of experience and skill, but this kind of shooting occurs but rarely, lasts only a short while, and usually yields few birds. It is so unusual, and the woodcock so highly prized, that the circumstances detract nothing.

The other pleasure of this kind of shooting is that of admiring a good gun-dog in all its beauty. In woodland, in scrub, in reed-beds, tall grass, and sedge, you see little of your dog, whereas here it is in full view. Woodcock have a strong scent and all dogs follow it avidly. Only dedicated sportsmen can appreciate all the charm of the scene when a dog, pausing frequently, finally goes right up to a sitting woodcock, raises its paw and stands trembling as in a fever, its eager eyes spellbound and seeming to turn green, fixed to the spot where the bird is sitting. It stands as if graven in stone, rooted to the spot, as sportsmen say.

8. HARES

As I have said, besides game birds there are also game animals, such as bears, deer, wild boar, wild goats, and hares. Of these I am well acquainted only with hares and it is these that I now intend to speak of.

In the province of Orenburg, and, I believe, in all others, three varieties of hare breed: brown hares, blue or mountain hares, and *tumak* hares. I do not include the "ground hare" or chipmunk, which is not used for food. The name *rusak* for the brown hare probably owes nothing to the fact that it lives in Russia, but more likely derives from the fact that even in winter its back remains gray or light brown (*rusyi*). The mountain hare, or *beliak* is so called because its fur is completely white (*belyi*) in winter. The *tumak*, being the product of mating between the brown and mountain hares, bears a name that describes its origin, as *tumak* means "cross-bred."[36]

The brown hare and the *tumak* usually frequent the steppe or treeless hills, while the blue hare lives in the forest. But exceptions can always be found: sometimes blue hares occur in the steppe and sometimes (for example, near Moscow) brown hares appear in forested areas, but they never spend the day sleeping in deep woodland, always on open ground or in thin scrub. An old brown hare is always larger and fatter than a blue hare of the same age, and is at the same time somehow better proportioned. The brown hare has sharper ears, and its limbs, especially its forepaws, are smaller and neater, which is why its tracks can always be told at once from those of the other kind. It is well known that the brown hare is incomparably faster than the mountain hare, with rare exceptions, but the fleet-footed *tumak* outstrips even the fastest brown hare. In summer the brown hare is the same gray color as the mountain hare, and they cannot easily be told apart, as the summer brown hare differs only in its black, slightly longer scut, black-tipped ears, and the ruddier tint on its breast and flanks, but in winter they are quite dissimilar: the mountain hare is snow-white, while the brown hare, especially an older specimen, has a pale yellowish breast and belly, and along its spine runs a fairly broad and very beautiful band composed of dark, yellowish and russet speckles in small spiral patterns or curls, rather like the fleece of the large Crimean mountain lamb. The *tumak* retains all the features of the gray and mountain hares, but in less distinct form: the yellow on the breast and belly is barely visible, the band on the back is narrow, without curls, and its coloration is neither bright, nor mottled, but grayish.

Hares are extraordinarily prolific breeders, especially the mountain variety, as brown hares are far less numerous, and *tumaks* are rare. In mountain hares the rut begins in January, and in late March, while there is still snow on the ground, the doe gives birth to her first young of the season.[37] In June comes the second litter, and in late September the third, or so peasant hunters tell me. For my part I am ill-equipped to dispute this and can only say with certainty that I have come across new-born leverets at all three seasons. Whether one and the same doe gives birth three times a year I do not know. Judging by the astonishing rate of reproduction of hares within a single year, it seems entirely possible. The doe, it is said, is pregnant for nine weeks and gives birth to up to nine young, born blind, apparently, and suckled for up to twelve days. There are naturalists, however, who maintain that gestation lasts four weeks, that the young number three to six, and that they are suckled for one week. I do not know who is right, but I am very doubtful about the supposed four-week term, as it is too short.

The appearance of the hare is well known, but the animal has one remarkable feature: its hind legs, which are much longer, stouter, and stronger than its forepaws and equipped with unusually tough, elastic tendons. This is the source of its extraordinarily agile leaps, sometimes up to seven feet, and of its marvelous speed.[38] By crouching down on its hind paws, that is, bending them fully at the joint, and pushing off from a firm footing, the hare is able to extend them with such speed and power that they literally hurl its body into the air; no sooner have its forepaws touched the ground than the hind paws, reaching forward far ahead of the forepaws, push off again with the same power, so that the running motion looks like a line stretched through the air. There is no doubt that the speed of these bounds is aided by a very strong spine. It is clear why hares find it awkward to run downhill and easy to run uphill. They always avoid the former, but when forced to do so by pursuit, mostly by borzoi dogs, they will often roll in a ball from the top of a hill to the bottom. The hare does not walk but bounds. It is even unable to stand on all four paws at once, and as soon as it stops running it sits up on its haunches, as its hind paws are so long. It is particularly adept at suddenly stopping in full flight and sitting up. I should add that the hare cannot turn its neck, so it cannot look back. If it hears a sound behind it or to one side it flings its whole body in that direction, using the power of its hind legs, sits on its haunches like a marmot, and pricks up its long ears. Hares are herbivorous animals, although they have very sharp teeth, which can inflict a painful bite if you grasp the animal clumsily: a live hare should always be held by the ears and hind legs. When there is grass, hares will eat it, as well as leaves and cereals. They are particularly fond of winter cereals. In winter they gnaw the bark of trees, especially young aspens and willows, and in the steppe they will rake away quite deep snow with their paws to get at the old grass underneath. Gardens can be severely ravaged throughout the winter if certain precautions are not taken.

The hare has a distinctive, piteous cry, like that of a baby. This cry is given when it is injured and in the clutches or jaws of a foe. During the rutting season it has a different cry, which hunters mimic in order to lure the animal toward them.

The hare is a timorous and defenseless creature. Its timidity shows in all its hasty movements and is recorded in the Russian saying "as timid as a hare." I myself have seen one trembling as it sat in its hiding-place, or "form," ready to spring out at any moment on hearing noises coming toward it. It has reason to fear animals and birds; only at night or in twilight does it emerge from its daytime refuge. For hares, nighttime completely replaces daytime and all night long they run about, feed, and frolic, and generally do everything that nature demands of them; at daybreak they select concealed places, lie down with their eyes open and sleep lightly, thanks to their distinctive short eyelids, until evening, with their long ears lying along their backs, constantly twitching their noses, which are fringed with sparse but quite long white whiskers. During the long nights of autumn and winter a hare may travel several versts, especially over open fields and hills, as every hunter who has tracked hares by following their trails knows from experience.

The Russian people speak of the hare as being cross-eyed. Its eyes are large and bulging, though they do not squint, as everybody knows, but, as the animal is timid and hurried in its movements and unable to look round, it sometimes darts straight toward somebody or something, stops suddenly, darts in another direction and again runs straight toward something. It may be because of these awkward movements that it is called "cross-eyed," and the epithet of "cross-eyed hare" is applied in jest to a person who hurries past something he has been looking for or dashes to the wrong place. Besides this, when in its "form," the animal sometimes rolls one eye upward under its lid, and sometimes both. Perhaps it does this to sleep, but at first sight it appears cross-eyed.

Everything that can kill hares does so: wolves, foxes, domestic and hunting dogs (which go after them in the forest on their own), and even stoats and weasels, as I have already mentioned. But in addition to those enemies that seek them by their scent on the ground, there are others in the sky above: eagles and large hawks are waiting to seize them the moment they are compelled to leave their daytime lairs, their "forms," for any reason. If the "form" is poorly chosen, with insufficient grass or shrubs to cover it (on open ground), it will be spotted even here by the extraordinarily keen-eyed steppe eagle, the biggest and most powerful of all birds of prey, so big that it looks like a hay-cock blackened by rain when perched on a marmot mound or hay-rick. Seeing the poor hare, it will fall on it suddenly from the clouds with a noise like the rush of an oncoming storm, carry it off a long distance in its long, sharp talons, land at a convenient spot and devour practically all of it, including its fur and small bones. As if this were not enough, the larger owls lie in wait at night to catch hares at their peaceful frolics.[39] One hunter whose opinion I trust has told me that golden and other eagles hunt hares by following their tracks. This is rather strange, since these eagles are creatures of the air, not the ground, but the proof of the matter is that these predators are sometimes caught in clam-traps set for hares at precisely the points where a number of hare-tracks meet.[40]

It is possible to shoot blue hares and even brown hares on occasion at any time of year, but the season proper, especially for blue hares, begins in spring, near larger and medium-sized rivers and on islands surrounded on all sides by meltwater. Such shooting can be very productive; there may sometimes be many hares on a small island, and, having been frightened by hunters, they run frantically this way and that, like a scattered herd of startled sheep. Some leap into the water out of fear and sometimes swim quite long distances. At this season they are killed in large numbers, but this kind of shooting has never appealed to me; it is rather like slaughtering penned cattle. I have always preferred shooting blue hares in spring, when they usually go to ground amid the snowdrifts that remain for a long time after everything around has thawed, as long white ridges on the edges of woodland and in scrub. The snow hardens, like ice, and easily supports a hunter's weight. Hares like to lie up among the snowdrifts during the day, after their nighttime forays in search of food. This shooting is best when several hunters work together: one, two, or three of them, depending on the breadth of the drift, should work their way along the ridge itself, while the others walk along the edges; the hares will spring up in a leisurely fashion, and, being reluctant to leave the snow, will run toward one of the hunters. When this shooting ends the hare season closes until autumn, although even in summer, when the hares in the forest suffer from ticks, they come out, especially in the early morning and evening, into open glades, onto roads, and woodland fringes. If you walk or ride along a forest road you can always shoot a few blue hares, always with several ticks that have buried themselves in their skin, fed on their blood, and hang like blue prunes. I have never gone out at this season specifically in search of hares, but have shot them when they chanced to appear. In spring and late summer, after hay-making, and in autumn, hares may also be shot after pursuit by hounds, and many take great pleasure in this social sport, especially in late autumn, when all the hares are white and when some larger form of game, such as a wolf or a fox, may suddenly spring from cover with the hares. I do not dispute the pleasures of this autumn shooting, but we all have our own likes and dislikes: I do not enjoy hunting that involves co-operation with others who may not be hunters at all, and I must admit that I am not fond of hounds or borzois so I do not like hunting with dogs.

The best blue hare–shooting takes place in late autumn, when the hares have turned white and can be seen from afar. Here the precondition is a long, wet autumn; if it is short and dry the hares do not have time to shed their summer coats, and snow often falls while they are still in their summer brown. In wet weather they dislike the damp and rub themselves constantly against trees, bushes, or haycocks, or simply roll on the ground. In the opinion of hunters, they turn white faster because the rubbing removes the thin, gray fur of summer and in its place grows the tougher white winter fur. They do not turn white all at once: first they become roan, then the outer part of the hind paws turns white, giving rise to the expression "a hare in trousers," then the belly goes white, followed by all the other parts. Reddish-gray fur remains only in a spot on the forehead and a stripe along the back. At last the hare is all as white as snow.[41]

In the distance an indistinct white shape shows up at moments against the dark ground: in the forest, in scrub, in open fields, and even in the steppe, where blue hares sometimes lie up, the experienced hunter's eye knows by some sort of sixth sense, even at a distance, that this is a hare, although comical errors can occur. It is curious that this kind of shooting should be so very popular among all true sportsmen, not to mention the ordinary hunter seeking a large bag. On the face of it, there is no particular attraction. You usually sight the hare from afar, you can draw close to it, as it sits tight in wet weather, knowing by instinct that a white animal has nowhere to hide from its foes on bare, black ground, and that even crows and magpies will fall upon it from all sides with such fury and uproar that in terror it will not know which way to turn . . . so you draw near, or you notice it unexpectedly at close range, take aim, fire and kill it. There is no more to it than that. What is so appealing, exciting or satisfying about it? . . .

Nothing at all, yet I myself, now considering the matter so calmly and rationally, well remember how in the past I passionately loved this shooting, despite the ceaseless drenching rain that sometimes damped my powder in the pan, despite the wretched flashes that sometimes drove me to despair (we then used flintlocks), for days on end—it is true that the days were short—I would walk dozens of versts, soaked to the skin, neither eating nor drinking, in search of white hares. . . . And I was not the only one. What were the reasons for this? I have discussed this many times with many other hunters. All agree that it is strange, and each has his own explanation: one would say that a hare is a large animal and that a hunter is always keen to bring home something big; another would speak of the pleasure of shooting hares in season, when they have changed color, so that the skin can be made use of and will not go to waste. There is some truth in this, but I suspect that there is another reason, an emotional one, so to speak, or a purely sporting one: the autumn shooting of white hares is not nearly so easy and straightforward as it may appear at first sight, as can be seen from the number of misses, particularly by novices before they develop the knack. These occur because the hare's "form" is almost always protected: it may be covered by small branches and twigs, if the hare is lying under the crown of a fallen tree—a favorite place. It may be shielded by tree-stumps, by long, dry grass, or by other litter of the kind that can always be found under bushes or in dense woodland. There is no need to explain that if the shot strikes any obstacle in its path it will be deflected and will miss its target. But beyond this, a shot can miss a hare lying on completely open ground in the steppe. In my opinion this happens because in the grass you can see only the top of the white fur, which the animal always raises as it huddles in its "form." If you take aim at the outer edge of the white fur, the shot will be too high, and it may sometimes happen (as has happened to me) that the shot blows off some white fur and scatters it in a semicircle round the "form," and the hare runs away. However, a hunter of experience knows this secret and aims lower; a close-packed charge of shot will fling the killed hare into the air and at close range on open ground there is no danger of missing. Add to all this the fact that you sometimes see something white in the distance and approach uncertainly, now taking it for a hare, now supposing it to be a piece of white bone; at times the white spot is hidden from view as your angle of vision constantly alters and various objects get in the way; finally, once quite sure that it is a hare, you rarely have the patience to approach closely, fearing that you may make a noise and spring it. So the hunter, especially the most ardent, will fire at long range. . . . This is the reason why so many shots miss, and this is why this kind of hare-shooting so excites hunters' passion, and why they so love it.

In a long, mild, damp autumn, in years when hares are plentiful, hare-shooting can be very productive: I myself have shot as many as twenty-four in one field—a whole cartload. In continuous wet weather blue hares come out of the forest to escape the water dripping from the trees and frequent its edges and even open fields. I remember many such autumns; sometimes, as you drive toward a small isolated hillock or a belt of woodland, you espy scattered whitish spots, even on winter crops—these are hares. In one such autumn, in 1816, on 28 October, I shot a blue hare of enormous size. It gave me a terrible fright: I was walking through the forest with a companion on a gray misty day, having shot many hares and hung them on branches for collection later. As dusk was gathering I suddenly saw the shape of a huge mountain hare, squatting on its haunches—as it seemed to me—three feet above the ground. Hunters tend to be superstitious, and I do not mind admitting that at first I was quite shaken; I stood without moving for a long time, thinking that I was imagining things, and that the optical illusion would vanish. At last I calmed down, screwed up my courage, and realized that the huge hare was not hanging in the air but sitting on the stout stump of a lime tree, as hares often do. It was sitting slightly sideways to me, its ears and forepaws twitching as it listened to the sounds, and had evidently not noticed me. The range was short, both barrels were loaded with large goose-shot, so I collected myself, took aim and fired. The hare gave an unusually piercing and piteous squeal and fell like a sack to the ground. . . . I fled and sought out my companion and with him and our driver returned to the spot where I had killed the freak hare: killed outright, it was lying beside the stump, and indeed it was a wonder! At least half as big again, if not twice as big, as the biggest full-grown brown hare! All over its body it had some kind of lumps under its skin, and in its cheeks, also under the skin, there were hard, fleshy protuberances almost the size of a fist. I kept the animal for a long time and showed it to hunters, but nobody was willing to eat the flesh of such a monster. A peasant hunter explained to me that this was a prize specimen of a kind that appears once in a hundred years. It is a great pity that I did not stuff it and even failed to weigh or measure the freak animal, in which excessive growth had reached the scale of abnormality.

But there is another kind of hare-shooting that, in my view, is even better sport, though less productive—it can even be tiresome and produce scant rewards: this is the shooting of brown hares in fresh snow. Occasionally *tumaks*, exactly the same in their habits as brown hares, may turn up among them. Here the skill that is required is that of tracking the hare, of following its trail to the end, to its "form," and shooting it there or as it runs. This skill can only be developed by practice. If in the early morning you pick up last night's trail from the moment the hare left its "form," in the fine powdery snow you can follow it until noon with little effort. At first the hare runs and gambols to warm up, then it feeds, then frolics again, before eating again and at dawn setting off to settle down for the day in its "form," which is usually one of several in different places, although there are exceptions. As it prepares to settle down the hare first "casts loops," two to four in number; that is, it circles round to its own tracks two, three, or even four times, leaps sideways, runs a little further, and finally, sometimes after another triple loop, it makes several large bounds and settles down in its "form" for the day. Sometimes the spot will not be to its liking and it will seek another. This is all variable, depending on the type of snow and the weather: if the snow is shallow and the weather cold, the hare travels a lot; if not, it travels little. Furthermore, the later the snowfall begins, the shorter the tracks, so if there has been a heavy fall that ceased at dawn (as quite often happens), you will find the hare where you see its tracks, as all earlier tracks will have been covered; this means of course that tracks are fewer. On foot this type of hunting is very hard work, so one should seek the trails on horseback, or better still in a light sleigh; it is not necessary to sort out all the tangled tracks, but to ride round them and count the entry and exit points: if there is an outgoing track missing, the hare is somewhere in the middle, although this does not often happen. Having found the last exit and established that the hare has started "casting loops," the hunter should follow the trail on foot with his gun at the ready and both hammers cocked, as the "form" will be somewhere close by and no time should be lost. One should not be overconcerned about the freshness of the tracks, but should check that there is no deviation to one side and that the hare is not lying nearby. It sometimes happens that it springs up and runs away without your hearing the slightest sound or noticing its movement, and you only realize your quarry has eluded you when you reach the "form" and see its departing tracks. However, the hare does not go far during the day before settling down again; after giving it a short time in which to recover, you can soon track it down again, but at its second "form" it will sit less tightly than at the first. A brown hare's favorite sites are beside marmot warrens, where it lies down right beside a burrow and takes cover at the first sign of danger; then there are snowdrifts along field boundaries and gullies, where it burrows a little way into the snow. If there is a breeze blowing over the snow the entrance may be completely blocked. Here the hare may sit so tight that I have sometimes had to kick away the snow to make the animal come out. . . . But what a joy it is to see a big, handsome hare leap out in a shower of snow and fly across the open field, and to end its flight with a well-aimed shot that sends it cartwheeling on before sprawling full-length in the snow!

Before the snow is deep enough for the hares to burrow in, brown hares will usually make their "forms" in bushy, overgrown dells, or along boundary strips where the snow collects under long grass. Sometimes they descend into frozen reedmarshes, where these are present, and select large hummocks for their "forms." In the open steppe they lie under clumps of feather-grass. Of course you cannot track down and kill many hares in a day at this season, and when winter sets in irrevocably, bringing snowfalls during the day instead of at night, and if the snow soon forms a crust that will bear the weight of a hare but not a hunter, so that it crunches underfoot and scares the quarry, this appealing sport becomes impossible.

Brown hares are very partial to bread grains, which is why they constantly visit threshing floors on the outskirts of villages, and even lie up on them for the day. They may be so fearless that, in spite of the peasants at work every day, the hum of activity and the clatter of flails, they remain peacefully in their "forms." These "threshing-floor hares" are fatter and sprightlier than others. I have often found them and shot them at threshing floors. Once in my presence a brown hare was caught right beside a threshing floor, in a huge pile of long logs in which it had taken refuge for the day: a peasant who had been drying the threshing floor noticed the hare going in early in the morning and blocked the entrance hole. Near Moscow, where cereals are threshed in autumn, hares visit hay barns and eat hay. Blue hares sometimes do the same. A grain-fed brown hare may sometimes grow so fat that without seeing one it is hard to believe: the hind quarters alone may yield up to two pounds of fat. And how much is left on the rest of the body? Hares like these have splendid flavor, and no blue hare, however fat, can ever compare with them. Generally speaking, hares have a pronounced, agreeable game flavor: the meat is very nourishing, even invigorating. Only fairly recently, in my own lifetime, ordinary folk would not eat hares; now in some places they are beginning to use the hind quarters as food, while rejecting the fore quarters, saying that these are like dog meat. Here I am speaking of the peasants of distant Simbirsk and Orenburg; those in the Moscow region are probably less strict in their observance of popular superstition.

The most potent enemy of hares of all varieties is man, and the shotgun is by no means the most dangerous implement of their destruction. Thousands are killed by borzoi dogs and borzoi crosses (much favored by Mordvin, Chuvash, and Tartar hunters), in snares or nets, and clam-traps.

Large-grade shot, Number One or Two, should be used for shooting hares. In addition to the fact that you often have to fire at long range, hares, though having little resistance to gunshot, are protected by their downy fur, which counters the effect of even large shot, while smaller shot gets lost in it. At short range, of course, shot of any size will kill a hare.

Besides the three varieties I have described, in the province of Orenburg one may occasionally encounter black hares of the same size and shape, but I have never seen one.

9. SMALL BIRDS

I should like to say a few words about some small birds that may be served as food and that have excellent flavor, especially when they are fat. Nobody would call these birds "game," and true fowlers seldom shoot them, unless it be to unload their guns or because there is no real game to shoot. Commercial trappers, however, catch them mostly for sale. I shall not describe these birds but merely list some of them: they include starlings, larks, waxwings, yellowhammers, bullfinches, and many others. In Okhotnyi Riad in Moscow they may almost always be found threaded on strings by their beaks and hanging in pretty clusters.[42] Chefs use them in sauces and pâtés, and gourmets speak favorably of these dishes containing "little birds."

Some hunters shoot and eat cuckoos; I have tried them and found them quite tasty. But incomparably superior to all others are the snow buntings.[43] Flocks of these little birds, similar in size and shape to the larks that everybody knows, appear in Orenburg province in winter and depart with the melting snow in spring. Their plumage is quite handsome: they are speckled or dappled with very varied color-shading, consisting of the following colors: bluish-gray to gray, dark to a reddish tinge, irregularly distributed over a brilliant white background; some individuals are almost pure white. In March, with the approach of spring, they begin to turn gray, and in summer they probably turn completely gray, but I do not know where they spend the summer and breed.

They bear the name *podorozhnik* on account of their habit of always clustering along roadsides, sometimes in quite large flocks.[44] They are especially fond of threshing floors. They feed happily on all sorts of grain, and I have always found their crops filled mostly with oats. When startled by travelers, snow buntings always fly a short distance forward and settle again on the road, repeating this maneuver many times, until at last, tiring of this repeated forward flight, they fly back, round the traveler and land on the road behind him. I have heard that they sing, and have tried keeping them in cages, but my attempts were always unsuccessful: the birds ate very well, but after a time began to limp, then turned on their backs and died. I cannot establish whether this was due to the warmth or the confinement of the cage. Once when some village boys netted a large number of snow buntings in January, I put about a hundred in a cold room, where they lived happily until late March. They were very plump and tasty. All were cooked for the table, so I do not know how they might have fared in warm air.

NOTES

Preface

1. As this book goes into its third edition, I must gratefully say that I have not been disappointed by the response from hunters and educated people generally. There have been many flattering responses. My modest work has been received much more favorably and accorded a much higher appraisal from all than I ever dared to hope.

2. Using a small pipe made from a goose quill or the bark of a lime twig, one may produce a note resembling the whistle of the hazel grouse.

3. Anyone who has walked on this crust in spring will be familiar with this phenomenon: whole glades seem to groan and suddenly sag. The unusual muffled rumble, with the shuddering of the entire surface of the snowy mass on which you are standing, has a powerful and unpleasant effect upon the nerves. The sensation is like an electric shock passing through a chain of people from a Leyden jar.

4. Aksakov's use of terms for certain species of waterfowl will be the subject of detailed notes in Category II. *Trans.*

5. The snipe is popularly known as "the wild sheep," because as it plunges vertically downward it partly folds one wing while flapping the other so hard that the wind resistance produces a sound like that of a lamb bleating. This is a view held by peasants and hunters alike, but an esteemed professor who has been kind enough to comment on my work explains the drumming as follows: "The bird flings itself downward at high speed with wings extended, making no movement with them. Wind resistance causes strong vibrations in the tips of the primaries and produces the sound."

[More recent studies have established that the sound is produced by the vibrations of the outer tailfeathers. *Trans.*]

6. The word for "game" (*dich'*) is closely related to the adjective *dikii* (wild). *Trans.*

Category I: Marshland Game

1. Russian has borrowed French *bécasse* for "common snipe" and uses *dupel'shnep* (from German, *Dopfelschnepfe*), *garshnep* (*Haarschnepfe*) and *val'dshnep* (*Waldschnepfe*) for the great snipe, jack snipe, and woodcock respectively. *Trans.*

2. See note 5 in the Preface on the source of this sound. *Trans.*

3. Aksakov gives all dates according to the Julian calendar in use at the time in Russia, rather than the Gregorian calendar, which was twelve days ahead. "Early April" therefore means 12 April or a little later by the new style. *Trans.*

4. By "social display ground" (Russian, *tok*) we mean a place where birds of certain game species gather in spring to mate and where the males, always far more numerous, fight.

5. The verb *tokovat'* is used of the snipe, but in a different sense from that given above, in imitation of the note. *Trans.*

6. This species is also known in English as the "double snipe." *Trans.*

7. Wildfowlers from the provinces of Penza and Simbirsk have told me that jack snipe are very numerous there and that it is possible to shoot forty or more in one field.

8. One hunter, however, did tell me that he had shot a very young bird, hardly able to fly, at Strel'naia, near Saint Petersburg, in a very wet marsh.

9. A fowler I know once shot four jack snipe on 6 November, beside springs, when there was already a substantial covering of snow.

10. The Russian name used here, *ogar'*, has since become the standard term for the ruddy shelduck. *Trans.*

11. N. T. Aksakov, a keen hunter and skilled observer to whom I am indebted for much information, tells me that he has found young greenshanks and nests in mossy bogs in large pine forests.

12. One fowler has told me that he once shot young snipe on 4 June, but this is quite exceptional.

13. *Chernysh* has become the standard modern name. *Trans.*

14. The same fowler tells me that green sandpipers breed in marshy spots within large forests.

15. The bill is not straight but downcurved at the tip. As for the coloration of the dunlin, Aksakov apparently knew the bird only in its breeding plumage and seems unaware of its very different appearance outside this season. *Trans.*

16. Kirikov points out that in the southwestern foothills of the Urals dunlin occur on both spring and autumn passage. S. T. Aksakov, *Zapiski ruzheinogo okhotnika Orenburgskoi gubernii*, edited by S. V. Kirikov (Moscow, 1953), 69. *Trans.*

17. Kirikov notes that K. F. Rul'e hesitated to identify this bird on the basis of the brief description, but the angle of the bill noted by Aksakov led M. A. Menzbir to conclude that the description does indeed refer to the Terek Sandpiper, now known as *morodunka*. Aksakov, *Zapiski*, 70. *Trans.*

18. Mashinsky quotes Menzbir as saying Aksakov was mistaken on this point, as this species nowhere congregates in huge numbers on passage. S. Aksakov, *Sobranie sochinenii v piati tomakh*, ed. S. Mashinsky, vol. 5 (Moscow, 1966), 465. *Trans.*

19. Aksakov is referring to the ringed plover (*Charadrius hiaticula*); in modern Russian, *galstuchnik*. *Trans.*

20. Aksakov's description of the ruff, particularly the division into two varieties, indicates some confusion, apparently due to the extreme sexual dimorphism of this species. Taxonomists do not distinguish any subspecies. *Trans.*

21. There is too little detail to allow more than the most tentative identification. Did Aksakov see avocets or black-winged stilts? *Trans.*

22. To my surprise this has happened to me several times and other hunters have had the same experience. The gun "hangs fire": this indicates that the powder in the touch-hole is slightly damp, it hisses, and the discharge is slightly delayed. There is no doubt that the muzzle will wander off target, usually dropping slightly. How then is it possible to kill a bird on the wing? All such cases only serve to demonstrate how widely the charge scatters.

23. Kirikov reports Menzbir's view, that this was a water rail (Rallus aquaticus). Aksakov, *Zapiski*, 82. *Trans.*

24. This word—also used in Polish with the same meaning—is well known in Russian, but with the meaning "seagull." *Trans.*

Category II: Waterfowl

1. Kirikov notes that Aksakov's description appears to be of the appearance of *Cygnus olor*, the mute swan, but his description of its voice suggests that he had also heard the call of *Cygnus cygnus*, the whooper swan, as the latter has a more resonant cry than the former. Aksakov does not distinguish the species of swans. S. T. Aksakov, *Zapiski ruzheinogo okhotnika Orenburgskoi gubernii*, edited by S. V. Kirikov (Moscow, 1953), 94. *Trans.*

2. In this respect waterfowl are quite the opposite of certain grassland birds; in grouse, partridges, and quail, the wingfeathers appear first, so that the young can fly while the body is still covered in down, whereas in waterfowl the wingfeathers develop last, so that a well-grown and feathered gosling or duckling displays the ugly sight of its naked, blue stumps.

3. After the night's roost, the crop is already empty. The digested food in it has passed into the intestines.

4. Strictly speaking, this term, without adjectives, could refer to either of the smaller "black geese," brant (*Branta bernicla*) or barnacle (*Branta leucopsis*). This description, however, points to the former. *Trans.*

5. The verse is from Aksakov's own poem of 1823, "Letter to My Brother." *Trans.*

6. A. Preobrazhensky (*Etimologicheskii slovar' russkogo iazyka*, Moscow, 1959) says "origin unknown" but tentatively posits a connection with the northern Sviiaga River. Max Vasmer, in *Russisches Etymologisches Wörterbuch* (Heidelberg, 1958), concurs. The form is not so distant from the more obviously onomatopoeic *svistun* ("whistler," cited by Vasmer) as to preclude an echoic element. See W. B. Lockwood, *The Oxford Dictionary of British Bird Names* (Oxford, 1993), 166, on the derivation of English "wigeon." *Trans.*

7. Some fowlers aver that wigeon and teal do in fact flight to cereal fields.

8. The first element of *plutonos, pluto-*, may be related to the verb *plutat'*, "to wander, roam"; *nos* = "nose, beak." *Trans.*

9. This is one of Aksakov's less accurate descriptions. It has been slightly amended in translation. Aksakov has, more literally, "rich-brown throat" [*zob*], and "light gray belly," which hardly match the chestnut belly, white breast, and bottle-green head and throat of this species. Could Aksakov have been momentarily thinking of the mallard drake (already described)? *Trans.*

10. Note a dialect English term for the garganey, "crick" (also "cricket-teal") used in East Anglia, and "imitative of the high-pitched rattle heard from the courting drake"; Lockwood, *Oxford Dictionary of British Bird Names*, 49. *Trans.*

11. Some fowlers hold to the view that teal never eat fish, and so can never smell of it. But this view is not always correct, or rather, not universally correct.

12. *Bucephala clangula.* Aksakov's nonstandard use of certain names can give rise to confusion here. Kirikov concludes that Aksakov's *nyrok*, which in standard modern terminology signifies the pochard (*Aythya ferina*), is the goldeneye (*Bucephala clangula*), for which the modern term is *gogol'*. Aksakov, *Zapiski*, 124. (Compare similar confusion in popular English terms for this and related species, noted by T. A. Coward, *The Birds of the British Isles and Their Eggs*, ser. 2, 5th ed. [London: Frederick Warne and Co., Ltd. 1936] 58.) In turn, Aksakov applies the term *gogol'* to the merganser family. See also the notes on *gagara* under 3I Great Crested Grebe. *Trans.*

13. It is not clear which species Aksakov is referring to here. *Trans.*

14. I have recently learned from a fowler who can be relied upon that he has found broods of tufted duck in the province of Orenburg. I can only explain my error by saying that I must have confused them with broods of wigeon or goldeneye: the females are very similar. [This last observation suggests further confusion. The females of the tufted duck and pochard may be said to resemble each other, but those of the tufted duck, wigeon, and goldeneye much less. *Trans.*]

15. Kirikov points out that *gagara* (in modern Russian, *gagara:* diver/loon) is apparently used by Aksakov for a bird of the grebe family, most likely the great crested grebe (modern Russian, *bol'shaia poganka, chemga*; *Podiceps cristatus*). Aksakov, *Zapiski*, 127. This matter is further complicated by an illustration from the third edition (1857), reproduced in Aksakov, *Sobranie sochinenii*, edited by S. Mashinsky, vol. 5 (Moscow, 1966), 150, showing not a great crested grebe but a very lifelike black-necked (or eared) grebe (modern Russian, *Chernosheinaia poganka; Podiceps nigricollis*). Note that, according to T. A. Coward, local English names for this species include "diver" and "loon." Coward, *The Birds of the British Isles*, 307. *Trans.*

16. Aksakov's original opinion was correct: grebes and goosanders (British name for the common merganser) are indeed different species, and

belong to different families. Grebes (*podiceps*) are not close to anatidae (ducks). Great crested grebes of both sexes have crests, but only during the breeding season. *Trans.*

17. K. F. Rul'e made the point that the toes of the grebe family are not fully webbed, as Aksakov states here, but rather lobed, as in the coot. Rul'e is quoted by Mashinsky in Aksakov, *Sobranie sochinenii*, 5:466. *Trans.*

18. Aksakov observes in a footnote that the peasants sometimes used the term *gagara* for the coot. Vladimir Dal' confirms the imprecision of popular usage, including *gagara* for "coot." In modern terminology, *krokhal'* is merganser. Vladimir Dal', *Tolkovyi slovar' zhivogo velikorusskago iazyka*, vol. 1 (Tokyo, 1934) (reprinted from the 4th ed.), 836. (The 1978 Moscow edition, reprinted from the 2d ed., does not include this word.) *Trans.*

19. Most authorities posit an echoic origin for this name. See notes 12, 15, and 18 above on Aksakov's use of it. *Trans.*

20. It is not clear which of two species Aksakov is describing: *bol'shoi krokhal'* (North American, common merganser/British, goosander), or *srednii krokhal'* (red-breasted merganser). *Gogol'* (in modern terminology, "goldeneye") is used in place of modern Russian *krokhal'* for merganser. Kirikov comments: "The descriptions of the plumage and particularly the upper mandible lead one to suppose that Aksakov used the word 'gogol" for the female merganser. At the same time, in describing this bird, he indicates certain features which are characteristic of grebes." Aksakov, *Zapiski*, 129. *Trans.*

21. Here Aksakov repeats and compounds his earlier error: the sexes of the sawbill species are quite distinct; only the female is described here; the "greater" species is *Mergus merganser*, the common merganser (British, "goosander"), and the "lesser," in modern Russian taxonomy "middle" (*srednii krokhal'*), is *Mergus serrator*, the red-breasted merganser. *Trans.*

22. It is easy to establish that the plaster is indeed the dung of the coot by comparing it with fresh droppings, which are always plentiful around the top of the nest.

Category III: Steppe and Grassland Game

1. The fruit of the wild peach consists of small beans the size of a small coin and heart-shaped. The nuts, which have the taste of bitter almonds and possibly their other properties too, are contained in a firm, hard shell, covered in a greenish furry skin. In Orenburg province, oil is extracted from them. The oil has such a sharp, penetrating taste and scent that one spoonful of it in a bottle of poppy-seed oil is enough to lend the whole bottle a powerful and agreeable aromatic taste. If more wild-peach oil is applied it produces headaches and stomach-aches.

2. Among Bashkir horses, amblers are very common. They almost always have large heads and humped backs and are not well built for speed, but they are very tranquil-natured mounts and the Bashkirs are fond of riding them.

3. Marmot mounds are the spoil-heaps thrown up by marmots while excavating their burrows, which are sometimes very deep, always have two entrances, and run for some distance underground. The main or front entrance is broad and well trodden by constant comings and goings. The back entrance is less obvious and used only in emergencies. These mounds—sometimes substantial hillocks if the marmot family is large—consist initially of black soil, but as digging progresses the marmots scrape out more clay and gravel, so that from a distance the mounds look red, until they become densely overgrown with pea-shrub and wild peach.

4. Ukrainian also has *drokhva*. The origins of this word are uncertain. A Turkic origin has been suggested but this view is not universally accepted. See Maks Fasmer [Max Vasmer], *Etimologicheskii slovar' russkogo iazyka*, vol. 1 (Moscow, 1964), 542. *Trans.*

5. Some wildfowlers hold a different view but I, judging by the evidence of other birds, do not believe the great bustard nests or rears its young in growing crops. It is probable, however, that it takes its young to them at an early age.

6. The Russian equivalent of "a bird in the hand is worth two in the bush." *Trans.*

7. A cold kvass soup with chopped meat. *Trans.*

8. The Russian name is related to the verb *vstrepenut'sia* (to rouse oneself with a start). *Trans.*

9. The standard Russian form *kronshnep* is borrowed from the German *Kronschnepfe*, now replaced by *Brachvogel*. *Trans.*

10. *Numenius arquata*, *Numenius phaeopus*, and *Numenius tenuirostris*. Menzbir queried Aksakov's assertion that the last-named was the most common. Quoted in Aksakov, *Sobranie sochinenii*, 5:466. In the twentieth century it has become very rare in the region. *Trans.*

11. Along the steppe roads of Orenburg, regular milestones are placed, tall and quite stout. I should add that curlew will readily perch on the boughs of dead trees and on tree-stumps.

12. The name is related to *kuritsa* (hen). *Trans.*

13. For this interesting description I am obliged to I. P. Akh-v.

14. There is no doubt as to the origin of the word but Aksakov may understandably be puzzled by its use for this species. It derives from *sivyi* (gray), and would seem more appropriate as a name for *Pluvialis squatarola*, the gray (or black-bellied) plover, a close relative of this bird, which Aksakov apparently did not encounter. *Trans.*

15. The description seems to be of dotterels (*Eudromias morinellus*), as suggested by Menzbir. Quoted in Aksakov, *Sobranie sochinenii*, 5:466. *Trans.*

16. Details are too scant to permit even tentative identification of this species. *Trans.*

17. For the hobby Aksakov uses the term *kobchik*, which, properly speaking, designates *Falco vespertinus*, the red-footed falcon. On the basis of a description under "Woodland Game," Menzbir concluded that Aksakov

was using this name for *Falco subbuteo,* the hobby, generally known by the Russian name *cheglok.* Quoted in Aksakov, *Sobranie sochinenii,* 5:466. *Trans.*

18. Wind-eggs are laid by the hen bird without copulation with a male. Such eggs are laid by all domestic birds, and probably by some wild birds, but young birds never hatch from them. I have tested this on the eggs of chickens, turkeys, and guinea fowl.

19. The Russian phrase is *pod-polot'.* Note that one of the English names of this species, also imitative of the call, is "wet-my-lips"; see T. A. Coward, *The Birds of the British Isles and Their Eggs,* ser. 2, 5th ed. (London: Frederick Warne and Co., Ltd., 1936), 354. See also Lockwood, *Oxford Dictionary of British Bird Names,* "wet-me-lip." *Trans.*

20. Other fowlers have told me, and I have read, that quail kept in cages will fight fiercely over food, but I have not seen this myself.

21. When a falconer's dog finds a quail and stands over it, the falconer raises his arm with his falcon perched on it as high as he can over the quail. On seeing the falcon, being afraid to fly up, a plump and heavy quail will flatten itself out in the grass, pressing down into it, and will often permit the falconer to pick it up.

Category IV: Woodland Game

1. Many settlements have lost all their water forever because of the destruction of the woodland that once shaded the headwaters of their streams or their springs. In some villages, wells have taken their place, while other villages have moved to new sites. I have seen an example of a substantial village situated on a beautiful spring-fed stream (the Bol'shoi Siuiush), which always used to power a mill, losing its water in the space of one year. The cause of this was very simple: during a winter of fierce snowstorms the peasants, in order to avoid traveling too far, felled for firewood the birch and alder carr that surrounded a circular patch of swamp, the source of more than twenty springs that formed the Siuiush. The winter was followed by a dry period and all the springs, now stripped of their cover of trees, dried up, as did the stream. Only two years later, when the vigorous alder had grown up again, did the springs begin to reappear, and only some ten years later did the stream begin to flow.

2. Popular speech refers pejoratively to the "bitter aspen." Its bark is indeed bitter, but hares are partial to the bark of young aspens.

3. An oak may live for many centuries; a lime tree more than a hundred and fifty years; a birch more than a hundred, and an aspen less than a hundred. A sign that a tree is old, even if it has green, but thin foliage, is the downward droop of its main limbs; this is most noticeable in birches when they reach the age of a hundred.

4. The golden oriole has another, quite different cry or squeal, which is harsh and piercing to the ear. Since these notes resemble the repugnant squeals of fighting cats, the bird also bears the popular name of "wild cat."

5. Kirikov points out that in Aksakov's home area, the wooded steppe of the south Urals, waxwings occur only in winter (S. T. Aksakov, *Zapiski ruzheinogo okhotnika Orenburgskoi gubernii*, ed. S. V. Kirikov [Moscow, 1953], 198). Rul'e commented earlier that waxwings, woodlarks, and hawfinches could not be found together as woodlarks are only summer visitors and hawfinches appear only in spring (quoted in S. Aksakov, *Sobranie sochinenii v piati tomakh*, ed. S. Mashinsky, vol. 5 [Moscow, 1966], 466). *Trans.*

6. A hollow tree taken over by bees is known as a "hive-tree" (*bort'*). Where bees are observed entering holes in a tree, the tree is hollowed out and grooves cut in order to extract them more easily and gain easy access to the honeycombs containing the aromatic green linden-blossom honey. In the province of Orenburg this was once a substantial industry, but the increase in population and ignorant greed for honey, which is often all taken with no thought for winter supplies, is destroying the bees—already at the mercy of bears, which are very fond of honey, of certain birds, and the fierce winter frosts.

7. In certain of the more heavily wooded districts of the province, where coniferous as well as deciduous trees grow, deer, lynx, and wolverines are found. Wild goats live in the more mountainous areas, and wild boar in the reeds and damp woodland of the Urals.

8. See Category III, note 17, on Aksakov's use of *kobchik*. *Trans.*

9. It is not true! The book *A Falconer's Way* makes clear that hobbies have been successfully used for hunting. This means that we do not know how to train them properly.

10. The alder is a tree which takes hold easily; it favors damp ground and usually grows thickly on the banks of small streams. It will also cover mountain slopes if the ground is damp enough. The alder grows to a considerable height and girth, but its timber is soft and brittle. Joiners nevertheless cut it into slats and use it for some kinds of furniture.

11. *Glukhoi*, besides the sense of "deaf," also means "remote"; *mokhovik* is derived from *mokh* (moss). *Trans.*

12. As noted by M. A. Menzbir, there are no black plumes in the capercaillie's tail. Quoted in S. Aksakov, *Sobranie sochinenii v piati tomakh*, ed. S. Mashinsky, vol. 5 (Moscow, 1966), 466. *Trans.*

13. Menzbir and Kirikov comment that the courtship and the display ground of the capercaillie are very different from those of the black grouse. Quoted in Aksakov, *Sobranie sochinenii*, 5:466. *Trans.*

14. These Siberian tribes are now known by the names of "Udmurt" and "Mari" respectively. *Trans.*

15. Black grouse consume astonishing quantities of acorns, with their cups and even twigs.

16. The quoted line is from Gavriil Derzhavin's *Evgeniiu. Zhizn' Zvanskaia*, much of which describes the charms of rural life on an estate named "Zvanka." *Trans.*

17. In unforested country, leks are in the open steppe, but high and open

sites are favored. Some fowlers assure me that they have seen something resembling spring courtship during a mild, late autumn; the males did not fight but gave their muttering calls as they ran through the grass or winter crops, distending their necks like turkey-cocks. In the province of Orenburg I have never witnessed the courtship of black grouse but near Moscow the males display every autumn; that is, they give their muttering calls as they perch alone in trees, and their eyebrows stand out bright red, as they do in spring. The females have no part in this performance.

18. The shooting of blackcock from hides at the leks is unknown in Orenburg province, as is shooting during the molt, which is widespread in other parts of Russia and can be very fruitful, particularly in the province of Kostroma, as hunters from those parts have told me.

19. I have asked those who are keen on this sport what pleasure there can be in killing young grouse that a dog can catch and that you can then take from it with your bare hands. Moreover, is it so difficult to hit a grouse, which flies like a hat, in absolutely straight lines, or lies flat on a branch above your head?

This question is disputed by most hunters, and some hotly defend the shooting of young grouse. While I respect the tastes of others, I cannot change my own.

20. The use of a troika, a team of three horses, to approach black grouse may seem strange to some, but this is the practice among hunters in the province of Orenburg in view of the distances there. I can say without exaggeration that I myself and other fowlers often traveled fifty versts before lunch, that is, before one o'clock, pursuing moving coveys of black grouse and sometimes mistaking their direction. If the snow is deep you cannot get far with only one horse, and we continued hunting until the snow was deep. Moreover, one often had to ride all day until it was completely dark. There is no doubt that it is preferable to use a single horse; in lightly wooded country and through bushes it is easier with just one, and the grouse have less fear of one horse than of two or of a troika, as they are used to seeing peasants hauling timber and hay with one-horse carts or sleighs. But for all this, lacking a troika of good strong horses in autumn, it is not possible to shoot black grouse in the numbers that I and other hunters used to record: three hundred grouse in a season was quite usual. In 1816, between 16 September and 6 December, I shot about five hundred by this means.

21. It has often happened that a black grouse withstood two or three shots and flew off unharmed. A reliable fowler tells me that he once fired seven shots at a male, which, after the seventh shot, clucked and flew off unhurt. I should add that the clucking call is regarded as proof that the bird is unharmed.

22. Near Moscow, along the Troitskaia Road, black grouse are shot using decoys in spring while there is still a hard crust on the snow, though in very small numbers, of course. I have never heard of this evening shooting in the province of Orenburg, and even now do not understand why they appear in this manner.

23. Both names are derived from the adjective *riaboi* (speckled). *Trans.*

24. Kirikov observes that "Aksakov's remarks concerning the habitat of the willow grouse and its range in Orenburg province are not quite accurate. It occurs not only in the forests (in lightly timbered marshland and in stands of birch and aspen), but also in the open, treeless tundra. In Orenburg province the species was absent only to the west of the Urals. It was present to the east of the Urals, and remains so." Aksakov, *Zapiski*, 225. *Trans.*

25. These terms are closely related to the generic term for "pigeon," (*golub'*). *Trans.*

26. In the province of Orenburg stooks are collected in small clusters, and if there is grass in the stubble or the weather is wet they are left for several days to dry. If the weather and the straw is dry the stooks are placed the same day on frame ricks and sometimes left for a long time.

27. In modern Russian *dikii* means only "wild," but an older sense, "dark gray," may possibly apply here. *Trans.*

28. Aksakov's supposition, a connection with Russian *gorlo* (throat), is confirmed by Vasmer and Preobrazhensky. Maks Fasmer [Max Vasmer], *Etimologicheskii slovar' russkogo iazyka*, vol. 1 (Moscow, 1964), 441; A. G. Preobrazhensky, *Etimologicheskii slovar' russkogo iazyka*, vol. 1 (Moscow, 1959), 147. *Trans.*

29. The poet is Nikolai Mikhailovich Karamzin (1766–1826). Aksakov quotes the last quatrain of a poem beginning "Dovolen ia sud'boiu" (I am content with my lot). It was first published in 1796 with another poem under the joint title "Dve pesni" (Two songs). N. M. Karamzin, *Polnoe sobranie stikhotvorenii* (Moscow, 1966), 148. *Trans.*

30. Aksakov uses the widely known term *Egipetskii golub'*, known in the nineteenth century by various scientific names no longer in use in the twentieth, including *Columba risoria*, *Columba aegyptiacis* and *Turtur cambayensis*. It seems likely that it refers to the domesticated variety known as the Barbary dove, a descendant of the Collared dove, now known as *Streptopelia decaocto*, of which several races are recognized. *Trans.*

31. The Russian name is *riabinnik*, derived from *riabina* (rowan or mountain ash). *Trans.*

32. Russian *mozzhevel'nik*, the same word as the name of the tree. *Trans.*

33. Aksakov's footnote to a later edition ran as follows: "The same esteemed professor whom I mentioned earlier has offered the following observations: (i) that the blackbirds I describe as two separate species are merely the male and female of the same species, and (ii) that the bird I described under the name of the 'water ouzel' (*vodianoi drozd*) does not belong to the family of ouzels, or thrushes, at all, and is known as 'the dipper' (*vodianaia oliapka*). I cannot with any certainty refute the first observation because, as I have mentioned, I have not had the opportunity to observe blackbirds at close range. They are not found in our province. As for the second, I must say that I have written only what I have observed

with my own eyes, and called the birds by the names used by the people of the province, both wildfowlers and ordinary folk. I am not concerned with scientific taxonomy."

The blackbird is *Turdus merula*.

Taxonomists have long separated the dipper from the true thrushes. *Trans.*

34. Such calls are given by mistle thrushes, fieldfares, and both blackbirds.

35. A reliable source informs me that in one particularly cold winter he shot eighteen fieldfares at the same spot, by a spring, almost all in flight, but this is unusual.

36. Aksakov feels it necessary to explain a word that not all his readers could be expected to know. Kirikov observes that Aksakov is mistaken in his taxonomy, since hybrids very rarely occur. The animal Aksakov calls *tumak*, he says, is merely a brown hare with slightly unusual coloration. Aksakov, *Zapiski*, 250. *Trans.*

37. Aksakov adds a note on another litter, born in April, and discusses the terms by which this and other broods are known. *Trans.*

38. Seven-foot leaps can be found in most ordinary tracks, but one hunter I know (A. S. Khomiakov) tells me that a brown hare will jump over deep ruts and crevices up to fifteen feet wide.

39. Hunters have told me that eagle owls and other owl species catch hares at night in the following way: they lie in wait on tracks followed by hares and seize the hare with one foot while clinging with the other to the branch of a bush or tree. The owl holds the hare like this until the hare's strength is exhausted, and then plunges the other claw into it to finish it off. My informants add that the hare sometimes manages to tear off the claw in which it is held, while the owl is still clinging with the other to a branch, and that some hunters have taken hares that had an owl-claw hanging from their flesh, torn off, and already dried up. I confess that I thought this most unlikely, but the hunter and expert A. S. Khomiakov, to whom I have previously referred, assured me that this was exactly so. Another hunter, Iu. F. Samarin, confirms it.

40. On 11 December 1854 I was brought a medium-sized yellowish-brown owl trapped in a clam set on a hare-run: apparently owls also catch hares by following their tracks.

41. Aksakov uses a threefold simile, adding, "as white as a harrier, as a spoonbill," and providing a footnote on these species: "The male harrier [pallid harrier? *Trans.*] is quite a large raptor: it is all white and in no way resembles its speckled, tawny mate, which is almost twice its size. The spoonbill [*kolpik*] is a white stork with red legs and beak. It is found near Astrakhan'." The latter description is less than fully accurate if "spoonbill" (modern Russian, *kolpitsa*) is really meant, but the white stork, which is not "all white," does not match the description either. *Trans.*

42. Okhotnyi riad is a well-known thoroughfare in central Moscow. The name means literally "Hunter's Row." *Trans.*

43. Russian *podorozhnik,* in modern terminology *punochka* (*Plectrophenax nivalis*). It seems clear from the description that Aksakov has this species in mind rather than its relative, *laplandskii podorozhnik* (*Calcarius lapponicus*), the Lapland bunting. *Trans.*

44. The name is derived directly from *doroga* (road). *Trans.*